CONGRESS BUYS A NAVY

POLITICS, ECONOMICS, AND THE RISE OF
AMERICAN NAVAL POWER, 1881–1921

PAUL E. PEDISICH

NAVAL INSTITUTE PRESS
ANNAPOLIS, MARYLAND

This book was brought to publication with the generous
assistance of Marguerite and Gerry Lenfest.

Naval Institute Press
291 Wood Road
Annapolis, MD 21402

Library of Congress Cataloging-in-Publication Data
Names: Pedisich, Paul, author.
Title: Congress buys a Navy : politics, economics, and the rise of American
  naval power, 1881–1921 / Paul Pedisich.
Other titles: Politics, economics, and the rise of American naval power, 1881–1921
Description: Annapolis, Maryland : Naval Institute Press, [2016] | Includes
  bibliographical references and index.
Identifiers: LCCN 2016021662| ISBN 9781682470770 (alk. paper) | ISBN
  9781682470787 (mobi)
Subjects: LCSH: United States. Navy—History—19th century. | United States.
  Navy—History—20th century. | United States. Navy—Appropriations and
  expenditures. | Civil-military relations—United States—History—20th
  century. | Shipbuilding—United States—History—19th century. |
  Shipbuilding—United States—History—20th century. | Sea-power—United
  States—History—19th century. | Sea-power—United States—History—20th
  century.
Classification: LCC VA58 .P43 2016 | DDC 359.00973/09034—dc23
LC record available at https://lccn.loc.gov/2016021662

♾ Print editions meet the requirements of ANSI/NISO z39.48–1992
(Permanence of Paper).
Printed in the United States of America.

24 23 22 21 20 19 18 17 16   9 8 7 6 5 4 3 2 1
First printing

TO ELLEN

CONTENTS

INTRODUCTION

This book presents the nitty-gritty activities that kept Congress in control of the structure and policy of the Navy while the executive branch moved about its myriad functions of varying priorities. Within the real time of national and world events, the following chapters present a view of the dynamics acting on the presidents and Navy secretaries, concurrent with congressional action at play in building a naval force from 1881 to 1921. The narrative covers contemporary national and international affairs and shows that the power of Congress held sway over the executive branch in naval development. The executive office experienced this incapacity because of the Navy's implacable managerial organization, the autonomy of its far-flung service, the firm attachment of its bureaus to the legislature, and the legislature's ultimate appropriations authority. Congressmen generally aligned with the Navy Department's eight semi-autonomous bureaus while also responding to their constituencies.

The main acts in U.S. political history often privilege the actions of the president and his cabinet because of the largeness and immediacy of events. On the other hand, congressional resolution developments are spread out over time and are rarely as monolithic as executive decisions. Records of votes cast and outcomes are, of course, available for research, but individual rationales, voting blocs, and agendas are often obscured, neither fully articulated nor recorded. Studies of the rise of the Navy prior to 1921 have laid out a valuable cornucopia of information on the record of naval growth and maritime force development, but they generally do not focus on the full placement of congressional responsibility. Therefore, the total raison d'être of the associated legislative decision-making has often remained in the background. In reality, contiguous legislatures dominated naval vitalization, beginning under the accidental presidency of Chester A. Arthur and ending under the presidency of Woodrow Wilson after the culmination of the First World War.

In the years following the Civil War, the peacetime Navy had deteriorated considerably. By 1881, the legislature applied virtually all of its naval appropriations to expensive repair work to maintain decrepit wooden and iron ships. The Forty-seventh Congress reversed that direction at the end of its final session in March 1883 and began building a new Navy by approving the construction of a few modern steam-driven steel warships. Initially, events in the Caribbean and South America, along with U.S. business interests in international trade, provided a stimulus for increased naval expenditures for ships and shore facilities. Under the circumstances, the legislative branch began the process of Navy expansion and the associated development of the United States as a world sea power. Successive congresses maintained close control of the Navy's force structure for the next forty years, through the U.S. involvement in the 1921 Washington Naval Conference.

By the legislative actions of the twenty congresses that met from 1881 to 1921, the Navy went from being an embarrassment to the United States to become one of the best in the world. During this period, six presidents molded a new administrative state and solidified the executive branch as the leading power broker in U.S. development. However, in the Navy's case, the office of the president did not rise to the same level of authority that came to pass in developing an enduring civil service system, reorganizing the U.S. Army, and establishing a significant executive branch bureaucracy.

Until 1934, congressmen, after being elected in November every two years in even-numbered years, formed their new legislature in early March. But unless called into special session by the president, each Congress normally met for its first session in December, thirteen months after its election. This biennial sequence meant that congresses generally had their long sessions begin in December of an odd-numbered year and end in the summer or perhaps early autumn of either a congressional or presidential election year. As a result, the immediate politics of election campaigns in general always weighed heavily on legislative decisions. The short post-election lame-duck sessions, which met from December to March and determined the next fiscal year's appropriations, also responded to the influence of the recent post-election returns.

Following the period of the weak potency of the administration of President Arthur, the presidents of the 1880s and 1890s began the reconstitution of executive authority. This was solidified by the wartime decision-making of President William McKinley and the "bully pulpit" of President Theodore Roosevelt. But the case of the Navy's structural advancement did not follow this progression. This book's exposition of naval developments shows that the role of Congress in building the Navy continued to supersede the rising primacy of the presidents and their cabinets.

The advent of progressivism in the late nineteenth and early twentieth centuries brought increased government involvement into the affairs of the country. The corresponding expansion of government necessitated a significantly increased bureaucracy in the executive branch. McKinley's hands-on Spanish War management, Roosevelt's exuberant global involvement, William Howard Taft's codification of the administrative state, and Woodrow Wilson's eventual military preparations added to the renewed presidential authority initially claimed by Grover Cleveland and Benjamin Harrison. Yet in the important circumstances of determining naval force structure during the period, political power did not so obviously shift away from congressional politics and move toward the presidency.

Notwithstanding credit traditionally given to presidents and naval leaders, Congress itself built an ad hoc Navy and controlled its administration. Yet biographies of Roosevelt, as well as those of Navy secretaries William Chandler, William C. Whitney, Hilary Herbert, Benjamin Tracy, John D. Long, and Josephus Daniels each favor those executive branch individuals with developing a new Navy. To more fully understand the evolution of a fleet that envisioned becoming "second to none," these chapters focus on the power of the legislature. An account of the sessions leading to annual naval appropriation acts shows the level of congressional interest and effective control of naval growth within the concurrent press of constant presidential demands and contemporary events. The appropriation acts themselves are the statutes writ large that in reality governed the Navy's destiny. The list of the usual suspects who controlled that legislation is as long as it is sometimes indeterminate. Over time, hundreds of lesser-heralded legislators voting on the floor of Congress actually built the Navy.

President Garfield won the presidency in November 1880 and took office in March of 1881. The Forty-seventh Congress that was elected with him did not meet until December of 1881 after his assassination that summer. Following an almost complete turnover of cabinet members, President Arthur had virtually no naval agenda. When that Congress finally met, it took no action on the recommendations of novice Secretary of the Navy William Hunt or the unintended president for any Navy reorganization or increases, since those issues were not high congressional priorities. Acting conservatively at the end of its final session in March 1883, the Forty-seventh Congress authorized funds for a few new warships without any reference to a strategic plan.

This was hardly an auspicious beginning, since the next Congress also waited until the end of its lame-duck session in March 1885, after the election of Grover Cleveland, to fund a few more vessels. Meanwhile the remnants of the Civil War Navy deteriorated to conditions of uselessness. Cleveland focused on national finances and the corrupt spoils system while the country was experiencing a monetary crisis and a great depression. He had no priorities for upgrading the state of the Navy. Rather, he called for increasing the Navy's business efficiency prior to embarking on any expensive program of new construction. His first two congresses filled the void by authorizing warship construction, again unconnected to any national naval policy. Their actions were consistent with the conservative priorities of the previous congresses.

President Harrison came into office primarily because of the revitalization of the Republican Party and its focus on balancing the tariff schedules in favor of big business. His hands-on management firmly controlled executive branch activities but not legislative action. For the Navy, his two congresses continued a course of authorizing a mix of small and large warships unrelated to any administrative scheme. When Cleveland returned to office in 1893, he again devoted his energies to monetary priorities, showing little concern for Navy developments. Meanwhile, each of his two contrasting congresses, the first with a Democratic Party majority and the second dominated by the Republican Party, took the lead in authorizing coastal battleships and cruisers for defense and commerce raiding.

The burning issues of the noisy Cross of Gold presidential campaign, which resulted in the election of President McKinley in 1896, did not extend to the military. However, international affairs soon escalated to a war with Spain. In reaction, the congresses elected in 1896 and 1898 increased the Navy budget considerably beyond the recommendations of the executive branch and increased warship appropriations to the highest level since the end of the Civil War.

After his unplanned ascendancy in September 1901 due to the assassination of President McKinley, President Roosevelt became an international player who needed a substantial worldwide naval force in order to give the United States a meaningful voice. But he could not unconditionally control Navy development. His first Congress lowered and then raised his budget requests for new ship construction in accordance with its concern over events in the Caribbean. Over time, Roosevelt has become the poster boy for the rise of the administrative state begun by McKinley and later expanded by Taft. Yet with all of his rough-and-tumble worldwide ventures, Roosevelt's congresses during his second term did not come close to doing his bidding for the Navy. By 1907, he had to stoop to publicly pleading for four battleships just so that he could get two. Eleven of the sixteen battleships of his Great White Fleet, which circumnavigated the globe from 1907 to 1909, had been authorized by Congress before he took office in 1901.

Ever the judge, President Taft ruminated over naval force structure while allowing the legislature to be his guide. He called two special sessions of Congress and expended considerable political capital to lower tariffs, but left executive decisions concerning the configuration of the Navy's line of battle in the relatively impotent hands of its General Board, created in 1900. Taft's interest in the Navy focused primarily on the budget. George von Lengerke Meyer, his Navy secretary, obliged by organizing efficiencies in management as well as in operations. His efficiencies proved to be temporary and were remanded by Josephus Daniels, Secretary of the Navy of the next administration. Congress continued to receive the Navy's recommendations and then mostly ignored them in favor of its own interests.

When Wilson took office, international issues were not a part of his platform of New Freedom for the people of America. However, he almost immediately faced crises with Mexico, Japan, and Caribbean republics. In August

1914, midway through his second year in office, the Great War erupted in Europe. However, neither Wilson nor his first Congress saw an urgent need for accelerating improvements of the Navy's fleet structure. Two years later, in August 1916, Congress authorized a massive three-year naval construction program for capital warships to command the seas. Yet when the United States entered the war less than a year later in April 1917, it was appreciably unprepared to fight the war at hand because of its serious deficiency in countering submarine warfare. Immediate appropriation measures by Congress and essential strategic planning by the Navy eventually corrected the significant lack of preparedness.

1

THE FIRST HUNDRED YEARS

Chronicles of the first one hundred years of U.S. Navy employment are consistent. In the beginning of the American Revolution, the Second Continental Congress agreed in principle that a naval force was necessary to protect the breakaway colonies. That defensive Navy consisted of a few ships, of varying sizes and armament, whose duties required them to individually disrupt British maritime commerce and protect the colonial coastline. After achieving independence the United States matured and gradually expanded from coast to coast, but hardly wavered from its initial defensive maritime strategy. Over time it formed and reformed various and often disconnected conglomerations of armed vessels to conduct successive naval engagements with France, Barbary Coast pirates, Great Britain, Atlantic and Caribbean pirates, Mexico, and its own separated Confederate States. Often with passion, military leaders, state governments, and presidents asked for capital ships. The legislative authority, which held the purse strings, responded conservatively by authorizing bits and pieces that never led to the formation of a true fighting fleet. In this untidy environment for much longer than a century, the U.S. Navy was neither formidable nor an instrument of world power.

In the beginning, colonial leaders recognized that they could never succeed in a fleet-to-fleet engagement with the Royal Navy. Instead in the fall of 1775, nine months prior to the signing of the Declaration of Independence, Gen. George Washington took the initiative by hiring privately armed vessels at government expense to capture British shipping. Operating under official letters of marque, private individuals had government authorization to outfit a ship for the purpose of plundering an enemy's commerce for profit. Shortly after Washington's action, the Continental Congress officially launched the U.S. Navy on October 13, 1775 by buying, rather than hiring, two small ships for raider duty in the Atlantic. Subsequently, Congress purchased additional merchant ships, operated armed vessels contributed by colonies, and oversaw a modest warship construction program for the newly formed United States of America.

While the Navy slowly developed throughout the revolutionary period, the majority of its fighting ships were independent privateers. These privately owned and operated armed vessels conducted legal piracy at the behest of their new federal government. Americans depended on *guerre de course* (attacks on unarmed or lightly armed ships for economic damage) rather than *guerre d'escadre* (battles between fleets). Both privateers and Navy craft captured lesser vessels and avoided direct battle with large warships.

By comparison, the British navy designated their fighting ships by class, the largest being "ship of the line" battleships with more than one hundred cannon. Dozens of these impressive warships sailed across the seas. The largest frigates of the original U.S. Navy carried twenty-six to thirty-two cannon and were no match against the king's fleet. The United States' armed vessels focused almost entirely on capturing prizes. Some of them successfully harassed the coast of England and British Caribbean shipping, but they were more of a nuisance than a significant threat to the Royal Navy. After the United States gained its independence, Congress sold the few ships that had survived the war and released the officers and crews.

The legislature, first under the Articles of Confederation and then under the Constitution, showed little interest in reconstituting a Navy until 1794. In reaction to the disruptions of U.S. commerce by the pirates of Algeria, Congress approved the construction of six frigates mounting from forty-four to thirty-six cannon.[1] A few years later at the beginning of the Quasi-War with France in the summer of 1798, Congress increased its naval authorizations, which led to a force of fifty armed vessels of various sizes. These warships were purchased outright, constructed under contract, or built in U.S. Navy yards. Subsequent additions included an authorization to build six capital ships of the line carrying seventy-four guns each.[2] This new Navy had a short life and was once again dismantled in 1801. The combination of treaties with Algeria and France and the policies of the incoming anti-federalist administration of President Thomas Jefferson led to a reduction of naval forces to a bare minimum. The U.S. government sold all but thirteen ships, keeping only six in commission and putting the other seven in "ordinary," laid up without masts, sails, rigging, cannon, or crew.[3] The "seventy-fours" remained unconstructed. Although originally authorized by Congress, succeeding sessions did not fund the shipbuilding projects.

The war with Tripoli in the first decade of the nineteenth century saw some renewed congressional attention toward developing a Navy that could protect U.S. commerce in the Mediterranean. But once again, legislative action did not lead to meaningful appropriations support and the government sent out only a few small squadrons consisting of one frigate each and lesser armed schooners and brigs. This unheralded naval force, constituted to protect U.S. shipping, showed a minor presence in the ports of coastal North Africa. By 1807 the British, engaged in all-out war with Napoleon, increased their attention to U.S. civilian maritime activities with blockades and impressments of U.S. seamen into the Royal Navy. To avoid confrontations, Jefferson chose to recall his small Navy to protect U.S. ports rather than escort oceanic shipping. He urged Congress to add as many as two hundred non-oceangoing gunboats to his maritime inventory to act as shore batteries. He rationalized that these small, lightly armed vessels could protect the United States against coastal adventures by the British or any other nation. Jefferson explained that the majority of the gunboats would remain in ordinary under shelter and be activated with rigging and crews only when necessary.[4]

President James Madison continued Jefferson's coastal defense policy until the United States declared war against Great Britain in the summer of 1812. The U.S. Navy then put a few medium-sized frigates to sea with a strategy once again focused on *guerre de course* and commerce protection. At the same time, significant land warfare along the Canadian frontier drew the United States into an effort to control the waters of the Great Lakes. Oliver Hazard Perry masterfully oversaw the rapid construction of a nine-ship fleet on Lake Erie that defeated a similarly constructed Royal Navy armada.[5] His hastily constructed vessels of fresh-cut timber opened communications for the U.S. Army engaging British and Indian land forces. But the unseasoned vessels had a temporary life sufficient only for the brief duration of hostilities.

The high seas U.S. Navy did not fare as well as its inland fleet. With little significant impact, its privateers experienced low-level success against British shipping throughout the war. In spite of excellent individual seamanship, U.S. warships could only swap losses with the Royal Navy and could not engage in a fleet encounter leading to anything resembling command of the seas. In one exceptional adventure, Capt. David Porter managed to permanently cripple the British whaling industry through his exploits against British whalers in the Pacific Ocean.[6] But in spite of his heroic efforts, Porter eventually lost his ship, the *Essex*, to a superior British naval force.

At the war's end U.S. citizens and politicians looked with newfound pride at their plucky Navy's effort, notwithstanding its marginal actual effectiveness. This time the government resolved not to dismantle its maritime force. During the recent war, Congress had authorized the Navy to construct four capital ships of the line. The first of these, the *Independence*, armed with ninety cannon, sailed in the summer of 1814 but played only a harbor defense role until the end of the conflict that winter.[7] Nevertheless, the Navy kept it in commission and in the late spring of 1815 sent it to the Mediterranean Sea to be a floating fortress against a new wave of North African piracy. Within a year, Congress approved construction of nine additional ships of the line to combat increased piracy in the Gulf of Mexico as well as in the Mediterranean. According to plan, the Navy staggered the launching of these thirteen ships over the next four decades. The guiding strategic principle consisted of keeping the ships in readiness in various stages of construction or as receiving ships in ordinary. As a result, only eight had entered the fleet by the time of the Civil War in 1861. The remaining five stayed either in the ways or dry docks, eventually to be burned or broken up.

The few large and heavily armed capital ships that saw sea service sailed as squadron flagships. In the years between the end of the War of 1812 and the beginning of the Civil War, the Navy's primary mission consisted of protecting U.S. commerce and whaling from piracy. The few expensive ships of the line and smaller but impressive frigates led the shallow-draft schooners, brigs, and sloops, which did the major pursuit of adversaries in inland waters. In his annual address to Congress in December 1819, President James Monroe explained the Navy's role as protecting U.S. commerce worldwide and suppressing the slave trade.[8] The United States sequentially established a few small squadrons in the Mediterranean, West Indies, South Atlantic, Pacific South America, and East Asia. This global pattern followed the lines of American commercial interests.

Although these small squadrons were no match for European powers in a fleet engagement, their regular deployment throughout the world established the U.S. Navy as a legitimate maritime force with its own personality. No longer wedded to its historical association with Great Britain, the U.S. Navy cultivated its own leaders and traditions. Selected groups of midshipmen, who routinely went to sea at the age of fourteen or fifteen, remained afloat after the War of 1812. They flourished under the tutelage of experienced captains, who autonomously operated on great ocean expanses, gave no quarter to hardcore pirates, protected maritime commerce, and often negotiated as the sole U.S. official ashore in distant foreign lands. The midshipmen in time became the captains who led the blockade and bombardment engagements during the 1846 war with Mexico, and who trained the Civil War naval officers. In the process, the U.S. Navy became a vibrant service with a unique cadre of men whose lifeblood depended on the unceasing challenges of seafaring life, even as the United States was at best less than a tenth-rate world power.

Meanwhile, Congress paid some attention to maritime organization and technical progress by approving the beginning of the U.S. steam-driven Navy. The first steamships, the *Mississippi* and the *Missouri*, launched in January 1840, had wooden hulls, two engine-driven side wheels, and full rigging for sails. Carrying only ten cannon each, they were not capital battleships, but did sail and steam as flagships to distant stations in the Mediterranean Sea and the western Pacific Ocean.[9] The Navy also began experimenting with iron-hulled vessels and screw propellers. Congress funded these new war machines during and after the Mexican War and continued to focus on commerce protection.

When the Civil War began at Fort Sumter in April 1861, the U.S. Navy's total inventory numbered ninety vessels of all types and design. However, less than half of them were in commission and capable of wartime operations.[10] The remaining vessels were serving as receiving stations or were in ordinary. The Navy immediately embarked on a program to purchase and build a large force for the primary purposes of blockade and shore bombardment. The new fleet contained numerous shallow-draft, steam-driven vessels not capable of conducting head-to-head engagements with capital ships. By concentrating instead on harbor and riverine accesses, this force contributed significantly to successfully isolating the Confederacy.

However, the Navy had considerable difficulty protecting its oceangoing commerce. The Paris Declaration of 1856 had declared privateering to be illegal. The United States did not sign the treaty because it considered the practice to be a legitimate strategy for its own protection. After the destruction of Fort Sumter, Confederate president Jefferson Davis immediately issued letters of marque to enlist privateers to his cause, while the United States assured the European nations that it would respect the Paris Declaration. Committed to blockade and inshore operations, the United States did not build a significant number of fast oceangoing cruisers to combat Confederate anti-commerce adventures and thus lost more than one hundred commercial ships.

After the end of the war, the U.S. government stood down its military and sold more than half of its warships. Once again the Navy would be a disparate group of small squadrons showing the U.S. flag throughout the world. Theoretically, ships in reserve would have the capability of rising up when needed. By the 1870s the legislature augmented its aging ships with defensive non-oceangoing artillery gunboats and rams. While the U.S. Navy fell to its lowest point since the days of President Jefferson, Congress concentrated on internal postwar economic recovery and did not develop its limited vision of a defensive maritime force.

From the doldrums of the 1870s came a new beginning in the 1880s. The Navy that became a major sea power by 1921 generally traces its birth as occurring during the presidencies of James Garfield and Chester A. Arthur. However, this beginning was certainly inauspicious and unheralded. In the event it only gradually moved from a tradition of homeland defense and commerce protection to become an international force. For the most part throughout the rise of this new Navy, Congress not only decided, session by session, on the force structure but also dictated its concomitant business and command organization. The president and his Navy Department could only accept what they were given.

2

A BEGINNING,
1881–82

By three o'clock in the morning following Election Day 1880, James Garfield was satisfied that he had won the U.S. presidency and went to bed. True to himself and his Campbellite background, he felt a sense of destiny rather than elation as he now anticipated the long haul ahead.[1] Since his early youth, he had followed the Second Great Awakening reform movement of Alexander Campbell that had become part of the Restoration Movement of Christian churches. Garfield became an enthusiastic Disciple of Christ as a student in the Geauga Seminary and in the Western Reserve Eclectic Institute, which later became Hiram College, located in the small town of Hiram in northeast Ohio.[2] After graduating from Williams College in Massachusetts, he returned to Hiram College as a teacher and at the age of twenty-five became its president. In his life, he diligently absorbed ancient Greek and Latin literature and also kept his Bible close at hand.

He began his political career at the age of twenty-seven by winning a seat in the Ohio State Senate in 1859. During the deepening sectional crisis, he solidified his position as an anti-slavery Republican through his support of Abraham Lincoln's campaign for the presidency. After the Civil War began in the spring of 1861, Garfield went to work building the Ohio militia but waited until the end of the summer to accept a commission as lieutenant colonel in a new Ohio volunteer unit.[3] He rapidly rose to the rank of brigadier general in early 1862 and became a U.S. congressman the same year. His actual combat experience was limited but he did distinguish himself in the Battle of Chickamauga in the summer of 1863. He used the title "general" for the remainder of his life. His subsequent eighteen years in the House of Representatives were years of dogged determination. His colleagues and constituents observed him as a fiscal conservative committed to Republican reconstruction of the Southern states.

He attended the Chicago convention of the hot summer of 1880 as a state delegate. He had not campaigned for his own candidacy, but his supporters had most certainly developed a well-organized movement before the convention began, in order to elevate him as a steady and more worthwhile dark-horse nominee than the announced leading candidates: Sen. James C. Blaine and Gen. Ulysses S. Grant, whose powerful backers were evenly split and remained at uncompromising loggerheads. Garfield deliberately chose not to propel himself into the fight and eventually gave a relatively weak endorsement to John Sherman of his home state of Ohio. After several days of stalemated balloting at the convention, the anti-Grant delegation of Wisconsin placed Garfield on the nomination list as the thirty-fourth ballot came to its alphabetic end. Almost immediately the evenly divided delegations shifted focus and on the thirty-sixth ballot settled on Garfield as a good compromise candidate from the important swing state of Ohio.

When he won the election in November 1880, the U.S. Navy was merely a declining remnant of its Civil War strength. The postwar government had discontinued almost all warship building, removed many existing vessels from naval service, and dismantled much of the Navy department's wartime civilian administration. As such, the Navy returned to its standard peacetime status as a widely dispersed maritime service sparingly supporting U.S. commercial and diplomatic interests in a few selected ports throughout the world. Wooden and iron ships with coal-fired steam engines continued to depend on auxiliary sail power, often used as the primary means of propulsion to save fuel. Prior to Garfield's inauguration in March, the outgoing Forty-sixth Congress passed a Naval Appropriations Act of $14 million. The money was earmarked for ship repair and administration, with unfunded authorizations for shallow-draft and low freeboard coastal defense monitors.[4]

Garfield had considerably bigger concerns than the latest assessments of the state of the Navy and its leadership. As he worked to construct his cabinet, he clearly understood the demands of patronage, having been an integral part of the system during his many years in Congress. At the time, the most important cabinet positions were the secretaries of State, Treasury, and Interior. The lesser appointments were the postmaster general, the attorney general, and the secretaries of War and Navy. The state of U.S. naval forces was simply not an area of collective interest. Shortly after his election, Garfield chose his friend Senator Blaine for secretary of state and then waffled and procrastinated for months until the very day of his inauguration in March to announce the remainder of his principle advisers. William Hunt, a judge from Louisiana, got the nod to be the civilian head of the insignificant Navy.

Garfield had chosen Hunt as a last-minute compromise appointee to balance his cabinet with someone from the South. Hunt had spent his early pre-Civil War years in a well-heeled household of established gentry in Charleston, South Carolina. His family proudly traced its heritage to the seventeenth-century Cavaliers (or Royalists) of English aristocracy, who opposed the Puritan Roundheads of Oliver Cromwell. Hunt's family was among the wealthy English émigré entrepreneurs of the West Indies who eventually made their way to the southern colonies prior to the American Revolution.[5] As a youngster, Hunt moved to Connecticut to receive his education in grammar school and at Yale College. While in New Haven he developed his lifelong abhorrence to slavery and the Southern concept of secession. After Yale, Hunt rejoined his aunts and uncles, who now resided in New Orleans, and took up the profession of law. He remained an abolitionist and unionist as the Civil War began some years later. Under local orders, he reluctantly served in the Confederate army for a few months as a lieutenant colonel drilling poorly equipped local guard troops.[6] When the U.S. forces took over New Orleans in 1862, in a show of animosity toward the Southern confederacy he personally entertained Adm. David Farragut in his home. This was Hunt's first official brush with a seasoned U.S. Navy leader.

After the war, as a Southern Republican, Hunt campaigned for the thirteenth, fourteenth, and fifteenth amendments to the Constitution, opposing Southern Democrats in Louisiana who vigorously struggled to regain control of the state. In 1876, as a participant in a decade of political turmoil and reconstruction, he appeared to have won sufficient votes for the office of state attorney general. In the hotly contested state and national elections, the U.S. Congress ruled that the national winner for president was Rutherford B. Hayes, the Republican candidate. The recount process included an electoral compromise that turned over the governments of Louisiana, Florida, and South Carolina to newly re-enfranchised Southern Democrats. This resulted in Hunt's failure to gain his state office. A year after Hayes' inauguration, Hunt's Republican Party loyalty brought him to Washington, D.C., to be a Court of Federal Claims judge. As a Southern lawyer in the capital, he was not part of the political machine dominated by northeasterners.

Hunt had led a life of privilege in New Orleans and he and his fourth wife smoothly integrated into Washington society. Not a philanderer, he was just unlucky with wives. His first wife died after only eight months of marriage and his second wife bore seven children before her death in 1864. His third marriage was a disaster, ending in divorce after three years. In 1871 he married his fourth wife, a New Orleans socialite with lifelong New York connections. She had a close, enduring friendship with Chester A. Arthur's wife, who died almost a year before he became vice president. As a political outsider, Hunt's sympathetic family bond held him and his wife in good stead with Arthur when the latter accidentally became president.[7]

Once in office, the unprepared Secretary Hunt, who only days before had thought he was in line for the Treasury, had to face the reality of a deteriorated and dispirited naval service. The outgoing Congress had expressed its dissatisfaction with the state of the nation's Navy and clamored for change. Washington Whitthorne, Democrat from Tennessee and chairman of the House of Representatives Committee on Naval Affairs, had stated in January: "The incoming administration ought to recognize that the United States had no Navy and begin to build from the bottom up what the country needed— a Navy commensurate with its great commercial interests."[8] For the past decade, the bulk of naval appropriations, directed by Congress and accompanied by considerable charges of corruption, had favored northeastern and California shipyards and did not contribute to maritime expansion. As a Southern Democrat, Whitthorne was echoing his compatriots' strong mind-set for developing international trade as part of their intense desire to establish an economically independent South.

The Navy deficiencies that Secretary Hunt inherited and Congress co-opted were related to postwar ennui and a spoils system dominated by political bosses. Although Whitthorne called for an improved naval service, the majority of Congress and the general population did not support either a large standing army or navy. For them, history had shown that voluntary military services would rise to the occasion as they had during the crises of 1775, 1812, 1846, and 1861. Accordingly, the Navy did not need to build up its fleet at this time.[9] In spite of Whitthorne's grumbling to the new administration, his legislative branch, not the executive, bore the brunt of responsibility for the business and state of maritime forces.

With close access to the internal administration of the Navy Department, the legislature worked within a Byzantine system of annual appropriations granted separately to each of eight independent bureaus of the Navy Department. In this organization established during the Civil War, the Navy officer chief of each bureau answered to the civilian Secretary of the Navy for management and operations but received funding directly from Congress.[10] The annual lump sum appropriated for the Navy budget consisted of eight separate, sacrosanct line-item allotments, rather than a single allowance to be distributed at the discretion of the Navy Department. Since the Civil War, the four bureaus of industrial activity had the titles of Construction and Repairs, Equipment and Recruiting, Steam Engineering, and Ordnance. As part of a deeply embedded spoils system, the military heads of these bureaus necessarily worked closely with civilian manufacturing and associated politicians. The other four bureaus of Yards and Docks, Provisions and Clothing, Medicine and Surgery, and Navigation dealt with civilian industry to a lesser degree. They were generally internally oriented, concerned with military port activities, ship maintenance, training, and personnel matters. Nevertheless, they too were beholden to congressional bosses for funding, manning, and survival.

The president, with the advice and consent of the Senate, appointed the military chiefs of the Navy bureaus to four-year terms. As the Navy had neither a single military head nor a general staff, the eight military bureau chiefs had no requirement for a unified voice. Under normal circumstances, the senior bureau chief who had the qualifications of a seafaring officer, regardless of his bureau, acted on behalf of the Secretary of the Navy in his absence but did not have chief of staff authority. The chief of the Bureau of Navigation, although it was not necessarily the most senior of the eight bureaus, held the most prestigious position as he controlled the movements of ships and, more importantly, was in charge of patronage-laden officer assignments.[11] Under the brief administration of President Garfield, the Navy began to be slowly but inexorably drawn into the global scene. Secretary of State Blaine had found an interest in foreign affairs when he moved from the House of Representatives to the Senate in 1876. As a fledgling imperialist and an influential member of Garfield's cabinet, he focused on the turmoil in Latin America and his vision of a dominant Monroe Doctrine as the guiding principle for U.S. international participation. Amidst the daily routine of dealing with the frenzy of office seekers in the spring of 1881, Blaine solidified his friendship and influence with Garfield. Together they shared the idea of a comprehensive plan of vigorous international involvement, especially in the Western Hemisphere.[12]

Both Blaine and Garfield began their national political careers as freshmen in the Thirty-eighth Congress of 1863 where Blaine, almost two years older than Garfield, rose rapidly in leadership positions that included speaker of the House, followed by his elevation to the U.S. Senate. He unsuccessfully sought his party's nomination for the presidency in both the 1876 and 1880 campaigns and later would be his party's losing candidate in 1884. Now in the administration of his colleague and friend, Blaine put on a new face and aggressively focused his attention on enhancing the international standing of the United States.

By contrast, Hunt could only play the hand he was dealt. His decaying Navy was far from capable of influencing foreign affairs. After a month in office, Hunt managed to disengage himself from the throng of job hunters to visit New York City for personal business and family pleasure. Touring the Brooklyn Navy Yard, he found it to be generally satisfactory but at the same time noted the dilapidated condition of some of the facilities. He stated to the press that he hoped to receive funding from Congress for necessary repairs.[13] But he knew that Congress would not meet until December, and the earliest that he could expect any infusion of money would be in the late spring, at least a year in the future. At this point he had not yet publicly faced the larger issue of fleet expansion, although it certainly was a concern in Navy circles.

On the occasion of the graduation of U.S. Naval Academy cadet midshipmen that June, the press advanced the subject of naval growth. At the commencement ceremony at Annapolis, principal speaker Sen. John T. Morgan of Alabama identified himself as a strong advocate of a defensive Navy. On behalf of the Board of Visitors, and in the company of Garfield and Hunt, he spoke of the importance of protecting the nation's maritime interests. As a former Confederate brigadier general, with interests similar to Rep. Whitthorne's, he dedicated himself to Southern economic expansion and independence from northern industry.[14] An unlikely bedfellow of Secretary Blaine, Morgan saw the potential that seaborne commerce could bring to his state in particular and to the South in general, reducing its subservient position in relation to the domination of the North. International shipping would greatly aid the recovery of the South's devastated agriculture industry. Also, the South's river system provided environmentally sound ports for iron ships, which were subject to significant hull corrosion in saltwater harbors. Supporting Blaine and his developing worldview, Morgan unceasingly promoted U.S. involvement in Latin America and the construction of a canal to join the Atlantic and Pacific Oceans. In his Naval Academy oration for public consumption, the powerful Southern politician emphatically declared: "I insist upon the necessity of the Government to build more ships to protect our commerce."[15]

A few weeks after the Academy event, Hunt announced the formation of a special Navy officer board of presumed experts to determine the needs of the Navy. Answering the growing body of politicians advocating commercial maritime expansion and protection, he and the president would use the findings to develop their annual recommendations to Congress.[16] To head his Naval Advisory Board, Hunt chose sixty-eight-year-old Rear Adm. John Rodgers, then the head of the naval observatory and a seasoned veteran of the Civil War and various Pacific and Atlantic Ocean commands. In his previous office as Court of Claims judge in Washington, Hunt's circle of high-society friends had included Rodgers as well as other senior Navy officers. Upon accepting his selection as Secretary of the Navy, he turned to them for advice both in filling important command positions and in the assignments of officers in general.

The fifteen-officer board, created in June 1881, appeared balanced, with nine line officers, three naval constructors, and three naval engineers.[17] Since its inception, the U.S. Navy classified its officers as being either in the line or staff. The term "line officer" had British origins denoting regular navy officers in command of battle-line ships. Staff corps officers performed technical functions in an advisory capacity both at sea and ashore, but were not eligible to command a ship of the battle line. In the U.S. Navy organization, line officers were the fighting officers in charge of warships. Staff corps officers were non-fighting specialists. Over the years, line and staff officers had developed a long-standing and serious rivalry for voice and control in naval matters.

Hunt charged his advisory board of line officer "sea dogs" and experienced staff officer technicians to present a plan for nothing less than the future direction of the Navy. As a Navy Department body of military officers, this special board appeared free of congressional attachments. Although Congress had the responsibility to determine the level of appropriations for any recommended warship construction, it would not participate in the internal proceedings of Hunt's board. Rather, this non-statutory body of Navy officers would act as an instrument solely for the Secretary of the Navy in determining his recommendations to the president and the legislature. In preparing their report, Hunt's experts would not give testimony in congressional hearings prior to drawing their own conclusions. Congress would receive only the consensus forwarded by the Secretary of the Navy.

ASSASSINATION AND DISRUPTIONS

On July 2, 1881, a few days after Secretary Hunt announced the formation of his board to report on the needs of the Navy, disgruntled office seeker Charles Guiteau shot President Garfield. Guiteau, a disorientated and unrequited supporter of President Ulysses S. Grant, was a truly unstable man with delusions of grandeur and a litany of failures. He believed that killing the president would somehow elevate him to a hero's status and earn him a place as a foreign ambassador of soon-to-be-president Arthur, a member of Grant's coterie of Stalwarts. The assassination tragedy played out for eighty days until Garfield died in September, while the mentally unbalanced Guiteau awaited his fate in prison. He would be found guilty of murder and executed in June 1882.

On the day of the shooting, Vice President Arthur was busy in New York State with his Stalwart cohorts, who were attempting to control the appointments of U.S. Senate seats. At this point in his career, Arthur appeared to be nothing more than a political hack who had never been elected to public office and had ridden on the coattails of his political bosses. His nomination as vice president was due to his affiliations and labors in the New York State spoils system, rather than to his role in national politics. Arthur was a first-generation Irish Protestant. In step with his Baptist minister father, he embraced the cause of abolition. He became a New York lawyer and successfully entered the world of patronage politics. His Civil War service as a brigadier general consisted of a year and a half of militia work with the New York State construction corps. While making a good income as a lawyer handling war claims, he became a privileged associate of political boss Sen. Roscoe Conkling and received a federal appointment to the very lucrative and patronage-laden position of New York City customs collector. The influential and dapper Arthur ran the customs house from 1871 to 1878 before being removed by President Hayes in response to supposedly serious patronage excesses. With no formal indictments or specific accusations against him, Arthur returned to his law practice and remained in Conkling's entourage. But misfortune struck in January 1880 when his beloved wife died at the age of forty-two. He grieved her death for the remaining six years of his own life.

Five months after his loss, he led the New York City delegation supporting a third term for General Grant at the unruly Republican convention of the summer of 1880, where he found himself a player in the struggles for power. Once Garfield won the nomination for president, the majority of delegates focused on New York for a vice presidential candidate who could help carry that vital state in November. Rising from his recent customs house embarrassment and defeat, a rejuvenated Arthur received reluctant support from Conkling and gathered the unanimous vote of his state's delegation to win the nomination.[18] Over the next few months, he campaigned separately from Garfield, who accepted Arthur's nomination but never embraced him as a friend or confidant. True to expectations, the two carried the important swing vote of New York State and won the general election.

The widower vice president did not maintain a residence in Washington, D.C. Rather, he temporarily lodged in the capital with political colleagues and kept his home in New York City, where he spent the majority of his time with his old friends and children. He appeared truly devastated by the assassination attempt. Upon receiving a telegram from Secretary Hunt and Postmaster Thomas James indicating that Garfield was indeed close to death, Arthur traveled back to the Washington apartment of Sen. John P. Jones, a fellow

Stalwart Republican from Nevada. Once in the capital, Arthur did not undertake any national business. After a week and half he considered the optimistic reports from the president's doctors that Garfield had a good chance of recovering from his wounds and decided to return to his home in New York City. Several weeks later, he received the news that Garfield had died in Elberon, a coastal town in New Jersey. The president had been taken to the sea coast to recover and avoid the summer heat of Washington. As the inevitable ranks of reporters waited outside his house on Lexington Avenue, a grave Arthur took his presidential oath of office at 2:15 a.m. on September 20, 1881. New York State Supreme Court Judge John R. Brady officiated.[19]

After the exhausting labors in New Jersey and Washington overseeing the myriad and emotional details of Garfield's funeral, Arthur gathered himself to conduct the business of his office and asked his cabinet members to stay on at least until Congress convened in December. In spite of his appeal, two members resigned within a month and two more were gone by the time Congress got down to business. However Hunt, with the lesser portfolio of the Navy and with his wife's sympathetic connections to Arthur, remained on the staff until the following spring. Cabinet turnover, combined with the immediate crush of the latest bevy of office seekers, left the overwhelmed president little time for the affairs of state. Essentially on its own, Hunt's advisory board delivered its report just a few months after enduring the scorn of the British, who sarcastically portrayed the U.S. Navy as consisting of "three mud-scows" and an old "canal-boat."[20] The majority of the board, led by Hunt's friend Rear Admiral Rodgers and conservative line officers, contemplated building a fleet composed of unarmored cruisers, rams, and Civil War–category coastal gunboats. Specifically, it recommended a long-term construction program of approximately $29.9 million for eighteen steel cruisers, twenty-four wooden cruisers, five steel rams, and twenty-five torpedo boats.[21] The mission of the various warships centered on traditional coastal defense and destroying enemy shipping and did not include engaging armored enemy warships on the high seas or close to foreign lands.

In late November, Hunt included the findings of his advisory board as part of the Secretary of the Navy's annual report forwarded to the House of Representatives. As a result of the advice offered by his Navy officer team, Hunt recommended to the new president an aggressive warship-building program to raise the Navy's low state. He ranked the U.S. Navy as no better than twelfth in the world, below China, Chile, and Denmark. Hunt wrote: "The condition of the Navy demands the prompt and earnest attention of Congress."[22] He explained that he had created the special advisory board in order to have one voice and that its recommendation for the eventual construction of seventy-two vessels of various sizes would bring the Navy to a satisfactory level over time. Hunt did not ask for a specific number or type to be immediately authorized. Rather, he left it for the legislature to consider how to spread out appropriations over the course of the next several years to create this new Navy.

In his own message to the opening session of Congress in December, Arthur called attention to the Navy report. Emphasizing the necessity to put the sea service on a footing adequate to meet the needs of the United States, he wrote: "I cannot too strongly urge upon you my conviction that every consideration of national safety, economy, and honor imperatively demands a thorough rehabilitation of the Navy."[23] In the initial stage of forming its annual naval appropriations bill, the House of Representatives duly examined the Secretary of the Navy's report in response to the president's plea. Deciding that the naval situation did require some movement, congressmen did not relinquish their role and took the lead in determining the extent of action required. After reviewing the majority report of the naval board forwarded by the Secretary of the Navy, congressmen challenged the recommendations and sought additional data.

In dissent to the Navy's majority recommendations, the board's staff officer minority, headed by aged Chief Naval Constructor John Lenthall, had presented an alternative view that called for a different fleet, which included large ocean-going ironclads of the European "first rate" category that could face the major navies of the world as equals. The disagreement between factions of the Navy board was part of emerging debates in both congressional and Navy circles as to whether the United States should enter into competition to become a full-grown maritime power or whether it should remain in isolation and continue to focus on coastal defense and *guerre de course* commerce raiding. Not surprisingly, congressmen insisted on reviewing the entire proceedings of the Navy board, rather than simply accepting the specific recommendations of either its majority or minority.

Before Congress had an opportunity to begin digesting, much less acting on, the Navy's report, President Arthur had already put into motion a plan to become directly engaged in negotiations involving war between Peru, Bolivia, and Chile. Prior to his departure from the cabinet in mid-December, Blaine had persuaded the new president to send diplomats and a warship to engage in the peace settlement process between Peru and Chile. The dispute focused mainly on the very valuable guano and nitrate deposits in the coastal territory bordering the two countries. The war had begun in 1879 and Bolivia was rapidly pushed aside, losing its entire coastline and causing it to become permanently landlocked. Showing concern about international business and Chile's belligerency, Arthur acted on Blaine's advice by choosing to support the vanquished Peru. Perhaps the United States could then become part of the negotiations to legitimize Peru's postwar government and ameliorate Peru's forced compensations of money and land.

Blaine had sent William Trescot to South America to act as a special envoy and minister to Bolivia, Peru, and Chile. Trescot, an experienced negotiator and acting secretary of state under President James Buchanan prior to the Civil War, was accompanied by Walker Blaine, who was third assistant secretary of state and also James Blaine's son. The two U.S. representatives carried instructions from Secretary Blaine to take a hard line against Chile should its government continue to hold Peruvian territory. At the time, the State Department avoided expensive telegraph communications with its diplomats in favor of slow seaborne mail service, which generally took a few weeks of one-way travel. As Trescot and his party traveled by sea to Panama, crossed the land bridge to the Pacific Ocean, and steamed to Peru, Blaine left office and was replaced by Frederick F. Frelinghuysen. Shortly thereafter President Arthur became aware of various business intrigues surrounding the U.S. support of Peru and took a more judicious path. He recalled the mission just as Trescot was meeting with Chilean authorities to further Blaine's agenda. The timing of the recall soured already stressed relations with Chile and, more importantly, highlighted the impotency of the U.S. Navy as the Forty-seventh Congress buckled down to its own business.

In reality, the U.S. Pacific squadron under the command of Rear Adm. George Balch was too weak to even consider confronting the modern battleships of Chile.[24] His flagship, the *Pensacola*, a wooden, 130-foot-long sailing steamer launched in 1859, presented a broadside of only one 11-inch and eight 9-inch Dahlgren smooth-bore cannon. By comparison, Chile had two armored battleships built in England and armed with powerful turret guns that had already wiped out the Peruvian navy. Supposedly the Chileans brashly threatened to send Balch's ship "to the bottom" if he tried to interfere with the progress of their war and negotiations.[25] This discomfiting incident forced both President Arthur and Congress to recognize that their warships could not protect U.S. interests abroad, even against the fleets of small South American nations.

Newly installed Secretary of State Frelinghuysen was a conservative politician and diplomat who initially did not follow Blaine's vision of U.S. international involvement. Coming from a well-connected New Jersey family, he placed himself in the midst of Stalwart politics as state attorney general during the Civil War and as a U.S. senator from 1866 to 1869 and from 1871 to 1877. His primary interest had been in strict Southern reconstruction, but as secretary of state he recognized the nexus of U.S. economic success with commercial expansion abroad. Once on the job, he moved closer to Blaine's international views as he attempted to fashion complex tariff reciprocity agreements with selected Latin American countries and with Spain. Also, he tried to involve the United States in construction of a Nicaraguan canal, in trade concessions with Hawaii, and in European commercial efforts in the newly established Congo Free State. But he could not convince Congress to approve any of his efforts, and in his three years with the State Department did not push for naval development as a requisite for global involvement.[26] Frelinghuysen died less than two months after leaving office in 1885.

Facing no clear national mandate for Navy development in spite of affairs in Peru and Chile, the Forty-seventh Congress convened its regular long session during the winter and spring of 1882. When it met, it took charge of the naval recommendations presented by Arthur and Hunt. As the House of Representatives began considering the needs of the Navy, it demanded access to all of the Navy board's records of arguments and conclusions. A few members of Congress in opposition argued in favor of Hunt's prerogative to submit only a Navy Department consensus. Supporting Hunt, Illinois Republican John R. Thomas contended that Congress had "no right to inquire what this clerk or that clerk" in the Navy Department "may have said," since the secretary had organized the advisory board for his own use. Thomas knew that the majority report was authored by line officers, and that the minority consisted of senior naval constructors and engineers. On the floor of Congress, he rather romantically put his faith in the officers who "command the ships," rather than side with staff officers living and working comfortably ashore. But Representative Thomas was only one of the few members of his naval committee who articulated this opinion. The others asserted that Congress had "not only the right but the duty" to ask for the fullest information.[27] Concurring with its naval committee, a majority of the House of Representatives required the Secretary of the Navy to submit the advisory board's minority findings. Congress, not the Navy Department, then weighed the available data.

Hunt did not have strong political backers for his proposed shipbuilding program and failed to get a consensus for congressional funding.[28] In April, while Congress remained undecided on the substance of the annual naval bill, President Arthur decided to reassign Hunt to the position of minister to Russia. At the time of his departure, Congress was engaged in economic regulatory issues, particularly the use of tariffs for protection and revenue, and would not enact naval appropriations legislation until August. Hunt sailed to Europe in May and no longer participated in Navy Department deliberations. He remained overseas until his death less than two years later. The U.S. government arranged the return of his body to the United States where he was eulogized by his successor in the Navy Department and interred in Oak Hill Cemetery, Washington, D.C.

3

POLITICS VERSUS PROGRESS, 1882–83

William Chandler, a wily politician, lobbyist, and highly successful lawyer, succeeded Hunt as President Arthur's choice for the Navy. Chandler, not Hunt, would preside over the department during the legislative sessions that eventually led to new naval construction. Raised in New Hampshire in a family with roots extending to the Massachusetts Puritans of the 1630s, he completed his law degree at Harvard and began his lifelong and lucrative parallel careers as a prosperous lawyer and an active politician. While a member of the New Hampshire state legislature, he provided Republican Party leadership in the first presidential campaign of Abraham Lincoln and then chose not to join the military during the Civil War. In the fall of 1864, Chandler came to work for the government in Washington as a litigator for Secretary of the Navy Gideon Welles, to prosecute thievery suspects in the Philadelphia Navy Yard.[1] The following spring, just prior to the assassination of Lincoln, Chandler accepted the position of solicitor and judge advocate general of the Navy Department. A few months later, he became first assistant secretary of the treasury under President Andrew Johnson and remained active in the controversial president's cabinet for more than two years until November 1867.

Chandler divided his time between his thriving Washington law practice of highly influential clients, his cabinet duties, and as a newspaper publisher in New Hampshire. His well-connected political activity included sixteen years as a leader of the Republican National Committee. Immediately follow-ing the presidential elections of 1876, his legal machinations in the state of Florida contributed significantly to the highly contested victory of Repub-lican President Hayes over Democrat contender Samuel J. Tilden. Thereafter, Democrats rightfully considered Chandler to be one of the major collabora-tors responsible for stealing the election from Tilden.[2] Continuing his political work as a flourishing, self-serving figure in the Capitol, Chandler labored for the candidacy of Blaine and then Garfield. His activity earned him President Garfield's nomination for U.S. solicitor general, an appointment rejected by a Senate wary of his lobbying activities and associates. A year later under a new presidential administration, the same Senate approved Chandler for the lesser portfolio of Secretary of the Navy.

As he took office in the early spring of 1882, a minority of fiscally con-servative New England Republicans, led by Sen. Henry Anthony of Rhode Island and Rep. James Briggs of New Hampshire, proposed significant busi-ness changes in the makeup of the Navy Department management.[3] These legislators focused on the Navy's bureaucracy, finding fault in the organization where the eight military bureau chiefs acted independently of each other. However, the majority in Congress disagreed. Concerned with their access to Navy administration, they preferred to maintain the status quo. In a mood similar to that of his New England associates, House of Representatives naval committee chairman Benjamin Harris of Massachusetts also complained of gross inefficiencies caused by Navy bureaucracy and pointedly declared the Navy unable to give unified advice on its own future needs. But he did not suggest congressional reorganization of the eight-bureau system or the cre-ation of a centralized general staff of military officers. Instead, Harris insisted on an internal effectiveness review to correct business deficiencies in Navy management and focused on expanding forces afloat by introducing legisla-tion to "increase the construction of vessels of war."[4]

In spite of the support from these leading members of Congress both the proposals for efficiency and for increases languished in committee. In the first case, the sponsors of the legislation to consolidate the Navy Department's bureaus hoped to reduce the several lines of responsibilities. But the majority in Congress disagreed with the sponsors. A centralized staff organization would result in the legislative branch losing direct attachment to the eight bureau chiefs, and the associated patronage. In the second case, with no discernible groundswell in his favor, Harris could not get his naval increase proposal on the floor for a vote.

In his new office, Chandler was cognizant of the patronage involving senior Navy officers' chain of command. With an unabated spoils system in place, congressmen and others in and out of public office besieged him with behests for appointments and assignments.[5] At the same time that Chandler broadened his understanding of the uniqueness of the Navy, he complied with these solicitations whenever he saw fit while keeping his own counsel. One of the more contentious applications of Navy benefaction involved Chandler's attempt to control officer assignments. As an ambitious politician and experienced lobbyist, he fixated on sponsorship connections and focused on Navy officer transfers as being especially important.

Chandler received affable encouragement from Rep. Charles Boutelle of Maine, who was equally concerned with the narrow patronage domain of Navy officer duty assignments, known as "detailing." A freshman congressman at the time, Boutelle later rose to considerable power over the next eighteen years as a leader of naval affairs and three-time chairman of the naval committee in the 1890s. Chandler and Boutelle shared political oversight of the Portsmouth-Kittery Navy Yard co-located in their states of New Hampshire and Maine. Boutelle, a former shipmaster and volunteer Navy officer during the Civil War, emphasized the political importance of firm control of officer assignments. Soon after Chandler took office, Boutelle entreated him to make "Officer Detail" part of the personal duties of the Secretary of the Navy.[6] Chandler was already in agreement with Boutelle's vision and took action accordingly.

The Navy officer in charge of detailing, Capt. John Grimes Walker, chief of the Bureau of Navigation, opposed Chandler for control of officer assignments. Walker had only recently been appointed to his position by Hunt and acted with a degree of independence in generating officer transfer decisions. Walker and the considerably older Rear Admiral Rodgers were active in Hunt's social circle as members of the prestigious Metropolitan Club. When he became Secretary of the Navy, Hunt had elevated Walker to the position of bureau chief and selected Rodgers to head the Navy's special advisory board. Sixty-nine-year-old Rodgers died in the spring of 1882 and shortly thereafter Hunt departed Washington for St. Petersburg, to begin his new political assignment as minister to Russia. Now their forty-six-year-old protégé held one of the top positions in Navy administration.

Walker could hold off some of the whims of Chandler's petty politics because of his own very considerable political clout. Walker had been raised by his uncle, James Wilson Grimes, an early Whig and Republican leader in the territory of Iowa who became its third governor and then U.S. senator. During Walker's Navy career, which included several years at sea in western Pacific and southern Atlantic waters as well as naval combat duty during the Civil War, he earned the respect and support of the well-known admiral David D. Porter, who became another of his sponsors. But as much as he enjoyed high-level Navy support, Walker derived his most effective power from his personal connections in Congress.

His elders included long-term friends James "Don" Cameron of Pennsylvania, chairman of the Senate naval committee, and William Allison of Iowa, chairman of the Senate Committee on Appropriations. Allison had married Walker's adopted sister in 1873.[7] Of the forty-five states represented in Congress at the time only six had more representatives and electoral votes than Iowa and only New York had more votes than Pennsylvania. After Walker's illustrious Navy career, he remained in government service as president of the Walker Commission of the late 1890s, where he examined possible routes for a canal across Central America. In 1904 he chaired the Isthmian Canal Commission, which supervised construction of the Panama Canal.

With his term as President Johnson's solicitor of the Navy Department seventeen years in the past, Secretary Chandler did not have a grip on the intricacies of day-to-day Navy management. But he did have considerable experience in Navy contract lobbying and legal work. Almost immediately upon taking office, he expressed his dissatisfaction with the existing bureau system and agreed with the minority of congressmen who saw a need to radically restructure the Navy organization. The secretary recognized his own bureaus as being partially responsible for unnecessary contracts and employment in the maintenance of old ships that had little military value.

Reinforcing his opinion, Henry Gorringe, an experienced mid-grade Navy officer on a leave of absence, composed a scathing assessment of the Navy bureaus as being subject to the logrolling influences of the worst type of politician.[8] He wrote in the prominent and widely read *North American Review* that millions of dollars each year were wasted by the duplicated bureau organizations, which seemed to work at cross-purposes to each other. Arguing that the bureau system was "beyond the reach and out of the influence" of the most competent officers of the Navy, he called for a permanent military advisory board of experienced seagoing officers appointed by the president to oversee the eight bureaus and directly serve the Secretary of the Navy.

Although Chandler showed little curiosity for naval warfare, he agreed with Gorringe that the Navy bureaus needed a coherent chain of command that answered to the civilian Secretary of the Navy rather than being bound by congressional patronage. Chandler sought further justification from his friend, mentor, and long-time client, Pennsylvania shipbuilder John Roach, who also strongly criticized the Navy hierarchy for its lack of centrality. Roach wrote to Chandler expressing his obvious preference to transact business directly with the secretary, rather than to operate separately through three or four military bureau chiefs associated with the various construction endeavors of his maritime construction company. He also echoed the findings of the Rodgers board submitted six months previously, and recommended constructing fast cruisers to protect commerce rather than capital ships to engage distant fleets.[9]

TOO MANY OFFICERS

Meanwhile Chandler used his cabinet position as best he could to accommodate requests from influential politicians of his party. He purposely elected to work within the prevailing spoils system while attempting to deal with his bloated officer corps. The sheer number of officers presented a problem. Congress had retained a relatively high number of Navy officers after the Civil War, in a situation somewhat different from that of the Army. During the war, the vast majority of U.S. Army officers were temporary volunteers who gladly accepted release back to civilian life at the end of the conflict. Although the population of the Navy was smaller than the Army, naval officers by necessity had to possess ship-handling skills, which entailed lengthy at-sea apprenticeships. As a result the Navy had proportionally more regular officers who retained their commissions after the fighting stopped. Congress permanently commissioned regular officers of both services and only Congress could reduce the force of regular officers through legislative action accompanied by some level of compensation or pension.

By 1882 many naval officers were on long-term leave or in a "without orders" status as the inflated officer corps only gradually aged out of service. Meanwhile, congressmen could not reach a consensus on Navy promotion or retirement ground rules to ease the overmanning problem. The options generally involved involuntary separations, which would lead to increasing the retirement list and payouts. Stand-alone Senate and House of Representatives proposals to curtail officer strength by reducing the promotion of Naval Academy graduates died in committee. The unsuccessful sponsors were Sen. George Vest of Missouri, who had served in the Congress of the Confederate States of America, and Rep. Alexander Stephens (D-GA), who had been vice president of the Confederacy.[10] These and other high-ranking members of the former rebelling states had by now received congressional pardons in accordance with the Fourteenth Amendment and were back in power.

Southern congressmen, especially Civil War veterans and former Confederate government officials, were particularly unsympathetic to Navy officer early retirement proposals. For the past decades, disability and pension payments for Northern veterans had increased exponentially. Confederate veterans were, of course, not included and they depended on the very limited largesse of their home states, which paid a tenth of the money granted to U.S. veterans and their families. After considerable deliberation, instead of acting on separate resolutions the Congress of 1882 decided to attach a Navy officer reduction clause to the annual naval appropriations bill. The House of Representatives, led by its appropriations committee, took this action rather than open a new debate with the Senate as a separate resolution. Primarily for financial considerations, congressmen agreed that the expense of bringing in new officers to a Navy without ships was unwarranted.[11]

In its August 1882 legislation, Congress set an arbitrary limit on the number of line officers and steam engineers in service. It reduced Navy line officer promotions to 1 for every 2 vacancies and established a baseline of 170 steam engineers with no further appointments of cadet engineers until that number was reached by attrition and retirement.[12] Yet even with that action, over the next decade and a half the line officer corps remained at a level where officers were unable to serve sufficient time at sea to meet the congressional requirement for promotion. Too many men, not enough ships! By slowing down accessions of new officers rather than increasing the retirement of older officers, Congress put off for another day decisions that could swell the pension rolls. Navy officers lobbied Congress without success against the reductions.[13]

In spite of the work of Hunt's advisory board and the subsequent inducements of Chandler, the Forty-seventh Congress adjourned its first session without directing the future path of the Navy or altering its military management. The Naval Appropriations Act of August 1882 merely approved but did not fund construction of "two steam cruising vessels of war" to be built of steel.[14] Production could take place only in the unlikely event that the Navy managed to divert money from existing obligations. This did not occur. To oversee future construction, Congress also directed the Navy Department to establish a second naval advisory board of both Navy officers and civilian experts. This new statutory board would examine the plans and specifications for ships recommended by Secretary Hunt's now-defunct ad hoc Navy officer board and recommend future legislative action.

Chandler chose Commo. Robert Shufeldt, an experienced line officer and diplomat, to head the congressionally mandated seven-member advisory group. Shufeldt had a solid seagoing background with typical long deployments to the West Indies, Brazil, the Mediterranean, and Africa prior to the Civil War. His wartime service included a hazardous diplomatic mission to Mexico followed by command of ships on blockade duty. After the war, he served on diplomatic missions to Nicaragua, Liberia, and Asia.[15] In March 1881, as part of his newly displayed worldwide focus, Secretary of State Blaine had sent Shufeldt to Asia as a naval attaché to open trade to U.S. interests. After successfully negotiating the first treaty between Korea and western nations, he returned home in late July 1882, eight months after Blaine left Arthur's cabinet.[16]

Back in the states, Chandler appointed Shufeldt to lead the Navy's new advisory board as a favor to Republican Stalwarts who supported Shufeldt's record of seamanship and diplomacy.[17] Although Shufeldt had a solid understanding of international politics, he was not closely apprised of the intricacies of steel shipbuilding or a yet-to-be-defined U.S. naval strategy.[18] Two relatively junior line officers, one chief engineer, one naval constructor, and two civilians completed the makeup of the new seven-member panel.[19] Lt. Edward Very, the line officer recording secretary, was the only member who had served on the previous board organized by Secretary Hunt. Even considering Shufeldt's diplomatic and seagoing experience, the board members were functionaries selected by Chandler rather than visionaries. Mandated by Congress, they were now in a position to supersede the advice of experienced officers serving as bureau chiefs who, not surprisingly disagreed with Shufeldt's plans and "took to quarrelling over the details."[20]

BUSINESS

In addition to its directions concerning future shipbuilding, the legislature also decided to require the Navy to investigate its own business practices. A provision in the appropriations act directed the Navy to establish a commission of a line officer, a staff officer, and a civilian to examine shipyard utilization under the Bureau of Yards and Docks. Congress charged this working group to report on the advisability of closing and selling any Navy yards.[21] Chandler selected the highly regarded Commo. Stephen B. Luce to lead the survey. Luce's investigative team consisted of Navy Chief Engineer Charles Loring and civilian A. B. Mullett. Loring was an experienced staff officer who was soon to begin a four-year tenure as chief of the bureau of steam engineering. Mullett was a political appointee, not associated with the Navy, who previously was the supervising architect of the construction of the Treasury Department building.[22] The shipyard commission had barely begun its survey when the legislature concluded its final session of December 1882 to March 1883. The results of Luce's Navy yard study would necessarily be carried over to the next Congress.

While putting off ship construction and Navy reorganization in its 1882 legislation, Congress reinstated the civilian position of Assistant Secretary of the Navy, adding to its civilian bureaucracy.[23] The legislature had originally established this office in early 1861 because of the exigencies of the Civil War. At the time, the Navy department's wartime work had become too big and complex to be managed by a single civilian head. For the job of assistant secretary, President Lincoln had selected former naval officer Gustavus Fox. With almost two decades of experience in the Navy and in maritime service, Fox brought considerable professionalism to the beleaguered office of Secretary of the Navy Welles. During the war, Fox facilitated the buildup of naval forces and centralized military control in the Navy Department under his personal administration. Although he was a civilian, he acted as a chief of staff of Navy operations. After the war, as the nation demilitarized, Congress decided that a civilian assistant secretary was superfluous and discontinued the position. Navy management then returned to its oligarchy of eight bureau chiefs.

In August 1882, while the maritime force was still in considerable decline, the legislature chose to expand the Navy Department's civilian bureaucracy instead of building ships. A minority preferred to formally establish a military rather than civilian hierarchy, to give Navy administrative responsibility to a single officer answering directly to the secretary. But the majority in Congress decided to return a civilian to the president's cabinet and retain the eight-bureau system of management. With a few months of on-the-job experience, Chandler did not support this reestablishment of the assistant position. Rather he expressed his apprehension that experienced military officers would gain power by controlling a novice civilian.

As the year progressed, Chandler claimed that he was unable to select a suitable individual to fill the position of a civilian assistant. On behalf of the president, he rationalized that the compensation of $3,500 per year was too low to attract a qualified person.[24] At the time the secretary received an annual salary of $8,000. Chandler disingenuously wrote that his department needed an assistant secretary, but a suitable candidate could not be found. Considering Chandler's attraction to patronage this was hardly a credible explanation. With no new ship construction under way, he further stated that the public interest would be best served by appointing not one but two additional civilians to the Navy Department. Accordingly, Chandler claimed that he wanted both an assistant secretary and a solicitor with high salaries in order to draw "from the ablest men in civil life."[25] He had been the Navy's first solicitor and judge advocate general at the end of the Civil War and now wanted to revive that post along with a highly paid assistant. Congress disagreed. With the position of assistant secretary unfilled, at the end of its lame-duck session of March 1883 the Forty-seventh Congress repealed its previous authorization.[26] Succeeding Congresses left the provision for a civilian assistant secretary out of their appropriation acts for the remainder of the 1880s.

Although Congress had authorized funds for increasing the civilian bureaucracy of the Navy Department, it persistently opposed increasing the military staff of the Navy. Some members even questioned the need for any Navy officer to serve in a shore-duty position.[27] In its appropriation acts of August 1882 and March 1883, it forbade shore duty for Navy officers except as provided by law or specially requested as being in the public interest by the Secretary of the Navy.[28] Congress' attempt to keep Navy line officers out of Washington was connected to restraining the power of the executive branch. Ships far away at sea had little local political influence, but a centralized Navy staff ashore had the potential to take on a life of its own and become independent of congressional benefaction.

Chandler's first annual report sent to Congress in December 1882 forwarded the details advocated by Commodore Shufeldt's advisory board to increase the size of the Navy. The document contained proposals involving ship speed, range, armor, and weapon standards, which had foreign policy implications beyond the use of technology. Chandler began his official statement by complaining about the well-known lack of ships in the Navy. He listed a total of only thirty-seven cruising vessels fit for service, with one first-rate, fourteen second-rates, and twenty-two third-rates. Of this meager total, thirty-three were wooden and only four of the smaller third rates had iron hulls. This was a poor Navy indeed. After eight months in office, Chandler appeared to be a committed advocate for an increase in the Navy. Choosing plain and deliberate language in his official report, he sarcastically wrote: "If the Naval establishment is not to be made effective, it should be discontinued, and the fifteen millions annually expended should be reserved to procure, in national emergencies, the assistance of foreign ships and guns."[29]

As an alternative to his mordant proposal, Chandler specifically recommended constructing the two authorized but unfunded steel cruisers and two of the ten second-rates previously recommended by Secretary Hunt.[30] The choice of unarmored cruisers reflected the continuation of senior line officer conservatism now led by Shufeldt. Those officers focused on destroying commerce and protecting U.S. coasts rather than on constructing fast, offensive, armored warships that could be used close to foreign shores anywhere in the world. The Shufeldt board also recommended completing five coastal monitors that had been lying incomplete in the "ways" for the past few years and were not part of Hunt's long-term program. Monitors were inshore vessels armed with turret guns, and functioned as movable shore batteries.

In March 1883, the outgoing legislature finally took action to construct new warships. The new Navy therefore marks its beginning with the lame-duck session of the Forty-seventh Congress providing $1.3 million to build one 4,300-ton steel cruiser, two 3,000-ton steel cruisers, and one 1,500-ton steel patrol gunboat.[31] In its first session, the legislature had approved but not funded one large 6,000-ton ship and one medium 4,300-ton ship. The funded resolution several months later whittled down Chandler's request for four cruisers (including the two previous authorized but unfunded ships) to three smaller cruisers and a gunboat. The choice to forego the larger ship was consistent with recently promoted Rear Admiral Shufeldt's focus on smaller commerce raiders. The legislature did not lay out a plan for future developments.

Carrying out the specific language of the Naval Act of 1883, Chandler "invited proposals" from American shipbuilders and specified the bidding procedures for the four ships. The Navy did not have its own steel shipbuilding capability. Accordingly, Shufeldt's board of confreres prepared the specifications and accepted civilian bids. Chandler's friend, Pennsylvania shipbuilder John Roach, bid on all four ships and was the lowest bidder on all four. Several builders had bid on one or more of the ships, while only one of them other than Roach bid on all four. Some of the high-bid losers expressed outrage that Roach would get all of the contracts, but overall the process itself complied with the existing bidding system. In fact, Roach had an excellent shipbuilding record.[32] But, his selection in the summer of 1883 was anathema to congressional Democrats, who saw continued collusion that extended as far back as the Civil War between Roach, Chandler, and corrupt Stalwart Republicans.

Roach had arrived in New York in 1832 as a penniless sixteen-year-old Irish immigrant. With little education and few skills, he learned the shipbuilding trade from the bottom up, working his way through several associated trades to establish his own factory. During the Civil War he prospered by manufacturing machinery and building ships, which included significant work for the Navy under the direction of Chief Engineer Benjamin Isherwood (who more recently had served on Hunt's advisory board). After the war when the Navy no longer needed ships, Roach kept his successful operations viable by shifting to toolmaking and civilian shipbuilding.

In 1868 he hired Chandler for legal services and lobbying to get "contracts, favors, and subsidies," and they became close friends. As part of the process of political machinations surrounding government contracts, Roach became a generous Republican Party donor and also established friendships with Hayes, Garfield, Conkling, and Blaine, among others.[33] However, his alleged connections with corrupt transactions under Secretary of the Navy George Robeson during the Grant administration put Roach at serious odds with the Democratic Party, and now their worst fears came to fruition. Nevertheless, he continued his loyalty to Chandler and proceeded on schedule with his contract for the so-called ABCD ships. Their official names were: *Atlanta*, *Boston*, *Chicago*, and *Dolphin*. The *Chicago* was the largest of the three cruisers and the *Dolphin* was the gunboat. All four vessels were "laid down" in Roach's yard by the end of the year 1883, as the new Congress convened.

With this relatively unheralded process, a closely divided legislature began to refurbish the Navy when Roach laid the keels for the three medium-sized, unarmored steel combatants and an auxiliary. The path ahead for Arthur and Chandler was neither clear nor without a considerable number of detractors. Any large-felt public spirit of navalism was certainly not evident in the fiduciary actions of the government. Navalism, in the sense of national Navy awareness and a desire to increase U.S. influence as a worldwide maritime power, may have been on the rise. But the majority of the politicians representing the people certainly did not open the purse strings. The incoming Forty-eighth Congress that met in December 1883 consisted of a Democratic-controlled House of Representatives and a Senate with only a thin Republican majority. Conditions were not conducive to visionary Navy advancement.

4

INCUBATION,
1883–85

The ship of the line *North Carolina* was a sight to behold as it stood magnificently in New York Harbor. Commissioned in Norfolk, Virginia, in 1824, it was one of the most preeminent and beautiful ships in the world. It simply exuded power and majesty in full sail with more than 80 cannon and 820 men. Drawing more than 21 feet of draft and measuring 200 feet long, it was mighty indeed. On its initial deployment, it served as the U.S. flagship in the Mediterranean for more than two years. In the 1830s it sailed around South America and cruised for two years in the Pacific, showing U.S. presence and protecting trade. In 1841 it was at home in New York.

That August, fourteen-year-old Midn. Stephen B. Luce entered the mystical and wondrous world of seafarers as he set foot on the *North Carolina*. When he crossed the quarterdeck of his first ship, he entered into a different and distant way of life uncommon to the average American. The young teenager shook the hand of Commo. Matthew C. Perry and reported to the captain of the ship, who passed him on to the midshipman of the watch, who led him to his new home below. One set of ladders after another led to the orlop deck, the lowest of the ship, where his guide assigned him a locker and showed him his billet: a steel hook where he would hang his hammock.[1]

For the next six months he literally learned the ropes and how the sails were furled, reefed, and set. He learned the duties of the men in the "tops" as well as those of the men who gave the orders. His new home in New York Harbor had no counterpart to his previous life ashore. His older shipmates had battled the seas, the British, and various pirates. Soon he would be one of them as he began his initiation into the realities of ship handling, ocean distances, solitude, different peoples, and strange places. Over the decades, he would rise to the rank of rear admiral and become a significant naval leader of the incubating new Navy while remaining relatively unknown to the public even in his own time. Sailors do their work far away and out of sight.

Luce's parents were descended from early American colonists. His father's line began with a passenger on the *Mayflower* and his mother's family emigrated from Holland in 1656 to become part of the Dutch settlement that later became the New York colony and state. Stephen was born in Albany, New York, in March 1827 and at the age of eight moved with his family to Washington, District of Columbia. Six years later he interviewed with President Martin Van Buren in the President's House to receive his appointment to the Navy. Stephen's father and family had known the president from their earlier days in Albany.[2]

Just prior to his fifteenth birthday, Luce boarded his second ship, the newly commissioned frigate *Congress,* for a two-and-a-half-year cruise throughout the Mediterranean Sea and various locations in the South Atlantic. The *Congress* carried 480 men and 48 cannon. Luce returned to Hampton Roads in the spring of 1845 and transferred to another sailing ship of the line, *Columbus,* outfitting in New York for a three-year cruise to China, Japan, and South America. Shortly after his next stateside return, Luce celebrated his twenty-first birthday, having spent the majority of the past six years at sea. After fourteen months of study at the newly established Naval Academy at Annapolis, Maryland, Passed Midshipman Luce returned to sea on board the 18-gun sloop of war *Vandalia*. His cramped quarters remained in the lowest deck of steerageway for his next three years of Asian and Pacific duty. On his return home at the age of twenty-five, he recorded in his journal that an English sailor had tattooed some figures on his arm.[3]

Luce finally had a short tour of shore duty followed by Home Squadron cruises in local waters and the Gulf of Mexico. In December 1855, he married his childhood sweetheart, Eliza Henley (grandniece of Martha Washington).

In spite of his years at sea, he obviously found some time to maintain a connection to life ashore. After his marriage and promotion to lieutenant, he returned to sea for three more years, moving up to officers' country on board the sloop of war *Jamestown*. The outbreak of the Civil War found thirty-four-year-old Lieutenant Luce instructing at the Naval Academy. During the war, he performed blockade duty, led the Naval Academy squadron on a show of force deployment to England, and later commanded ships in joint Army and Navy actions in the coastal waters of Georgia. His postwar career as a senior officer consisted of training and diplomatic assignments while in command of steam-sailing ships in the Pacific, Atlantic, and Mediterranean.

In the course of his many years at sea beginning with his midshipman training, he had become a scholar and a voracious reader of the classics. Typically, Navy officers of the time were quite well versed in Greek and Roman studies because they had the time and the books on board ship. In his maturity, Luce continued his intellectual pursuits as a forward-looking thinker contemplating the place of the U.S. Navy in the modern world. In November 1881, during Hunt's secretariat, Luce advanced to the rank of commodore while commanding the newly formed Naval Training Squadron on board the now hoary wooden sailing ship of the line *New Hampshire* in Newport, Rhode Island. His squadron represented the Navy's earliest attempt at systematic professional training of enlisted personnel, rather than depending on the rough-and-tumble system of apprenticeship training before the mast.

By now he was a leader and spokesman whose "progressive ideas" were inspiring a new generation of post–Civil War Navy officers.[4] In 1873 Luce had helped establish the U.S. Naval Institute, an unofficial professional organization of officers, and he would soon become the first president of the new U.S. Naval War College. An outspoken critic of the Navy bureaus, Luce agreed with Representative Whitthorne in 1878 that the Navy was improperly organized.[5] At the time, he gave his full support to a House resolution calling for a mixed commission to investigate the organization of the naval service. Later, he excoriated the self-serving bureau system for its lack of unified naval policy and progress, and called on Congress to regulate Navy Department administration because the existing system was simply incapable of efficient management.[6] Carrying out the congressional resolution of

August 1882, Secretary Chandler appointed Commodore Luce as a logical choice to lead the congressionally mandated investigation of shipyard business practices in relation to the Navy's bureaucratic structure.

After a year of investigation, his shipyard commission reported to the incoming Forty-eighth Congress in December 1883. Luce singled out the organization of separate bureaus as the root cause of gross improprieties in ship repair. In Navy yards each bureau maintained an independent establishment, each having its own head, officers, and foremen, whose chain of command led directly to its bureau chief in Washington. Shipyard workers were hired by the bureaus rather than by shipyard commanders. Luce wrote that this system fostered both patronage and debilitating duplication. Unlike civilian manufacturing of the period, which generally operated a plant with a single structure of authority, each Navy Department site inefficiently contained several plants with parallel hierarchies. Each industrial bureau was "constantly striving to do all its own work" and "had its own body of artisans, its own machinery, its own steam generators, and its own peculiar method of doing business."[7] According to Luce, nothing less than a complete overhaul of the bureau system would bring the Navy Department in line with sound business practices.

CONGRESS IN ACTION

But as part of its oversight, Congress persistently eschewed change in the Navy's organization. Instead it remained committed to the bureaus and their patronage-laden Navy yard operations. In spite of the Pendleton Civil Service Reform Act of early 1883, effective civil service reform for the Navy still lay in the future. While the legislative branch pondered fleet expansion, Luce determined the condition of each facility to decide whether it was advisable, in the interest of efficiency, to sell any plants or property. In effect closing Navy yards could divert future naval business to private industry. Legislators placed themselves in the middle of deliberations concerning the ramifications of using private contractors versus government facilities for ship construction, prior to approving any increases beyond the ABCD warships.

Luce's Navy yard study had in fact targeted several small yards for sale as being inefficient. With congressional approval, Chandler closed the Pensacola, League Island, and New London shipyards, diminishing the prospects for government shipbuilding and maintenance. As a result of the study the Navy

Department also reduced the operations at the Boston and Portsmouth yards, and decreased civilian overall employment by about one thousand workers. But over the next few years Congress reevaluated the Navy's position and provided appropriations to bring the affected yards back into the government system.[8] Not surprisingly the legislature straddled the issue, eventually settling on a division of Navy work between both government and civilian shipyards. This decision was a diffident compromise acceptable to the majority of northeastern Republican industrialists and Southern Democrats. Ultimately the congressional perturbations did not affect the Navy's eight-bureau organization.

Congressmen who had Navy yards in their districts felt it their right and duty to oversee and direct the Navy Department's personnel assignments for unnecessary repair of decrepit ships. These Gilded Age legislators had full expectations that they would get what they wanted. In spite of his complaints concerning organization, Chandler often forwarded congressional requests to his military bureau chiefs for action in their specific areas of interest. While not necessarily corrupt, those officers were certainly susceptible to patronage, since their bureaus depended on Congress for separate line-item appropriations to maintain their organizations. Also in the interest of patronage, congressmen sometimes bypassed the Secretary of the Navy altogether and dealt directly with the military bureau chiefs and their assistants. Navy officers in charge of business management and contracts simply could not ignore the interests of the legislature. Their own jobs depended on Congress, as the Senate gave its consent to all presidential appointees to Navy bureau chief positions.

When the Democratic House of Representatives of the Forty-eighth Congress met in its first session of December 1883 to July 1884, Chandler renewed his efforts to reorganize naval administration. Focusing on Commodore Luce's recent condemnation of the eight-bureau system, Chandler requested legislation to consolidate the Steam Engineering and the Equipment bureaus within the Construction and Repairs bureau.[9] His action would consolidate the three current manufacturing organizations under the single head of construction. This proposed reorganization of the bureaus sparked opposition within the Navy Department as well as within Congress. Chandler's plan would elevate a naval constructor staff officer to be in charge of both a steam engineer staff officer and the line officer who headed the equipment bureau. Almost immediately, leading line officers, steam engineers, and congressmen pleaded their cases supporting the various officer corps affected by the proposal.[10]

The legislature reacted by tabling any bureau consolidation plan. Chandler could not persuade Congress as a whole to examine changing the Navy's long-standing management system. Both parties in the House of Representatives spoke against his efficiency plans and favored the status quo hierarchies for Navy ship construction and repairs operations. The Senate likewise showed no interest in Chandler's consolidation scheme. Neither congressional body would consider reducing the number or the independence of the military bureau chiefs who had access to appropriations, contracts, and patronage.[11]

With the construction of the ABCDs barely underway, the actual growth of the Navy's fleet was nonexistent. Many of the old, useless ships on the register had officers and crews who found themselves to be without duties as their ships were progressively decommissioned and stricken from the record. As long as the officer corps remained top-heavy and overmanned for sea service on a dwindling number of ships, the legislature was in no mood to consider creating any new military positions ashore. Yet Captain Walker, as chief of the navigation bureau, needed additional officers to handle his increasing range of responsibilities. His bureau controlled the movement of those naval vessels capable of getting under way, issued all officer assignments, and ran the Hydrographic Office and Naval Observatory. Additionally, in 1882 he became responsible for the newly established Office of Naval Intelligence and in early 1884 Chandler added the Naval War College, with Commodore Luce as its first president. Walker temporarily filled his shore-duty manpower deficiencies with officers who were on long-term leaves of absence, awaiting orders to ships.

By using long-term temporary assignments, he managed on his own to bring the number of officers on staff duty in Washington, D.C., to more than 160 by the late 1880s, compared with only 15 in 1869.[12] Congress was not blind to the growth of positions ashore and continued to direct the Secretary of the Navy to justify the movement of officers. A growing number of congressmen endeavored to resolve the tension between the tasks of the executive and the recalcitrance of the legislature to establish new Navy positions. This minority of mostly progressive members of both houses of Congress sought expansion in Navy administration. But, unable to agree on structural changes in shore assignments, Congress acted by default, essentially turning a blind eye toward Walker's actions increasing shore-duty manning.

As part of his cabinet life, Chandler routinely received requests from other politicians expecting special treatment in the posting of a friend, relative, or associate, and passed these on to Walker's bureau for action. But to Chandler's chagrin, Walker did not readily give in to Chandler's caprices and, more often than not, made his own choices. Because officer assignments often involved the special interests of his patrons, Chandler tried various methods of pressuring Walker in order to get personal control of officer detailing. After a year and a half of dispute, in a move that Walker reported to his friend Senator Allison as being "typically vicious," Chandler created a Board of Detail under the direct dominion of the Secretary of the Navy.[13] The board members were the four line officer bureau chiefs, which included Walker. As one member of a board of four, Walker was now constrained to compromise with the other three members as well as with Chandler. The Board of Detail had a short life and was terminated when the cabinet of President Grover Cleveland took over in March 1885. Walker continued to serve as Navigation Bureau chief until he received his promotion to the rank of acting rear admiral in late 1889 and took command of the Navy's newest squadron. He and Chandler remained at serious odds throughout their years of association with each other.

Rep. Samuel S. Cox (D-NY) chaired the House of Representatives naval committee of the Forty-eighth Congress and vigorously opposed Navy progressives. He originally had served as a representative from Ohio in the 1860s and positioned himself as a small-government and small-Navy advocate. After the end of the war, he moved his law business to New York City and returned to Congress as a representative from New York State for the next twenty years.[14] Embellishing on his grandfather's friendship with Thomas Jefferson, Cox supported decentralized government and leniency for the South. As chair of the naval committee, he favored reducing the scope of the Navy's military organizations and argued against both creating additional officer positions and the pervasive creep in shore-duty assignments. Cox sponsored a resolution requiring the Navy to furnish "the names and number of the officers on shore-duty in Washington, with a memorandum of the service on which each was employed" and "certify in all orders for shore duty" that these were required in the public interest.[15] He insisted on carrying out the letter of the "no shore duty" provision passed by the previous Republican Congress.

The Democratic-controlled legislature also balked at approving the ship increases called for by Arthur and Chandler. In his last year in office, President Arthur had sent a special message to Congress in March 1884, asking for three steel cruisers and four gunboats.[16] But the legislature would not release the purse strings and continued to express caution concerning expenditures. In June perennial Republican candidate James Blaine defeated Arthur for the Republican presidential nomination. Shortly thereafter, the Democratic Party settled on newcomer Governor Grover Cleveland of New York as their nominee. Ending its session a month after the conventions, Congress could not reach a consensus on naval appropriations and simply passed a contingency budget to be resolved in its lame-duck session after the national elections.

GROVER CLEVELAND

Cleveland had a reputation for being an honest man. His ancestors were English indentured servants who arrived in the colonies in the mid-1600s and remained in New England, participating in various business ventures, with each generation having at least one minister. Grover's father, Richard, preached the Congregationalist tradition during the Second Great Awakening of the 1830s. Although Richard married a woman of means, his religious calling led him from place to place, with neither financial success nor a permanent homestead. Stephen Grover Cleveland, the fifth of nine children, was born in Caldwell, New Jersey and then lived in small towns in western New York State. After his father's death, seventeen-year-old Grover (who had dropped his first name) went to work in New York City as an assistant teacher in the New York Institute for the Blind. Enduring a year of hardscrabble subsistence, he decided to seek his fortune elsewhere and set out on an uncertain path, which led him to the legal profession while working for his maternal uncle in Buffalo.[17]

Cleveland much preferred law to the ministry and teaching. Under the tutelage of his uncle, he worked with steady deliberation in his career of choice. Within a few years he became self-sufficient and began to participate in the ward politics of the conservative unionist elements of the Democratic Party.

His older brothers both volunteered for duty during the Civil War while he stayed home to support his mother and two younger sisters. In 1863, while serving as assistant district attorney in Buffalo, he was drafted into the Army and in order to care for his family decided to hire a legal substitute. After the war he returned to a successful private law practice and reached a comfortable level of financial success.

Cleveland began his three-year meteoric rise to the presidency in October 1881 with his acceptance of his party's nomination to be mayor of the bustling and rowdy city of Buffalo. At the time, citizens clamored for change from the corrupt politicians who had the city locked up under their control. In the fifty-six years since the opening of the Erie Canal, Buffalo had become the gateway to the Great Lakes and the west. City managers simply could not keep up with the explosive infrastructure growth and a population of transient canal and industry roustabouts who thrived on saloons and saloon politics. Inaugurated as mayor in January 1882, Cleveland wrested control from the dominating cartels and within a year gained widespread recognition for his honest competence and results cleaning up the city and canal. By the fall of 1882 he found himself a successful candidate for governor of New York State. Once in office, Governor Cleveland relentlessly appointed officials based on merit and refused to patronize the well-oiled Democratic organization of Tammany Hall in New York City. In less than two years, his reputation spread nationally, leading to his nomination for the presidency. Only Blaine and his political machine stood between Cleveland and the executive residence in Washington, D.C.

The resultant presidential campaign became especially nasty as both sides did their best to prove malfeasance and moral turpitude by the opposition. Republican leaders self-righteously wallowed in the news that Cleveland had a liaison with a widowed woman named Maria Halpin, who supposedly bore him a son. The accusations were sordid, involving legal actions, maternal neglect, and a third-party adoption. Cleveland faced the grubby allegations directly and truthfully. He explained his honorable level of support for both the mother and child in spite of his uncertainty of the child's paternity. Although many voters believed his account, the opposition chanted its distaste in its famous campaign jingle: "Ma! Ma! Where's my Pa? Gone to the Whitehouse, Ha! Ha! Ha!"[18]

Not to be outdone, some Democratic leaders latched on to salacious accounts concerning Blaine, who supposedly was not married when his wife became pregnant during his early days of teaching in Kentucky, before they were wed in a Pennsylvania ceremony. Blaine professed that just prior to leaving Kentucky on the occasion of his father's death he was in fact married in Kentucky in the company of a few close friends and the second marriage took place as an official but unexplained secret family event. In spite of his protestations, Democrats delighted in keeping Blaine's story in the news until he began to bring lawsuits against the offending newspapers. Blaine also had to deal with his involvement in past financial scandals that weakened his candidacy.

Cleveland won the election with a plurality of slightly more than 23,000 of the 9.9 million votes cast. To no avail, Chandler had attempted to gain support for Blaine by bringing the North Atlantic fleet into Brooklyn just prior to the November elections. He was hoping that increased shipyard work for a deteriorating Navy might enhance the standing of local party leaders in the swing state of New York, but his tactic failed.[19] The deciding issues for the voting public involved character and change rather than distinct political choices, and now Cleveland faced the enormity of national governance. Examining the state of the Navy as a strategic military force or instrument of national policy was not part of his deliberations.

In the Forty-eighth Congress' lame-duck session of December 1884 to March 1885, prior to Cleveland's inauguration, Rep. William McAdoo (D-NJ) attempted to reopen the issue of the bloated Navy officer corps. McAdoo, a future Assistant Secretary of the Navy, introduced a bill intended to both stimulate promotions and restructure the officer organization.[20] Sympathetic to the perturbations of sea and shore duty manning, his plan allowed officers stuck in the middle of the "hump" to advance by elevating a few senior officers to a new rank of vice admiral and retiring some others involuntarily. In spite of his efforts, his bill did not come out of his naval committee for discussion. The legislature would not consider either raising the peacetime level of military rank structure or increasing the number of Navy officer retirees.

Congress waited until the final day of its last session in March 1885 to authorize funds for two additional steel cruisers and two gunboats.[21] Over a four-year period, two Congresses during the administrations of Garfield and Arthur had now approved new construction of eight steel warships. This pace of Navy shipbuilding contracts was insufficient to replace decrepit ships going out of service. On the day after the Forty-eighth Congress adjourned, Cleveland assumed office and the Navy once again came under the review of a new president, a new secretariat, and a new Congress.

Cleveland's public focus was on open government. His issues concerned the spoils system, the gold standard, and fiduciary efficiency in government. Accordingly, he chose his cabinet members from his trusted Democratic Party supporters and men of stature. His top three choices were Thomas Bayard for the State Department, Daniel Manning for the Treasury, and William Whitney for the Navy. Bayard was an elder statesman and three-term U.S. senator from Delaware. He would take the lead against U.S. protectionism and foster closer relations with Great Britain. Manning, a respected rags-to-riches businessman and journalist from New York, was Cleveland's right-hand man for money policy. Whitney, often accused of being too close to corporate and railroad finance, strived to establish Navy administration under efficient business management.[22]

The new Secretary of the Navy was a successful and wealthy New York lawyer who had become a kingmaker in Cleveland's campaign for the presidency. Born in western Massachusetts, Whitney's family hailed from the Boston Puritans of the 1630s. When he was a young teenager, he moved with his middle-class family to Springfield and then to Boston where his father engaged in politics. Whitney graduated from Yale and then from Harvard Law School during the Civil War. He developed a profitable law practice in New York City and married Flora Payne, the daughter of a wealthy entrepreneur.[23]

During the presidential election run, he had contributed large amounts of his own money to the contest. In spite of his wealth he remained faithful to liberal Democratic causes and supported honest business practices, putting him at serious odds with the patronage-driven Republican Stalwarts of New York. Whitney was certainly in line for a cabinet position and post-election speculation predicted that he would become secretary of the Interior. Instead, in February 1885, less than two weeks prior to Cleveland's inauguration, Whitney accepted the appointment as Secretary of the Navy. Similar to his predecessor, he had no previous experience or interest in the Navy. Whereas former Secretary of the Navy Chandler had a well-deserved and unflattering reputation as a "political" secretary, Whitney's supporters came to identify him as an honest "business" secretary, immune from political pressure.[24] His attempts to reorganize the Navy were initially concerned with financial efficiency rather than with building an internationally competitive sea service. But in spite of his considerable efforts to change Navy management, he could not overcome congressional intransigence.

After the Democratic Party had carried the 1884 elections, Whitney, as a leader of the successful campaign team, received many letters both extolling the victory and asking for favors. In early December, three months prior to his Navy assignment, New Hampshire politician and unabashed capitalist Frank Jones reminded him that there would be the usual scramble for office and that the "patronage of the government" must be "regulated and disbursed" to benefit the victorious party that had been out of the Executive Mansion for twenty-four years.[25] Jones had served in the U.S. Congress in the 1870s and now owned the largest brewery in the country, with New England operations in Boston and Portsmouth. Similar patronage exhortations poured in from all quarters during the interregnum as Cleveland and his cabinet prepared for office.

In keeping with its continued desire for Congress to guide the process of naval planning, the outgoing legislature of March 1885 had empowered the incoming Secretary of the Navy to replace the members of Chandler's statutory advisory board. Its annual appropriations act granted the new board increased control over all decisions relating to building new warships, including the important authority to enter into contracts. Whitney appointed Chandler's nemesis, Captain Walker, now in his fourth year as navigation bureau chief, to head the reconstituted board. Two other line officers, two naval officer constructors, and a civilian engineer completed the board's six-member composition.[26] For the senior constructor position, Whitney could not ignore Chief Naval Constructor Theodore Wilson, who had also served on Hunt's board, was an experienced voice with Congress, and was then serving as head of the construction bureau. Unfortunately for Whitney, Wilson emerged as a staunch opponent of bureau consolidation proposals. Although Wilson was perhaps an "old-line bureaucrat" and "ultraconservative" aligned with Republican Party traditionalists, both Cleveland and his successor, President Benjamin Harrison, recognized his expertise in naval construction and kept him as bureau chief for a total of twelve years.[27]

Congress charged this third naval advisory board with a wider scope of authority than either of the first two temporary boards established by the Secretary of the Navy. For the first time, the Navy's board for warship construction now contained two military bureau chiefs, Walker and Wilson, who were already in positions of authority in the Navy Department. As heads of independent bureaus, the military chiefs had significant competing interests among themselves, but at least could arrive at a consensus instead of being directed by lesser officer ad hoc committees. Recommendations concerning the future of the Navy were now vested in the established Navy officer hierarchy, while the legislature maintained oversight of the procurement process.

The existing Navy bureau system continued to pose a challenge for Whitney. In one of his first actions to strengthen his position, Whitney selected William Calhoun, a prominent New York accountant, to examine the Navy's management and financial practices. Within a month after Cleveland's inauguration, Calhoun reported glaring inefficiencies and, similar to Luce, castigated the Navy bureaus for duplications and the lack of centralized accounts.[28] He recommended establishing a single accounting office to oversee all of the bureaus' financial activities. As a follow-up to the independent audit, Whitney appointed a panel of Navy officers to recommend ways to enhance the Navy Department's administrative efficiency.[29] Eventually he made the logical decision to assign the Bureau of Provisions and Clothing, headed by Paymaster James Fulton, the responsibility of overseeing the financial activities of all the bureaus. A few years later, during the next administration, it became the Bureau of Supplies and Accounts, to recognize the full scope of its operations.

Whitney certainly did not inherit a budding new Navy. The total increase in oceangoing warships when he took over consisted of authorizations for only five cruisers and three gunboats, none of which had been turned over to the Navy. The ABCDs were still under contract with Roach's company and the specifications for the remaining four ships had not yet been advertised for bids. The ABCDs had been designed by competing naval officer interests and disagreeing congressional committees, did not fit into any strategic scheme, and were not close to the capabilities of foreign warships already underway. Additionally, the Navy bureaus continuously submitted alterations at each stage of construction. This was new territory for U.S. naval engineers as they tried to tie together some combination of useful endurance, speed, firepower, offense, and defense.

The initial concepts of the successive Rodgers and Shufeldt boards fixated on a traditional U.S. Navy designed for coastal defense and commerce raiding. However, civilian mail steamers were already faster than the specifications for the contracted Navy combatants. Slow raiders were obviously not effective against speedier opponents. Also, the embryonic Navy was essentially unarmored, making it vulnerable versus equal-sized armored foreign warships, and was not designed for combat close to foreign shores. Whitney did not focus on the long-range strategic view. Rather, in keeping with Cleveland's record and determination, the secretary looked for sound business adjustments in shipbuilding and maintenance enterprises.

Whitney's first significant opportunity to exercise entrepreneurial decision-making presented itself with the upcoming acceptance and commissioning of the gunboat *Dolphin*, scheduled to be turned over to the Navy in the summer of 1885. For Whitney, the *Dolphin* was a Republican product of a questionable bidding process built by a questionable contractor, and the ship was flawed. In fact it had encountered engineering failures during its trials and Whitney decided to challenge its contract. With President Cleveland's assent, Attorney General Augustus Garland offered a legal judgment based on Whitney's evidence that the contract had not been met. The Navy refused to accept the *Dolphin*, and the fate of the cruisers *Atlanta*, *Boston*, and *Chicago* remained in question. With large sums of money at stake, seventy-year-old Roach felt that he faced an unwinnable situation and decided to cut his losses. Chandler, his principal advocate, was gone and his antagonist, Whitney, was calling the shots. Roach was also seriously ill with mouth cancer and not up to another fight. He put his shipbuilding company under "assignment" and turned over his yard to the Navy to complete the four ships with its own work force.[30]

5

SOME MOVEMENT, 1885–89

President Cleveland concentrated on reform to bring the government in line with sound business practices. Along those lines, he approved Whitney's movement to formulate organizational changes in naval administration in spite of resistance by the Navy bureau chiefs. But similar to the stonewalling experienced by Chandler, when the new legislature met in December 1885 it declined to take any action that would alter its close relationship to the Navy bureaucracy. The weak naval committees of both houses of Congress were superseded by powerful party bosses interested in local issues and patronage.

Members of the respective naval committees were generally not prime movers. The speaker of the house and the Senate majority leader selected their respective committee chairmen and members according to the politics of their party. Each branch of Congress had established a Committee on Naval Affairs in the early nineteenth century, after the War of 1812 with Great Britain, and used it to collect information on naval matters and make recommendations for naval legislation. In general, congressional chairmen of important standing committees attained their positions through seniority and presided with almost absolute authority.[1] By the 1880s, places on the minor naval committees were not highly sought after.

When the Navy began its slow redevelopment, the House of Representatives naval committee lacked stability. From 1881 to 1889, committee membership averaged a turnover rate of more than 55 percent each congressional term, while the biennial turnover rate of the entire House was less than 45 percent.[2] As they gained seniority, congressmen often left the low-ranking naval committee for more important positions affecting policy or appropriations. For example, Robert Davidson of Florida left it to chair the more prestigious and consequential railroad committee after his party won the majority in 1883. Similarly in 1887, second-term representative Thomas Norwood of Georgia and the outspoken Joseph Sayers of Texas also left the weak naval committee in favor of foreign affairs and appropriations respectively. As these strong Southern representatives gained seniority, they moved upward to take positions of greater influence rather than deal with the relatively minor business of naval affairs.

The Democratic Party had regained the majority in the House of Representatives in 1883 during President Arthur's last two years. Well-traveled representative S. S. Cox, of Ohio and New York, reluctantly accepted the naval affairs chairmanship after failing to get the appointment to chair foreign affairs, one of the "good places" on the standing committees.[3] With twenty years' experience in Congress, Cox had never previously served on the naval committee and initially refused to accept the position, considering it unimportant. After a single term as its chairman, he left Congress to be President Cleveland's minister to Turkey. When he returned to the Democratic Congresses of 1885 to 1889, he did not receive any subsequent committee chairmanship appointments.

The Senate naval affairs chairman, powerful Republican James "Don" Cameron of Pennsylvania, had been away in Europe during the first session of 1883. In his absence Eugene Hale of Maine, who later would become a prime mover in naval development, only midway through his first term in the Senate accepted the temporary chairmanship of Senate naval affairs.[4] The committee's most senior member, Henry Anthony of Rhode Island, in his twenty-fifth year in the Senate, was mostly ineffective in the Forty-eighth Congress, being virtually on his deathbed. Navy committee member John Miller of California put his time and effort into the Senate Foreign Relations committee, which he chaired.

Upon his return from Europe, Cameron decided to retain his naval chairmanship as he realized its gradual increase in importance. He was the son of former senator Simon Cameron, secretary of war under President Abraham Lincoln. As a young man, Don Cameron accepted the position of secretary of war from 1876 to 1877 in the final year of the Grant presidency. Cameron was the consummate powerful politician, succeeding his powerful father in the Senate and then serving for twenty years. He was a railroad man who favored big business, especially by supporting high protective tariffs.

As another discordant reality for the Senate naval committee, the seven states with Navy yards were not equally represented. Government yards were located in California, Virginia, Pennsylvania, New York, Massachusetts, New Hampshire, and Maine, with the latter two sharing the Portsmouth-Kittery facility. But only Pennsylvania, New Hampshire, and Maine maintained continuous membership in the naval committee throughout the entire 1880s and 1890s. Dominated by these three states, the committee did not represent the majority of regional interests and did not command complete authority on naval matters or growth. Even with the committee's gradually growing shipbuilding authorizations, Navy expenditures stood at less than half the Army's budget by the early 1890s. This occurred because the government committed significant manpower to maintain Army forts throughout the western frontier.

There was good reason for the lack of standing of the House of Representatives naval committee. Before President Cleveland's administration, the House Committee on Appropriations approved all money bills and sent them to the Senate for joint ratification. The House naval committee served primarily as a body of advisers concerning Navy business and generally only proposed legislation for changes in naval administration that did not involve significant monetary allocations. But during the first session of the Forty-ninth Congress of 1885–86, the Democratic House radically reduced its appropriations committee's role in originating bills. The rules committee held that its appropriations committee had too much power and gave several standing committees authority over appropriations in their own areas.[5] Although the rule was not specifically aimed at the Navy, the House naval committee gained stature and a stronger bond with the Navy bureaus once it could structure its own money bills.

On the other hand, the Republican-controlled Senate kept the benign status of its naval committee for a longer period. For the remainder of the nineteenth century, the Senate Committee on Appropriations retained authority to receive and review House naval appropriation bills. Only after the war with

Spain did the Senate also change its rules by giving its naval committee appropriation oversight. This action ushered in a unique period in U.S. history when both the Senate and House naval committees formed money bills for the Navy. After the buildup of the new Navy and the end of the First World War, the Budget Act of 1921 reverted financial responsibilities back to the respective appropriation committees.

Even with its newfound fiscal responsibility, in December 1885 the House naval committee of the first Cleveland administration remained in an early stage of developing prestige. The practice of the speaker of the House giving the naval chairmanship to "the member of the majority with the longest uninterrupted service on the committee," was not yet followed.[6] Under the new rules of financial oversight, Speaker of the House John Carlisle (D–KY) chose an outsider and appointed fellow Southerner and future Secretary of the Navy Hilary Herbert of Alabama to succeed the reluctant Cox as the leader of naval affairs.[7]

Over the years, Herbert became a strong Navy advocate and eventually guided important naval legislation through the House of Representatives. But when appointed to chair naval affairs in December 1885, he was a fifth-term representative who had previously served on law and judiciary committees. He had no experience with the Navy Department and, similar to his predecessor, had never been a member of the naval committee. Eight years later, Herbert left Congress to become Secretary of the Navy when Cleveland was reelected after his four-year hiatus. As a result of the considerable naval legislation passed during his three terms as chairman of the House naval affairs committee and four years as Secretary of the Navy, Herbert shares among several others the sobriquet of "Father of the New Navy." Various contemporary and modern historians have also acclaimed Secretaries Hunt, Chandler, Whitney, and Benjamin Tracy, as well as Herbert, as being the "Father of the New Navy." Success has many fathers.

In Herbert's case, the selection did not fit the mold purported by critics who characterized congressional chairmen as powerful autocrats.[8] Herbert was a loyal Southern Democrat who protected the solid South from renewed federal reconstruction attempts by negotiating with progressive Northerners. By not opposing Northern industries, he leveraged lucrative construction contracts for Southern naval bases. This father of the new Navy was a dedicated partisan and regional politician, a far cry from the modernizing progressive supposedly rising in that era.

Herbert's formidable regional inclinations were shaped by his Southern and Civil War experiences. He was born in South Carolina in 1834 to an unrepentant slave-owning family with lineage tracing to the Virginia colony of the mid-1600s. At the age of twelve he moved with his family to Greenville in southern Alabama. In keeping with his legacy, while at the University of Virginia he became an ardent and lifelong supporter of states' rights before establishing a law practice in his Alabama hometown.[9] He began his extensive war experiences as a captain in the Confederate army during the retreat from Yorktown and the Battle of Fair Oaks on the Chickahominy River, where he was taken prisoner in June 1862. Repatriated in a prisoner exchange two months later, he led his men in the bloody Battle of Antietam and then wintered over in Fredericksburg. He fought at Gettysburg in the summer of 1863 and after three years in the thick of the war was severely wounded in the Wilderness Campaign of the spring of 1864, where he permanently lost the use of his right arm.[10]

Herbert retired from the Confederate army with the rank of colonel and returned to his law practice in Alabama. He married Ella Smith of Selma in 1867 and ten years later won election to the U.S. Congress as a fiercely loyal Southerner. Rather than confront the politicians in Congress who took issue with Southern Democratic post-Reconstruction governance, he worked out regional alliances that kept outsiders from interfering with conservative Bourbon politics. Herbert focused his energy on industrial development attractive to northern Republicans as part of the congressional compromise process in building the Navy. His book *Why the Solid South?, Or Reconstruction and Its Results*, written later in life in defense of his politics, shows his strong desire to protect the independence of the new South.[11] His wife died in 1885 just prior to the beginning of his fifth term in Congress and his appointment to chair the naval committee.

When Herbert's new Forty-ninth Congress convened in December 1885, Secretary Whitney recommended consolidating the Navy's eight bureaus into three divisions. In a way similar to Secretary Chandler's previous scheme, he desired to restructure his department's work among the logical divisions of Construction, Personnel, and Finance.[12] In his first annual report, Whitney did not mention increasing the Navy force or establishing a warship baseline.

Instead, he focused on reorganization in keeping with the first nine months of work by Cleveland's cabinet to streamline the government and clean up the spoils system. Whitney also explained why he took away the ABCD contracts from Roach and noted that new contracts for completing the four authorized ships were now advertised.

THE NAVY AND CONGRESS

Whitney's first official statement forwarded to Congress was the fifth annual Secretary of the Navy report since Hunt and Rear Admiral Rodgers presented baseline recommendations to the House of Representatives in December 1881. Hunt had left office the following spring and Rodgers had died shortly thereafter. Their list of seventy-two vessels of various unarmored wooden and steel warships remained in suspension as an unrevised standard for the successive board of Rear Admiral Shufeldt. Whitney's new advisory board for warship construction was still a work in progress. Cleveland endorsed Whitney's businesslike proposal to consolidate the bureaus and took the additional step of making a strong statement to Congress to consider Navy Department administration changes before proceeding with naval increases. In his first annual message to Congress, Cleveland wrote: "I earnestly commend the portion of the secretary's report devoted to this subject to the attention of Congress, in the hope that his suggestions touching the reorganization of his Department may be adopted as the first step toward the reconstruction of our Navy."[13]

The priority to consolidate the Navy bureaus was a business issue that would rationalize executive-branch naval activities. Some well-placed progressive Navy officers, such as recently promoted Rear Admiral Luce, supported Cleveland and Whitney. The majority of line officer bureau chiefs also favored the consolidation plan because it appeared to them that seagoing officers would have a stronger voice. In spite of the potential loss of congressional patronage Sen. William P. Frye of Maine, a close friend of former secretary Chandler, followed Chandler's lead from the previous administration and introduced a bill to combine the functions of selected bureaus in order to "prevent abuses in the Navy Department." Contemporary media pointed out that consolidation would also increase presidential power.[14]

Navy advisory board member Chief Naval Constructor Wilson, the current influential head of the construction and repairs bureau, dissented from the majority line officer opinion that favored restructuring. He expressed his concern to the House of Representatives about removing staff officers, expert specialists like himself, from the top decision-making positions. Wilson judiciously highlighted the negative effects consolidation would have on the power of Congress. He inaccurately predicted that in the future, congressmen would allot appropriations to fewer bureaus, reducing direct congressional jurisdiction of funds.[15]

Captain Walker, now in his second four-year assignment as head of both the navigation bureau and the advisory board, strongly disagreed with Wilson and in turn reiterated the "unsatisfactory results" of Navy management by the bureau system.[16] House naval committee chairman Herbert sided with Walker's evaluation and supported Whitney's scheme. For Herbert, this movement was a necessary correction of gross inefficiencies and scandals in Navy management during the post–Civil War Republican era. Many members of the new Democratic majority in the House also sought to alter the basic civil-military foundation controlled for years by Republican industrialists. However, neither the full House of Representatives nor the Republican Senate approved Navy reorganization legislation.

The bill to consolidate certain bureaus of the Department of the Navy managed to survive into the second session but eventually died unresolved.[17] As the arguments proceeded, Charles Boutelle of Maine disagreed with the majority report of the House naval committee and stated that consolidation was anti–staff officer, especially considering the growing importance of senior steam engineers, and that line officers would have too much sway in the business arena when their expertise was more appropriate to high seas operations.[18] His position was consistent with his apprehension about losing access to important bureau chiefs who possessed contract and employment authority. In reality, he reacted as a champion of congressional prerogatives and successfully led the House against changes in Navy organization and against the recommendations of the president.

Boutelle vigorously argued that consolidating the four bureaus of Engineering, Yards and Docks, Construction and Repairs, and Ordnance would not eliminate the discrete tasks currently handled by each bureau chief. He pointed out that Whitney's proposal would require new sub-divisions of bureaucracy to oversee current bureau functions that would continue to exist. Boutelle blamed civilian and military leadership, not the system itself, for inefficiencies. He insisted that the present organization best met wartime requirements and that downgrading the bureaus would have the deleterious effect of reducing congressional access to Navy Department administration. Under Whitney's plan, military heads of the proposed new subdivisions would answer to three military division chiefs. Congress would then be forced to deal with the civilian secretary and fewer Navy officers of a centralized military body.[19]

Rep. Thomas Reed of Maine added his voice supporting the existing congressional patronage system. Reed, a volunteer Navy paymaster during the last year of the Civil War, was now in his fifth term in the House and, along with Boutelle, looked after the interests of the Portsmouth-Kittery shipyard. He reiterated the potential loss of congressional appropriation management under the proposed Navy reorganization plan and embellished the apprehensions of Chief Naval Constructor Wilson. For Reed, combining bureau functions would limit House fiscal control, increasing the discretionary power of the Secretary of the Navy and the executive branch.[20] By retaining the existing bureaus, Congress could continue to control the apportionment of funds to each bureau and control the development of naval forces.

Contrarily, both Herbert and Whitney had lobbied extensively in the first legislative session for the consolidation plan. To no avail, Herbert laid out the extravagances and defects in the Navy's way of doing business.[21] But according to a bipartisan majority in Congress, the proposed reorganization ran counter to their interests and would result in a loss of congressional oversight. As the arguments came to a whimpering conclusion in the second session, the combined efforts of the chairman of the House of Representatives naval committee, the president of the United States, the Secretary of the Navy, and several senior Navy line officers could not convince the Forty-ninth Congress to dislodge the status quo of the bureaus.

Although Congress did not support changing the Navy Department bureau system, the subject of establishing a general staff that would be superior to the bureau chiefs remained active among progressive line officers.[22] They called for a general staff to prepare campaigns and oversee fleet movements and communications. For several years, arguments promoting a Navy general staff initially consisted of debates by insiders. Professional publications such as the U.S. Naval Institute *Proceedings*, the *United Services*, and the *Army and Navy Journal* contained in-house dialogues. Occasionally, senior Navy officers also spoke out against their own bureau system in more public forums, and called on Congress to revamp the Navy's administration in favor of a streamlined organization that gave increased voice and management authority to experienced sea-going officers. But despite the sustained criticisms of the bureau system within the Navy itself, the legislature continued to table discussions of a general staff until after the turn of the nineteenth century, and kept the bureaus intact until the 1960s.

President Cleveland had larger issues at stake. In his first year in office, he devoted most of his energy to implementing fairness in retaining competent government administrators rather than orchestrating a traditional clean sweep of public offices in favor of his victorious political party. Of 126,000 federal employees at the time, 110,000 were chosen by the president and his entourage. Only 16,000 had their jobs protected as being "classified" in the new Civil Service System.[23] Cleveland put into action at a national level the same tenacious effort against patronage corruption that he had done as governor of New York State.

In his second year in office, Cleveland spent most of his energy on sound money issues and the tariff. He opposed silver speculation, which he saw as dangerous to the country's well-being. But he could not resolve the silver-gold standoff. Eastern businesses and banks demanded a sound money system based on the gold standard. This was in reality a deflationary policy due to the rising value of gold as demand exceeded supply. The situation had the effect of increasing the burden of debts without actually increasing interest rates. The debtor class of westerners and farmers looked to a market-driven silver policy as the basis for money. This would become inflationary as silver prices decreased due to increased mining, which would give relief to farmers and others who acquired annual debt. Cleveland was unable to stop the U.S. use of bimetallic currency, which continued until 1900.

In spite of his steady workaholic habits, he found time for a personal life. Without much fanfare, Cleveland quietly conducted a courtship with Frances Folsom, the young daughter of Oscar Folsom, his deceased former law partner. Frances was eleven years old when her father died and Cleveland kept in contact with her mother. He privately showed his romantic intentions toward Frances when she was a student at Wells College in upstate New York. In June

1886 they married in a reserved White House ceremony attended by only a few dozen of the president's close friends and the Marine band led by John Philip Sousa.[24] Irrespective of their twenty-seven-year age difference, the marriage was solid and joyful. The attractive and effervescent Frances lit up both the White House and Oak View, the president's country home on a twenty-nine-acre estate north of the capital.

In addition to attending to his new bride, Cleveland faced the problems associated with national growth and finances while Whitney attempted to control Navy issues. Whitney continued unsuccessfully, into the late summer of 1886, to focus on reorganization, while Congress authorized funds for its own selection of warships. Prior to adjourning on August 5, Congress approved new construction for three cruisers, one torpedo boat, and an experimental ship that threw dynamite projectiles, and ordered the completion of four monitors approved but unfunded by previous congresses.[25] Also, Congress directed the use of domestic steel and the construction of a warship in a government shipyard. A few months later in his second annual report sent to the House of Representatives in December 1886, Whitney continued to call for administration changes. He also commented that the ABCDs were in fact too slow, noting the obvious: that foreign powers already had faster merchant ships under way. Without listing specific warship needs, Whitney "hoped" for additional ships but did not refer to a new baseline goal.[26]

President Cleveland's second annual message to Congress followed Whitney's by a few days. In his rather large thirty-one-page document, Cleveland covered a wide range of various topics of both international and domestic interest. His one-page Navy section again reviewed the obsolete condition of the naval service and gave the status of new construction in progress, but offered no specific recommendations for the composition of a new fleet. He also reported the difficulty in contracting appropriate steel for the two armored cruisers authorized in the previous session. The fair purchase of quality steel for naval construction would remain a major problem over the course of the next fifteen years.

The outgoing Forty-ninth Congress adjourned in March 1887 without agreeing on what to do with the national financial state of affairs, but did add ships to the Navy's ongoing construction program. It provided appropriations for two cruisers, two coastal gunboats, and the completion of five monitors.

Congress also included a mandate to build unspecified ships on both coasts.[27] It was acting, albeit slowly, on dictating the relationships of the developing military-industrial complex to the government.

As it ended its lame-duck session, it finally took action on the Gun Foundry Board's recommendations of the previous year. Its naval act included authority to use armament appropriations to establish naval gun manufacturing at a Washington, D.C., site. Government factories for manufacturing modern naval guns did not yet exist. The Forty-seventh Congress that had authorized the ABCDs in 1883 had also established a commission to investigate the feasibility of a government foundry to manufacture guns.[28] The growing steel trusts were engaged in extensive railroad and commercial construction and had only limited capacities for manufacturing military naval stock. Retooling for small quantities of unique warship hardware did not initially appeal to private industry. Congress, therefore, looked to the government to fabricate heavy ordnance. Rear Adm. Edward Simpson, a line officer with considerable experience both at sea and with the Bureau of Ordnance, headed the congressionally mandated Gun Foundry Board. Since the retirement of Rear Admiral Shufeldt in February 1884, Simpson had also headed the second advisory board of Secretary Chandler.

The Gun Foundry Board, which included three Army officers, held sessions at the League Island Navy Yard in Pennsylvania and continued to meet at Simpson's call. Together, the members also traveled to Europe, visiting England, France, Germany, and Russia to observe the work of steel manufacturers. On their return they examined the state of U.S. steel making. In its terminal report to the Forty-eighth Congress, the board favored the Washington Navy Yard as the best location for a government gun factory.[29] In the process, three Congresses with changing leadership over a six-year period debated the measure before the Forty-ninth eventually decided, in early 1887, to use a government facility rather than a civilian contractor for naval guns. Progress occurred at a slow pace.

On the more visible budgetary issues of concern to President Cleveland, the Republican Party, backed by bankers and industry, had no interest in reducing the federal surplus. But the president and progressive Democrats felt that high protective tariffs lined the pockets of the rich by causing large profits while promoting inefficiency and patronage at the expense of the working man, who was forced to pay taxes on commodities and bear the burden of tariff-driven high prices. To Cleveland, reducing tariffs was the obvious solution. But most Republicans and some Democrats saw Cleveland's stand as one of noxious free trade, seriously harmful to the nation's economic well-being. The incoming Congress would not convene until late 1887, with the bulk of their work to be conducted in the spring during the 1888 presidential election season.

In his third annual report sent to Congress in December 1887, Whitney noted that the president had approved the construction of a cruiser by Union Iron Works, a West Coast civilian shipyard in San Francisco. Then, differing from his past reports of generalities, he presented an explicit request for new ships to the incoming Congress, which was again composed of a Democratic House and a Republican Senate. He wrote that: "It has not been the custom of the Department of late years to specify the form and characteristics of vessels recommended to be built."[30] He then pointed out that the Navy did not want unprotected torpedo boats and at the same time praised new submarine and torpedo developments, even though Congress had not yet approved any submarines. He specifically recommended appropriations to build two large, armored vessels and three cruisers of the fastest types.

With no introductory explanation, he inserted in his text an interesting and somewhat out-of-context sentence that read: "A public feeling seems to exist for the creation of a naval reserve."[31] Most probably this was Whitney's recognition to Congress that perhaps a national spirit of navalism was in fact emerging. Navalism may cover a range of definitions, but in this case was presumably associated with a public attitude supporting some level of increased maritime involvement and advancement. A feeling toward establishing a military organization of Navy Reserves certainly was within that concept. Whitney may have been influenced by the yachting society of his peers, who might have been interested in part-time gentlemanly service while wearing the Navy uniform of coast watchers.

Cleveland's focus was not on the Navy as he sent his third annual message to Congress in December 1887. He devoted his relatively short ten-page summary entirely to the single issue of tariffs and the associated budget surplus. He had made up his mind that this was the most important problem of the

United States and he would commit all his energy to reducing the burden of taxes during the approaching presidential campaign. He expressed great concern that the working man paid considerable hidden taxes because of high prices caused by protective tariffs. Cleveland then charged Congress to reform the tariff system and end the treasury surplus.

As Congress convened, past Secretary of the Navy William Chandler joined the legislature as the junior senator from New Hampshire. His Republican Party recognized the value of having a former Navy secretary and experienced Washington insider serve on the naval committee, but the committee had no vacancies. To make room for Chandler, party leadership obliged Henry Dawes of Massachusetts, in his thirtieth year in Congress and noteworthy chairman of the Indian affairs committee, to leave the naval committee in favor of Chandler.[32] The politically astute Chandler now had considerable influence in the Senate while Whitney continued his attempts to reshape Navy organization.

In spite of the navigation bureau's efforts to place officers in shore duty positions, the military bureau chiefs found themselves in managerial situations of increasing complexity without sufficient administrative support. The Department of the Navy needed a larger bureaucracy simply to function. At the same time that Congress authorized new ships, it continued to debate personnel requirements and manning level realities. Minority bipartisan alignments could not overcome entrenched congressional aversion to any increases in the Navy's shore establishment.[33] The issue of establishing new positions for naval administration would languish for several more years. Meanwhile, Captain Walker's navigation bureau continued its unilateral steps to prevent staff manning shortfalls.

ANOTHER ELECTION

The great tariff debates that occurred in the spring and summer of 1888 took place concurrently with the conventions and campaigns for the fall presidential election. Cleveland's call to run again as the Democratic candidate was of course expected and he was officially anointed as their candidate. The selection of his vice president was more problematic. Cleveland had been without a vice president since his running mate Thomas Hendricks died in December 1885, having been in office for less than a year. After some relatively brief political maneuvering the convention settled on Allen Thurman, an elderly Peace Democrat from Ohio, to run for the second position. In his long career as a politician, representative, and senator he had often sided with Southern Democrats opposed to emancipation, the civil rights act, and government interference in state affairs.[34] Leading Democrats mistakenly felt that he, as a seventy-five-year-old senior statesman and orator for small government, could help carry the critical state of Ohio. In reality he was not a good choice because of his lukewarm stand on Cleveland's tariff reform and his frail appearance.

By contrast, the Republican convention was a lively event, with several organized candidates vying for the nomination. This time around, perennial candidate Blaine allowed that he was finished with the rough-and-tumble necessities of campaigning and did not run. Initially, Benjamin Harrison of Indiana was a distant fourth in the number of contenders, but with the help of Blaine's men rose to the top. His strengths consisted of the tenacity of his chief adviser, Indiana's attorney general Louis Michener, and his platform of supposed worker protection, which to him meant continuing high tariffs. Harrison's principal kingmaker was Matthew Quay, reigning Republican leader of Pennsylvania and the anointed successor to lead Simon Cameron's exclusive political cabal.[35] As such, he ran a daunting campaign with seemingly bottomless funds to promote protectionism and anti-British sentiment to capture the votes of Irish labor. Quay also vigorously attacked Cleveland's tariff policy, once again raising the bogeyman of free trade as an abomination to both workers and business.

While the president focused on the supply of money, his reelection organization proved to be woefully inadequate for the campaign. Democratic national chairman William H. Barnum was closely associated with a sizable anti-Cleveland protectionist faction within his own party. Barnum's campaign assistant Calvin S. Brice, a big-business developer in Ohio, was also similarly tepid on tariff reform, which of course was Cleveland's foremost issue of the campaign.[36] At the expense of his reelection, Cleveland approved a compromise tariff act, which was passed in July after the spring and summer congressional debates.

The annual Navy act passed in September showed continued congressional management of the shape of the Navy and was not associated with tariff legislation or the election campaign. Congress ignored Whitney's request to fund a naval reserve while it approved four cruisers and three gunboats. It also authorized two commissions of three officers each to determine locations for new navy yards on or near the Gulf of Mexico and on the northwest Pacific coast.[37] By using such special officer boards for administration and fact finding, Congress continued to appropriate the expertise of Navy Department officials for its own deliberations. The commissions would directly assist legislators in determining locations for naval expansion. With a statutory Navy Advisory Board and temporary commissions essentially working for the naval committees of both chambers, Congress maintained its oversight.

In November, Cleveland lost the election. The vote count was close and questionable. Cleveland won a considerable plurality due to the high number of votes from the Democratic South, which included some degree of illegal local disenfranchising of black voters. But the key electoral swing states of Indiana and New York went to the Republicans, amid highly probable accusations of money for votes in strategic districts. Harrison, on the other hand, credited God rather than his party for winning the election.

The president-elect presented himself as a deeply religious man dedicated to the value of hard work for success in the abiding Puritan ethic. In spite of his famous grandfather William Henry Harrison's record as an Indian fighter, successful governor, and tragically short-term president, Benjamin Harrison led a relatively humble early life as an ordinary citizen. He had enjoyed a happy childhood in a typical debtor-class farming household in Ohio, replete with daily devotions and religious instruction. He worked hard for his local education and advanced to study at Miami University of Ohio, where he professed his call to the Presbyterian Church. Matriculating in the discipline of law rather than the ministry, Harrison maintained that all of his work was for the glory of God. In his commencement oration at the age of nineteen, he articulated his lifelong position on work and poverty. He denounced England's dole to its country's poor as a ruinous policy leading to a downward spiral of debilitating lethargy. For Harrison, the success of the United States on the other hand depended on deliberate work for measured rewards.[38] Even with a strong anti-welfare mind-set, he later made a singular, politically expedient exception by supporting very liberal pensions for Civil War veterans and their widows.

After graduation he moved to Indianapolis to establish himself as a lawyer. He soon married his fiancée, Caroline Scott, the daughter of a Presbyterian minister. As Harrison settled in his new city, he became involved in the Republican Party, won election as city attorney general, and a few years later campaigned for Lincoln. Answering the call of Oliver P. Morton, governor of Indiana, Harrison enlisted in the Army as a second lieutenant in 1862 and wrote to his wife that he wanted to bear himself "as a good soldier of Jesus Christ."[39] After a year and a half of garrison duty he joined the hot war with General Sherman, advancing to Atlanta. He showed his mettle in battle and rapidly rose to the rank of brigadier general. In his postwar work back home, he supported radical reconstruction and progressed as an influential lawyer and political figure known for the power of his oratory. He took a strident law-and-order position against burgeoning railroad strikers as being part of an un-American revolution, while at the same time expressing empathy for laborers who worked for their daily bread. In 1880, he had stumped for Garfield and got credit for carrying his state of Indiana. Harrison defended high tariffs as necessary protection for both the labor force and industry, and served one term in the U.S. Senate, which led to his move to the presidency.

Cleveland and his cabinet had four months to turn over their offices to the victorious Republicans, who not only won the White House but also won the majority of seats in both the House of Representatives and the Senate. In his final report of December 1888, outgoing Secretary Whitney extolled the progress of the Cleveland administration to the departing Congress and concluded that the United States must build fast armored warships to keep up with foreign powers.[40] He did not refer to the long defunct and outdated recommendations of the Hunt and Chandler boards of 1881–85, or those of his more recent advisory board of 1885–89. Without an agreed national policy, the Navy Department did not propose a new schedule or a baseline of specific classes of warships for particular purposes. Congress, therefore, remained the authority for Navy organization and annual warship increases in accordance with its own view of national dynamics. The lame-duck session of the Fiftieth Congress ending in March 1889 added another dynamite cruiser, a ram, and other smaller vessels to the Navy inventory.[41]

In sum, during the second four-year period of Navy development that took place under the Cleveland presidency from 1885 to 1889, two Congresses selected a potpourri of warships unconnected to any coordinated executive branch national strategy. Their total of nine cruisers, two dynamite boats, seven gunboats, one torpedo boat, one ram, and nine non-oceangoing monitors reflected a continuing focus on local coastal defense and limited commerce raiding. Considering that the Navy's ship inventory was still in decline, the legislature was certainly not funding a major rehabilitation. The two dynamite boats were experimental vessels that the Navy believed were sound defensive warships at the time, but their weapons range was limited and required the ships to be dangerously close to the target. The use of a ram in modern steel-ship warfare was problematic at best.

Of the nine cruisers authorized since 1883, only three were of the armored category. The two largest armored cruisers, the *Maine* and the *Texas*, were later re-designated as second-class battleships. These two were just over 300 feet in length, carried approximately 390 men, and weighed between 6,300 to 6,700 tons. Their major armament consisted of less than a dozen each of 6- to 12-inch naval rifles and an assortment of smaller guns. In reality, these re-designated cruisers were not capital warships on the international scene.[42]

6

A TURNING POINT, 1889–93

I ncoming President Harrison appointed Benjamin Tracy Jr. to join his cabinet as the Secretary of the Navy. Tracy was born in 1830 to a middle-class family whose ancestors came from the Plymouth colony of Massachusetts. After the American Revolution, his family migrated to the growing southern tier of New York State and settled in the vicinity of the Susquehanna River along the border with Pennsylvania. Tracy had a happy childhood and solid year-round schooling where he cultivated a permanent friendship with Thomas Platt, an older classmate and eventually a powerful figure in New York politics. Tracy briefly taught school and then began his lifelong career in the field of law. As a portent of subsequent poor health episodes, he became ill in 1860 and, with sufficient means, convalesced for over a year with his wife and children on his father's farm.[1] In the fall of 1861, several months after the outbreak of the Civil War, the recovered Tracy became a member of the New York State Assembly.

The following summer, he volunteered for military service with the rank of colonel and spent the next year and half in command of a regiment guarding the nation's capital. He and his troops finally saw action in May 1864 in the violent Battle of the Wilderness in Virginia. In his first day of combat, he led a successful charge in close quarters, but shortly thereafter succumbed to exhaustion and spent the next two days resting in an aid station behind the lines. Rejoining his troops, he participated in dispiriting skirmishes a few days later with only small gains and high casualties, and again physically yielded to the strain of battle. After a total of seven days on the front, his condition worsened and his Army surgeon judged him unfit for duty due to a heart condition. Tracy returned to his home in Elmira, New York, for recuperation. Four months later, he resumed Army duty as commander of the disreputable U.S. prisoner of war camp for Confederate soldiers at Elmira, where he remained from October 1864 until the end of the war.[2] Inheriting a poor state of affairs at the under-maintained prison, Tracy showed concern for the prisoners. In spite of poor funding and low priority, he managed to somewhat improve conditions as the war came to an end.[3]

Upon his return to civilian life, Tracy rebuilt his lucrative law practice and reentered the political arena of the Republican Party. Opposing New York Party boss Roscoe Conkling, Tracy joined the movement against provisions of the Fourteenth Amendment that would give citizenship to former slaves and disenfranchise Southern leaders. Instead, he aligned with President Andrew Johnson to disallow black citizenship and to rehabilitate Southern politicians as soon as possible. As a reward for his support, Johnson appointed Tracy as U.S. district attorney for the Eastern District of New York, a position that he held for the next six years. Johnson later promoted him to the rank of brevet brigadier general backdated to March 1865 "for gallant and meritorious service during the War." Tracy would use the title General Tracy for the rest of his life. Thirty years after the Civil War and after he left Harrison's cabinet, President Cleveland awarded him the Medal of Honor "for distinguished gallantry in action at the Battle of the Wilderness."[4] Cleveland acted at the behest of Tracy's brother-in-law and former law partner, Gen. Isaac Catlin, an influential New York lawyer, politician, and Cleveland supporter.

As Tracy's law practice and work as a federal prosecutor flourished, he amassed a comfortable financial estate and became a noted breeder of trotter race horses. After a period of work as an associate justice of the Court of Appeals, his health deteriorated again in the winter of 1882–83, causing him to give up his law practice. He convalesced for two years with his family and took a long tour of Europe. Upon his recovery and return to New York City he reentered the field of law, partnering with Frank H. Platt, the son of his close friend Thomas Platt, and once again involved himself in state politics. At the 1888 Republican Convention in Chicago, the New York delegation—led by Thomas Platt, who expected to be rewarded with a cabinet appointment—swung behind Benjamin Harrison. The Republican Party not only won the presidency but also won the majority of seats in both the House and Senate.

With little notice, a few days before the March 1889 presidential inauguration, Tracy received his appointment to lead the Navy. Harrison had already rewarded Blaine by appointing him secretary of state. Tracy had no connection with the Navy and expected to be selected for the office of attorney general. Harrison chose Tracy for the lesser Navy portfolio as a compromise candidate in order to fill the unofficial New York State quota in the new cabinet, without siding with the competing interests of political bosses. Tracy assumed his position as the fourth Secretary of the Navy identified with the development of the modern steel fleet. However, neither he nor Congress at the time linked the current naval progress as the beginning of a significant new era. Similar to his immediate predecessors, Tracy was a naval neophyte. In spite of his unfamiliarity with maritime operations, he approached his new job with the considerable vigor that characterized his subsequent four years in the president's cabinet. He began by befriending his military bureau chiefs and learning the business of the Navy.[5]

In his long inaugural address, President Harrison spoke of his priorities as he laid down his policy for administering the country. For him, steady U.S. progress was the result of direct government action in the Hamiltonian sense rather than the small-government policies of Thomas Jefferson. Harrison in essence announced that he would be an activist president with governmental involvement in the life of the citizens. Consistent with his campaign rhetoric, he strongly defended high protective tariffs as essential to American well-being. Considering commercial maritime trade enlargement, he said that the United States needed both distant coaling stations under national authority and modern warships to ensure trading equality across the seas.[6]

Although not obvious to Harrison at the time, the patronage system for appointments to government jobs was beginning its decline. The Pendleton Civil Service Reform Act of 1883 had provisions that permitted the seated president to convert federal jobs to the new civil service classification structure based on a merit exam. This mechanism allowed the outgoing president to designate selected appointees as holding civil service positions that could not be reassigned by the next administration. The practice occurred to some extent when Arthur left office in 1885 and to a greater degree when Cleveland turned over the government to Harrison in 1889. The new president's fortuitous choice for the position of Civil Service commissioner was thirty-one-year-old Theodore Roosevelt, who considered his appointment to be the end of his short-lived political career in New York City.[7] Nevertheless, he approached his task with the typical vigor shown in his later years and he did not hesitate to take on political bosses.

Shortly after his inauguration in March 1889, Harrison learned that a violent hurricane in Samoa had sunk three U.S. Navy and three German navy ships in harbor. The single British ship that survived carried the news to the United States via Australia. In the ensuing months, the United States managed a recovery process that included a treaty with Great Britain and Germany to jointly take over the governance of the Islands of Samoa. During recent years the United States and others had shown interest in the islands as a coaling station for increased maritime commerce. Now, in his first month in office, Harrison turned the hurricane disaster into an opportunity to gain a legal foothold in the central Pacific.

Closer to home, in spite of his testy relationship with Secretary Blaine, Harrison accepted Blaine's initiative to organize an assembly of Latin American nations under U.S. leadership. This diplomacy resulted in the creation of the Bureau of the American Republics, which eventually evolved into the Organization of American States. But in spite of Harrison's and Blaine's diplomatic reaches, the small U.S. Navy did not have a meaningful sea power presence in either the Pacific or Atlantic theaters. To increase American influence, Harrison sanctioned Tracy to take an aggressive lead to change U.S. naval strategy from focusing on warships for coastal defense and commerce raiding to the development of armored ships with open-ocean offensive capabilities at least on par with the world powers. This watershed change in naval philosophy had been in the minds of progressive Navy leaders for several years and became a serious executive department interest by the end of the year 1889.

DELIBERATIONS

The proximate events leading to this transformation began with Tracy's study of the Navy in the spring of 1889. The crisis involving the Samoan hurricane illuminated the reality that an expanding Navy, not just commercial carriers, depended on coaling stations in faraway places. As such, Tracy realized the importance of developing a coherent mission and a support plan for future naval employment. Within a few months of the hurricane disaster, followed by his initial exposure to Navy Department affairs, he began to settle into his new city. To handle the challenges of his job, he recognized the necessity of becoming an integral part of the Washington scene. He purchased a large residence to house his family and to establish the requisite social-political ties, especially with Navy leaders. In order to augment his government salary of $8,000 per year and buy a suitable home for entertainment, he raised $60,000 by selling several of his valuable race horses.[8]

Once ensconced in his new mansion and Navy office, Tracy decided to use his cabinet position to rearrange Navy Department administration while staying within the sacrosanct bureau system. He issued a general order in June that resulted in inter-bureau transfers of responsibilities. Because ships and shore services were rapidly replacing oil lamps with electric lights on a large scale, he consolidated the growing electrical services, currently developing in various bureaus, into the Equipment Bureau. He also gave that bureau the responsibility for the Naval Observatory and the Hydrographic Office. The Navigation Bureau, in turn, gained in stature by becoming the executive arm of the Secretary of the Navy for all matters concerning the Naval Academy, fleet movements, operations, and personnel.

Applying reason to the process of ship manufacturing, Tracy created a Board of Construction consisting of the chiefs of the five bureaus of Steam Engineering, Ordnance, Equipment, Yards and Docks, and Construction and Repairs.[9] This board was the current advisory body whose lineal predecessor in 1881 had reported the recommendations that began the process of building a steel Navy. No longer an ad hoc committee, the board that recommended ship designs, construction, and equipment now included five of the eight bureau chiefs. Senior Navy officers generally agreed with Tracy rearranging bureau duties, although many preferred that he move further by creating a military general staff.[10]

However, the redistribution of bureau responsibilities did not address some of the Navy's deeper problems. Tensions caused by diverse officer specializations continued to gain traction. Ships went to sea with staff corps officers who performed duties as steam engineers, paymasters, surgeons, and chaplains.

More numerous line officers commanded ships and performed navigation, deck seamanship, and gunnery functions. When serving ashore, the line officers commanded shipyards and training stations as logical extensions of their exclusive qualification to command ships at sea. Similarly, line officers headed the four bureaus associated with navigation, ordnance, ship equipment, and Navy yards.

As the Navy's fleet evolved to ships driven by steam propulsion rather than sail, the role of steam engineers obviously increased in importance. However, line officers maintained their position as the seamen who maneuvered the new warships. Steam engineers had dominion over ships' propulsion plants and machinery but remained ineligible to command a ship and its crew. As large ships with complex machinery began to be contracted for the new Navy fleet, the rivalry between the engineers and line officers deepened. Steam engineers questioned the rationale of line officers having total command authority and sought equality in rank and responsibility.

Tracy necessarily schooled himself in the unique responsibilities, hierarchy, and language of the naval service in order to better understand his challenges. He often met with congressional leaders and some of the more outspoken Navy professionals, such as seventy-five-year-old Adm. David Dixon Porter and recently retired Rear Admiral Luce, along with several of the new breed of upcoming progressive officers. Contributing to Tracy's education, Luce publicly exposed Navy weaknesses by publishing "Our Future Navy" in the widely read *North American Review*.[11] Tracy agreed with Luce's assessment that the U.S. Navy was not capable of engaging major world powers and that the United States needed battleships, not gunboats and unprotected light cruisers. Luce referred to Britain's five-year plan for the construction of ten battleships and sixty cruisers during the period of 1889 to April 1894. Taking action, Tracy created a one-time in-house Policy Board, separate from the activities of the statutory Board of Construction, to write a total plan for Navy requirements for the secretary in terms of warship classes and capabilities, including a time frame for annual appropriations from Congress to increase the Navy. Eight years had passed since Secretary Hunt formed his Naval Advisory Board to determine the needs of the naval service. Tracy now charged his department to establish a baseline for an offensive Navy fleet.

He submitted his first annual report to the new Fifty-first Congress in December 1889, a few months prior to receiving the conclusions of his policy board. Tracy began by noting the Navy's inadequacies. The fleet had only 11 armored cruisers, 2 of which had been reclassified as second-class battleships. The remaining 31 vessels of various classes in service were unarmored. By comparison, Great Britain had 367 warships in service and France had 260. Tracy stated that the standing of the U.S. Navy was meaningless as being less than twelfth in the world and was not ranked as a naval power. His report called for congressional action to build two fleets of battleships, with eight in the Pacific and twelve in the Atlantic. This was a major departure from previous Navy secretaries, who had focused on small, unarmored fast cruisers for *guerre de course* commerce raiding and coastal protection. Tracy asked for his program to be accomplished in five years and wanted eight armored battleships to be funded this session. President Harrison concurred.[12]

While Capt. Alfred Thayer Mahan had not yet published his ground-breaking study *The Influence of Sea Power upon History*, he certainly was part of Tracy's inner circle of Navy progressives. Mahan had already completed a two-year term as president of the Naval War College and a recent assignment on a commission to select a Navy yard site on the northwest coast. Then on special duty in Washington, D.C., he was a strong voice for change. Also, a spirit of navalism seemed to be on the rise among some lawmakers, although the majority of them were not amenable to funding radical changes in the naval force structure. In its 114 years of life, the United States had never sought to build an offensive fleet of ships of the line. Progress toward that goal had come piecemeal and slowly.

Mahan had begun his seafaring career in 1859 as an eighteen-year-old midshipman, cruising for two years in the South Atlantic Station on board the ship of the line *Congress*, one of the last venerable sailing frigates of the old U.S. Navy. Shortly after the Civil War began, Mahan was promoted to lieutenant and transferred to a screw steamer for a year of blockade duty along the coasts of the Carolinas and Florida. Following eight months ashore in Newport, Rhode Island, at the relocated Naval Academy, he spent the next year and a half deployed on board another screw steamer and then a sidewheeler in Atlantic and Gulf waters. Several months after the war ended, recently promoted Lieutenant Commander Mahan shipped out again on another sidewheeler for ten months of peacetime service in the Gulf of Mexico. In January 1867, he boarded a screw steamer for a two-year cruise in Asian waters. In early

1871, he returned to sea for a special six-month relief mission to the Mediterranean to bring supplies to the victims of the Franco-Prussian War. After a year at home, Commander Mahan deployed again in 1872 to the South Atlantic Station at Uruguay. In 1883 he took command of the *Wachusett*, a Civil War–era screw sloop-of-war armed with ten cannon, and sailed in the Peruvian waters of Callao Harbor and the Pacific Ocean for the next two years.[13]

With his many years at sea and in distant lands over a twenty-seven-year period, Mahan had cultivated a worldview interconnected with the status of nations that ruled the oceans. During his two years in Peru, he continued his readings on the course of empires throughout history. He spent considerable time in the British library in Lima engaged with the three-volume work *The History of Rome*, written in the 1850s by the noted German historian Theodor Mommsen. From his reading and experiences, Mahan continued to advance his concepts concerning the historical significance of maritime supremacy in relation to the state of competing nations. This led to his authorship regarding the influence of sea power, theorizing that it was responsible for sustaining great empires.

To Mahan and other Navy progressives, sea power meant the ability to control maritime outcomes on distant shores by concentrating sufficient force to withstand any challenge. Not having control of the seas leaves a nation open to attack by an adversary. Contemporary U.S. political leaders did not readily accept this theory, which Mahan put together in 1889 and published in 1890. Indeed, many government leaders continued to pursue their own isolationist view for successful national survival, which for them depended primarily on maritime defense. But forward-looking Navy officers were already advancing the notion of command of the seas as a requirement for international success. Agreeing with his admirals, Tracy became a proponent of developing an offensive Navy, even if he did not specifically articulate the theoretical relationship between sea power and empire.

RESPONSES

However, neither the Secretary of the Navy nor the president of the United States controlled the budget. In order to build an offensive Navy, Congress with its many diverse constituencies had to be convinced to fund expensive armored battleships with the endurance to operate on distant shores. Concurrently, the legislature also needed to agree upon a policy that would justify an offensive maritime strategy. The Fifty-first Congress acted cautiously regarding the Navy. Early in its opening session in December 1889, Senator Hale introduced a resolution authorizing the shipbuilding program of eight battleships as requested by Tracy. The proposed bill immediately evoked intense opposition from Senator Chandler, who strongly criticized battleships as being unnecessary for the Navy. Leading members of the House of Representatives also balked at funding such a sweeping warship construction program.[14]

At the same time, lobbying by naval officers for equitable pay, promotion, and new retirement arrangements became a serious distraction. As the legislature moved into the work of its first session, congressmen challenged the legality of officer organizations that were attempting to influence lawmaking. Totally in character, Chandler, in his third year in the Senate, jumped on the bandwagon to limit the prerogatives of Navy officers. He introduced a resolution requiring Tracy to report on the lobbies that did not have Navy Department authorization and were designed to pressure Congress. Chandler and other senators expressed concern about the legality of officers paying lawyers to press their case in Congress rather than petitioning directly themselves.[15]

In his official reply to Chandler's Senate resolution, Tracy listed six separate groups organized specifically to influence Congress: first, officers for legislation favorable to the line; second, engineers for legislation favorable to engineers; third, ensigns of both the line and staff to advance the interests of ensigns in all corps; fourth, mates for the passage of a bill for their relief; fifth, medical officers, paymasters, and engineers for legislation of interest to the naval service as a whole; sixth, an organization dedicated to passage of the Cowie Bill for reorganization and efficiency.[16] Congress did not take further action on the issue.

Thomas Cowie, then assigned as a storekeeper at the Torpedo Station, Newport, Rhode Island, was a thirty-two-year-old "passed assistant paymaster," a rank approximately equal to Navy lieutenant of the line. He authored an officer composition plan that proposed an equivalent rank structure for staff and line officers and better opportunities for promotion for all officers based on an expanded early retirement system. His supporters unsuccessfully pushed for some level of legislative acceptance and action on the proposition.[17] Cowie would later become the Navy's paymaster general and then head of the Bureau of Supplies and Accounts.

As both chambers began vigorous debates on what Congress could afford for the Navy, the report of the Navy Policy Board, headed by Commo. W. P. McCann, was unintentionally leaked to the public. The commentary represented the thinking of younger Navy officers whose work had not yet been fully vetted and approved by the Navy Department. Tracy himself had not had the opportunity to fully digest the findings prior to their untimely release. Congressional reaction to the report was immediate and extremely negative. The policy board offered a controversial and politically charged interpretation of the international scene of expanding empires and then presented a solution composed of an idealistic building program that would result in the U.S. Navy being "second only" to Great Britain. The construction program called for 35 battleships, 35 cruisers, 100 torpedo boats, and other miscellaneous vessels, for a grand total of 192 ships at a cost of $281 million.[18] That fiscal year's budget for the Navy, including previously authorized shipbuilding, stood at $21.6 million.

Personal disaster struck for Tracy as he grappled with the untoward release of his policy board. During the early morning of February 3, 1890, his grand house caught on fire. President Harrison immediately heard the news and hurried to the scene, where he found Tracy unconscious. Harrison helped revive Tracy and had to inform him that his wife of thirty-eight years, his second daughter Mary, and his French maid had died in the blaze. The president then took Tracy into his home to temporarily live with Harrison's extended family, already in residence. The funeral for Tracy's wife and daughter took place in the East Room of the White House as the capital mourned. During Tracy's convalescence, he bonded with the president and his wife and, in turn, became the president's chief adviser for the remainder of his time in office. Tracy returned to work eleven days later on Lincoln's birthday.[19]

A few weeks after the fire, Congress passed legislation for an assistant secretary of war to help manage the large appropriations for river and harbor improvements, as well as to help administer Civil War pensions.[20] Some five months later, the legislature decided also to authorize a civilian assistant for the Navy. The progressive-leaning majority of Congress chose to re-establish the position of Assistant Secretary of the Navy rather than increase the Navy officer bureaucracy.[21] In reality, the authorizations for civilian assistants for the War and Navy Departments were relatively low-level events in the military expansion process. The new positions did not affect the power relationship between Congress and the bureaus of either the Army or the Navy.

As Tracy recovered, he necessarily distanced himself from the growing controversy of the policy board, letting McCann's proposals die without formal review. Democratic senator John McPherson of New Jersey severely criticized the very formation of the policy board as an abomination consisting of officers lacking in experience and unqualified for the task. For him, it was a "foolish scheme" and a wrongful departure from the longtime policy of the U.S. government.[22] McPherson had been a member of the Senate naval committee for the past twelve years and supported building a fleet of cruisers and harbor defense vessels. He would become chairman of that committee during the second administration of President Cleveland.

At the end of June 1890, concentrating on Navy material increases, Congress authorized the largest single amount of funds for new ship construction since the Civil War. The $23 million appropriation included $15 million to build a total of three coastline battleships, one protected cruiser, one torpedo cruiser, and one torpedo boat.[23] Although the legislature was beginning to move away from an isolationist view, this allocation fell a good deal short of Tracy's and Harrison's requests for eight armored battleships and five torpedo boats. Intentionally sidestepping the issue of constructing an offensive fleet, Congress continued to use the word "coastline" to infer the battleships' usage rather than capability. Actually, the three large ships were the first full-sized armored battleships of the U.S. Navy that could realistically be employed in offensive roles.

After Congress authorized the position of Assistant Secretary of the Navy in July, Tracy looked to his Navy officers, who provided counsel in choosing Naval Academy professor James Soley to fill the office. However, the legislature, showing its concern for increasing the power of Navy officers, had stipulated that the president appoint a civilian for the assignment. As a professor at the academy, Soley held a commission in the Navy with the equivalent rank of commander. In order to assume the $4,500 per year position of assistant secretary, he necessarily resigned his commission, relinquishing his eligibility for military retirement. Showing his favor for Soley, retired Rear Admiral Luce expressed his confidence in the selection as "one that marked an important end in the history of naval administration."[24] The admiral and other leading senior officers hoped that he would function as a Navy chief of staff.

Unfortunately, under the current peacetime structure, Soley could not devote his efforts to centralizing Navy administration. Instead, he acted as a ninth Navy bureau chief in charge of the Office of Naval Intelligence and the Naval War College rather than becoming an agent for change.

By now Tracy was President Harrison's closest confidant on issues beyond the state of the Navy as Harrison pushed an unprecedented number of bills through a relatively compliant legislature. Congress approved antitrust regulations, a complex tariff system, silver purchase for monetary backing, and significant increases in military pensions for Civil War veterans. However, Harrison had been unable to win over farmers and laborers to approve his expanded government policy. With only one-third of its members up for reelection, the Senate managed to maintain a Republican Party majority in the November midterm 1890 congressional elections. However, the resultant Democratic Party sweep of the House of Representatives resulted in the replacement of nine of the thirteen members of its naval committee. This new, solidly Democratic working group opposing the president would control the Navy budget when it met the following year.

Tracy made a strenuous effort to gain approval for his principal programs from the friendly outgoing Congress as it met in December 1890 for its three-month lame-duck session. In his second annual report, he presented a lengthy recap of the Navy's progress, emphasizing the need for constructing battleships. Additionally, he made pleas to improve the officer promotion system and to establish a Navy militia. He pointed out that during the Civil War the enrollment of sailors went from 9,000 to 50,000. Finally, he reiterated the significant lack of steam engineers to man the growing Navy.[25]

In contrast to Tracy's appeals, President Harrison's annual message to the outgoing Congress barely mentioned the Navy. In two short paragraphs in his lengthy and self-congratulatory twenty-two-page report, he simply noted the government's energy in new naval construction and the esprit de corps of the officers and seamen in the naval service. His other sections included a long recap of successful international relations throughout the Americas, Europe, and Asia, and a full explanation of his positive views of the value of the recently passed tariff legislation.[26]

During the lame-duck legislative session, key issues concerned voting rights for black Americans and silver coinage. First, Rep. Henry Cabot Lodge introduced an elections bill that would give the federal government authority to monitor voting procedures in the South in order to protect the rights of black citizens. Not surprisingly, Southern Democrats bitterly opposed any interference in their election procedures. Second, westerners introduced a bill that would allow silver coins to be accepted using the same mechanism currently in place for gold. With a growing silver supply from western mines, silver currency was inflationary and benefitted the debtor classes of farmers and laborers. Eastern Republicans strongly opposed silver coinage, favoring the sound money of the gold standard, which privileged banks, industry, and lenders. Harrison supported the elections bill and threatened to veto any silver coinage act. Debates on both issues stalemated without legislative action at the end of that session.

Congressional Navy issues concerned the dwindling number of steam engineers for assignments to operate the machinery of an increasing number of modern ships. The legislation of 1882, limiting steam engineer officer accessions, had set an arbitrary number of 170 to be reached by attrition. The quota turned out to be too low, and within a few years the Navy indicated that it did not have enough qualified engineers for shipboard duty. Several congressmen in both houses of Congress agreed and pushed proposals to cease the reductions required by law. But their bills, introduced in their first session, remained in their respective naval committees and never made it to the floor for discussion or vote.[27] As the lame-duck session progressed, Senator Chandler joined in the legislative efforts to help the engineers and reported that the current limit was simply inadequate for the needs of the Navy.[28] However, his bill also remained in committee as the final session ended.

The legislature labeled the Billion Dollar Congress adjourned in March 1891. However, the Republican-friendly Fifty-first Congress did not come close to funding the Navy's building program supported by Harrison and Tracy. In spite of congressional billion-dollar largesse, the Navy's share over the course of two sessions amounted to $54.6 million. Although Congress had begun the first steps toward building an offensive Navy, it did not follow through with sufficient appropriations to continue the process. As it adjourned, it added only one protected cruiser of the approximate size of the second-class battleships *Texas* and *Maine*.[29] It also allocated the relatively small amount of $20,000 to the Bureau of Ordnance, for arms and equipment for naval militia regulated by the Secretary of the Navy. Officer personnel issues concerning the steam engineer shortages, rank stagnation, duty ashore assignments, staff officer status, and retirement restructuring were put off for the next Congress, which was scheduled to meet in December 1891.

MOVEMENT

Meanwhile, Tracy focused on halting the Navy's patronage-laden spoils system, which loomed with the impending congressional power shift, by establishing civil service in Navy yards. Breaking the hold of multilevel bureaucrats, he gave shipyard commanders authority to hire from approved lists of qualified candidates. Civil Service commissioner Roosevelt praised his action, noting that only the Indian agencies suffered more than the Navy under political patronage.

Concurrent with the views of Harrison and Blaine, Tracy concentrated on obtaining coaling stations for the Navy and merchant marine. His motivation included the maritime commercial interests of his longtime business associates on the East Coast, as well as his growing attention to a naval fleet that could effectively use the seas any place in the world. In the spring of 1891, Tracy aggressively tried to influence the government of Haiti to grant the United States exclusive rights to a coaling station at Port-au-Prince. Routine diplomatic efforts escalated when Tracy ordered Rear Adm. Bancroft Gherardi, the commander of U.S. ships then visiting Haiti, to conduct gunnery drills nearby to intimidate the Haitians to give in to the U.S. request. When the Haitian authorities did not react, Tracy sent another group of ships under Rear Admiral Walker, to put further pressure on the island nation. Tracy soon realized that the presence of such a large U.S. force was unproductive and drew significant negative U.S. press coverage. He withdrew both naval groups and refocused on Navy administration at home. The United States failed to get a coaling station in Haiti or any other port in the Caribbean.

During the summer, Tracy again attempted to resolve the problem of a top-heavy officer corps and the dismal outlook for the promotion of junior officers. In June, he appointed a board of officers to make recommendations to Congress regarding the stagnated Navy officer structure.[30] Its chairman was Capt. Robert L. Phythian, who was then superintendent of the Naval Academy and had commanded the *Trenton*, the largest steam frigate of the Navy built after the Civil War and a flagship of the Asiatic fleet. The Phythian Board considered increasing the rate of promotions by increasing the number of retirements and changing the rank structure to provide additional senior positions. This was similar to Representative McAdoo's proposal seven years earlier. Additionally, the board introduced a measure to promote some high-ranking officers by a selection process rather than by seniority. The recommendations faltered because of the sticking point about increased retirements.

In the autumn of 1891, the United States faced an escalating revolutionary crisis with Chile. Harrison sided with its incumbent president and Tracy kept a fleet nearby to protect American commercial interests. The *Baltimore* (C 3), a 4,400-ton protected cruiser with a crew of 380 men, maintained a presence in the vicinity. In mid-October a group of sailors from the *Baltimore*, while on shore leave in Valparaiso, got into a series of fights with local citizens. A mob of Chileans and complicit local police killed two U.S. sailors and wounded seventeen others.[31] The victorious revolutionaries in Chile rejected the U.S. demand to conduct an investigation, declaring the event to be an internal affair, and the situation festered.

When the incoming Democratic Congress gathered in Washington in December, its priorities concerned tariffs and money, not the state of the Navy. After a two-year hiatus, Rep. Herbert of Alabama once again received the chairmanship of his naval committee. Having headed naval affairs for four years during the Cleveland administration, he was no longer a naval neophyte. But his personal relations with Tracy remained problematic. During the Civil War he had been permanently disabled at the Battle of the Wilderness in May 1864 by wounds received fighting against the U.S. Army. Tracy briefly fought at the same battle at the same time against the Confederate army. Twenty years later the former enemies by necessity now worked with each other on Navy issues.

Tracy's annual report, forwarded to the new Congress, began with an optimistic appraisal of the delay in the delivery of ship armor and followed with a lengthy, up-to-date recounting of the violence against the crew of the *Baltimore*. The crisis continued into the winter and would not be resolved until January when Chile recanted and gave in to U.S. demands, including the payment of indemnities. Considering the confrontation, Tracy stressed the need to continue building large ships and asked for two battleships of the new *Indiana* class.

This approval would result in a total of five 10,000-ton armored warships for the Navy and was considerably less than his request two years earlier for a fleet of twenty ships of that category. He also asked for one large armored cruiser of the *New York* class and an unspecified number of small and fast torpedo boats for riverine service. In keeping with his "control of the sea" concept, he stated that the Navy did not need gunboats or unprotected cruisers for defense.

Tracy also reported that since March, after the previous Congress had authorized $25,000 for a Navy militia, 6 states had established a total force of 1,147 men. He expressed the importance of continuing and expanding this voluntary service. In closing, Tracy noted that the findings of the Phythian Board, appointed in June to examine the promotion stagnation of officers, were now available to Congress.[32] Reactions to the Phythian Board report were varied. The press incorrectly reported that a majority of officers favored promotion by seniority and were concerned that selection board favoritism would adversely affect any attempt to promote or retire officers. This conclusion was the product of media supposition and was not backed by any poll of the officers involved. In fact, leading senior officers tended to support some form of a selection process as recommended by Captain Phythian and advised Congress on the benefits of competition.[33]

Following the advice of progressive naval officers, congressmen introduced bills based on the board's recommendation to restructure the promotion and retirement system of the Navy. Alignments solidified along regional rather than party lines. Progressive northeastern Republicans in the Senate, led by Hale and naval committee chairman Cameron, joined with Southern Democrats in the House of Representatives, led by Herbert and freshman Archibald Williams of North Carolina, in support of Navy reorganization legislation.[34] However, the majority of the full legislature did not support the restructuring resolutions, which again died in their respective naval affairs committees. Congress as a whole would not consider a plan that put selective military promotion in the hands of the executive department, nor would it open debates to change the Navy pension system.

The majority of the legislature also would not consider raising the quotas of engineers or adding any new shore-duty billets for officers.[35] Opponents of an expanding Navy, especially congressmen from inland states, continued to contest the cost of bringing in any additional officers. William Holman of Indiana, chairman of the House appropriations committee and a strong adversary of big government and naval growth, objected to any increase in Navy spending. Members of the new Populist Party Jeremiah Simpson of Kansas and Tom Watson of Georgia joined agrarian Democrats led by Benton McMillin of Tennessee and agreed with Holman. With little sympathy for further expansion of the Navy, they vehemently argued to retain the engineer ceiling and also refused to add even one new shore duty position to assist the beleaguered chiefs of the eight bureaus.[36]

By late spring 1892, Harrison faced political opposition from various sides in his fight for renomination. Three days before the Republican convention opened in Minneapolis on June 7, Blaine resigned as secretary of state. Without campaigning, the "Plumed Knight" made himself available as an unannounced candidate in case a groundswell occurred in his favor. With considerable effort and backroom dealing, Harrison managed to maneuver sufficient support to win his party's selection on the first ballot. However, many delegates remained disgruntled by the heavy-handed fundraising and lobbying excesses of his campaign managers. His Democratic opponent would be former President Grover Cleveland.

For the past two years, Cleveland had been speaking out against Harrison's policies supporting protective tariffs, silver coinage, and the treasury surplus. The McKinley Tariff Act of 1890 heavily favored industrial and financial sectors at the expense of working citizens. The act had energized the Democratic Party to manage a successful sweep of the congressional elections that year and helped affirm Cleveland's run for the presidency in 1892. His most serious concern was the maneuvering of David Hill, who saw himself as a more viable Democratic candidate for the presidency. He had succeeded Cleveland in the New York governor's office and then won election to the U.S. Senate. In order to collect delegates for his presidential nomination, Hill gathered Democrats who favored silver coinage and protective tariffs, issues that were an abomination to Cleveland. At first Hill appeared to be assembling sufficient backing, especially among Southerners who wanted the soft inflationary money of silver currency. Cleveland held his ground against Hill's machinations by maintaining his fervent commitment against both free silver and high tariffs, which he felt hurt the working people. When the Democrats met in

Chicago on June 21, Cleveland won his party's nomination on the first ballot and prevailed in getting a platform supporting lower tariffs.

Congress was still in session and Tracy spent his time lobbying a legislature not amenable to his programs. Its Naval Appropriations Act of July 19 authorized one coastline battleship and one armored cruiser.[37] After vigorously working with the legislature since it had opened its session in December, Tracy could not get relief for steam engineer officers or make progress on any other pressing personnel matter. Congress left the issues on the table to be resolved after the upcoming elections and the commencement of its lame-duck winter session.

Cleveland's managers ran a calm but vigorous campaign led by his former Secretary of the Navy William Whitney. Cleveland helped his own cause by his determined focus on economic issues. Although he chose not to campaign directly, he wrote many letters and talked with Democratic leaders about the need for unwavering leadership regarding the principal business of reducing protective tariffs and maintaining sound currency. The canvas of 1892 showed no resemblance to the dreadful historic mudslinging of the 1884 campaign or the lethargy of Cleveland's failed 1888 run for reelection. This time around, it was Harrison who lacked vigor and a cohesive team. The active campaign season ended due to the illness of Harrison's wife Caroline, who died of tuberculosis on October 23. Cleveland ceased his activities as an act of propriety and let the polls speak for the people, who elected him with a wide margin.

Harrison and Tracy still had four months in office and a lame-duck Congress to work with until the turnover in early March. In the beginning of Tracy's fourth annual report of December he wrote: "While the authorizing of new ships rests wholly with Congress, the recommendations of the Department have a large influence on the results."[38] In this final report, Tracy attempted to get positive movement from Congress. He claimed that his first report of December 1889, three years previously, had indicated a radical departure in U.S. policy to build offensive battleships and cruisers for the Navy. That was something of an overstatement: President Harrison certainly had not articulated a significant policy change. In his final report, Tracy did not request a specific number of ships to be authorized at this time. Toward the end of his rather lengthy account of the state of the Navy, he also noted that a large naval review would take place in April to celebrate the four-hundredth anniversary of Columbus's first voyage to America.

Harrison's lengthy fourth message to Congress gave a glowing recap of all his accomplishments. His section on the Navy restated the number of vessels put in commission during his tenure and, without specificity, hoped that Congress would consider the Secretary of Navy's recommendations. Harrison focused primarily on the success of protective tariffs as being responsible for bank prosperity and high wages.[39] Referring to the harbor at the Pearl River in Hawaii, he encouraged friendship with the friends of the United States that in mid-January would overthrow Queen Lili'uokalani.

In the beginning of its final session, the Fifty-second Congress finally dealt with Tracy's steam engineer officer shortage and passed a bill to stop the decrease. Meanwhile, the cadre had dwindled to 189 officers, which was 19 more than the unrealistic maximum set by law 10 years previously. According to the new act, 1 engineer officer could now be appointed from the Naval Academy for each vacancy that occurred, effectively raising the quota to 189 based on the number in service at the time.[40] Members of both houses of Congress also recognized that as long as officers were available and on duty, the legislature could not curtail the necessary officer movements ashore. With that realization, Congress provided for a Navy officer assistant to the Bureau of Navigation while modestly increasing the Navy warship inventory by authorizing defensive gunboats and an experimental submarine boat.[41] The legislature only cautiously began to legitimize the Navy's expansion.

In summary, the third four-year period of new Navy growth during the 1889–93 administration of Harrison and Tracy saw increases in ship authorizations. However, the expansion was not close to the level requested by the president and his Secretary of the Navy. As a milestone, two Congresses approved building ships of the largest class and funded a total of four coastline battleships. The legislators also added three armored cruisers, torpedo boats, and gunboats to the Navy inventory. The United States was slowly taking a course toward oceanic expansion but fell far short of the executive branch recommendations. The naval acts also specified that warships should be built in shipyards on the Pacific, Gulf, and Atlantic coasts. As such, the growing state of California would soon be the site of major Navy construction.

7

REASONABLE PROGRESS,
1893–97

President Cleveland hesitated until the end of February to select a cabinet that met his requirements of talent and political balance. Initially, he unsuccessfully sought a representative from the influential New England maritime states to head the Navy Department. As an alternative, Cleveland appointed Rep. Hilary Herbert to manage the Navy portfolio.[1] With eight years on the naval committee and six as its chairman, Herbert was by far the most seasoned naval authority since before the Civil War to become the Secretary of the Navy. Overall, the new president had considerably larger concerns than the state of the Navy.

He inherited a country in a serious depression bound up by protective tariffs and a monetary system that was hemorrhaging the U.S. gold supply. He delivered his rather brief inaugural address of March 1893 with an emotional focus on the instability of U.S. currency, which threatened to seriously draw down the health and success of the nation. Additionally, he emphasized the need for civil-service reform to ensure government competency and financial fitness. Cleveland also devoted a paragraph to the inescapable responsibility to treat American Indians fairly and lead them to independent citizenship. He closed his speech with a pledge to lift the burden of unfair tariffs and his awareness of the duties of his office.[2] His concise address made no mention of the state or future of the Navy.

Cleveland's first crisis concerned the proposed annexation of Hawaii, which had been advancing for several years. American missionaries and their descendants had developed a growing presence in Hawaii since the 1820s. The immigrants converted islanders to Christianity, constructed a written language, and provided education to a population that was being decimated by disease and alcoholism introduced by merchants and whalers. The expatriate Americans also established and controlled huge plantations encompassing a large majority of the land. By early July 1887, the offspring of American missionaries and settlers had become sufficiently influential in the Hawaiian legislature to force a new constitution on the reigning King Kalākaua. Favoring the foreign settlers, the constitution disenfranchised significant numbers of Hawaiians who did not have substantial wealth or landholdings and granted voting rights to non-Hawaiian residents. The ultimate goal was U.S. annexation.

A few years later, Kalākaua's successor, Queen Liliʻuokalani, prepared another constitution to return the government to the native people of Hawaii. Predictably, she ran into intransigent opposition from the ruling legislature and withdrew her proposal with a promise to bring it up in the future. Hawaiian annexationist leaders viewed her promise as a barely veiled threat to break up the existing legislature. Consequently, they set up a Committee of Public Safety and asked for protection from the U.S. Navy squadron, which was conveniently anchored in the harbor. On January 16, 1893, 160 Marines came ashore to protect the Hawaiian government from its own queen. The Committee of Public Safety then deposed the queen and established a provisional government that requested U.S. annexation. President Harrison's on-scene ambassador, John S. Stevens, immediately recognized the new government and, with determined haste, its commissioners sailed across the Pacific to the United States to present their case for statehood. On February 16, outgoing President Harrison agreed with the treaty proposal and sent it to the Senate, which cautiously chose to withhold action until after the inauguration of President Cleveland in early March.

The new president decided to send James H. Blount, a former ten-term Democratic congressman from Georgia and former chairman of the House's Foreign Affairs Committee, to Hawaii to appraise the situation. After arrival, Blount condemned the actions of Stevens, returned the Marines to their flagship (the protected cruiser *Boston*, one of the ABCDs of the new Navy), and recommended restoring the queen's government. In view of the necessity for long ocean transits, several months had passed between the queen's deposition and Blount's findings. Cleveland reluctantly acknowledged the legitimacy of the current government with the realization that a restoration attempt by the United States at this time would be an act of war. U.S. annexation of Hawaii remained simmering for the next five years.

Back in Washington, the cabinet began its work in the new administration. Although quite popular in Congress and praised by both the North and the South, Herbert was certainly a lesser light in Cleveland's organization and not a close adviser.[3] Navy growth was far removed from the issues of the day. Herbert, as well as other cabinet members, first faced considerable challenges concerning the patronage necessities of appointments. In spite of the growing civil service system, the new officials were inundated by requests for government job placement, a situation exacerbated by the Democratic takeover after four years of Republican government. As a result, the incoming administration got little accomplished during the first few months in office.[4]

For the position of Assistant Secretary of the Navy, Herbert selected his own man, former congressman William McAdoo of New Jersey. Before leaving Congress in 1891, McAdoo had been a member of the House of Representatives naval committee for eight years and chairman of its subcommittee on militia in his final term.[5] Noted for his technical knowledge of naval matters, he maintained his connections with his former congressional colleagues as he worked within the executive branch. As assistant secretary, he expended considerable effort on his pet projects to expand state naval militias and establish a federal Navy reserve force. Although these programs perhaps promoted some navalism, they remained localized affairs confined to the Great Lakes and coastal states. Navy militia organizations and proposed reserve formations often involved the efforts of a small group of congressmen and proved to be a minor part of the larger national debates concerning naval increases and organization.

Herbert added oversight of the newly formed naval militia to the duties of his assistant secretary, rather than give the responsibility to a military bureau chief. He preferred to maintain civilian control in the Navy Department as much as possible. Similar to Tracy, he continued to treat his assistant as a ninth bureau chief responsible for naval intelligence and the Naval War College.[6] McAdoo also supervised various naval boards and ship construction in the Navy yards. Akin to his predecessor, he concentrated on administrative details rather than attempting to alter the power relationships within the Navy Department.

During Herbert's second month in office, the United States sponsored an international naval review that formed at Hampton Roads, Virginia. The event had been meticulously planned by the previous administration to celebrate the four-hundredth anniversary of Christopher Columbus arriving in the New World. Herbert accompanied President Cleveland on board the *Dolphin* and cruised from Virginia to New York Harbor for the formal review to be held in late April. The review was a proud moment for the president and the U.S. Navy. As the *Dolphin* steamed in front of the anchored international fleet, each ship "manned the yards and saluted the President as he passed by."[7] After the events in New York, Cleveland and most of his cabinet traveled to Chicago for the May 1 opening of the Columbian Exposition, commonly called the Chicago World's Fair.

Upon returning from his trip to Chicago, Cleveland noted that he had a troublesome spot in his mouth, which he suspected would require treatment. Meanwhile the existing financial panic continued, with severe inflation and significant gold loss to Europe. In mid-June, the president's physician found a "malignant growth as large as a quarter of a dollar in Cleveland's mouth and called for a surgical procedure."[8] Cleveland made preparations for an operation to be done clandestinely in New York Harbor on board the yacht of prominent stockbroker Elias Benedict, and also decided to call on Congress to repeal the Sherman Silver Purchase Act of 1890. On June 30, the president summoned a special session of Congress to convene in August.

A day later, Cleveland underwent surgery while on board Benedict's yacht slowly steaming in the East River. The procedure removed the malignant growth along with teeth and parts of his palate and jaw, but remained totally confined to the inside of his mouth with no external evidence of surgery. Within a few days he was able to walk around the yacht, and his condition remained secret from the public for years. Fitted with a prosthesis for his jaw, he recuperated rapidly and was back to work within a month, albeit fatigued.

During that summer, Herbert traveled to Newport, Rhode Island, with the intention of shutting down the Naval War College as a superfluous training facility. But in transit on board the *Dolphin*, he experienced an awakening while reading Mahan's second book about naval strategy and the importance of an offensive navy, *The Influence of Sea Power upon the French Revolution and Empire.* A key issue for Herbert's volte-face was his realization of the futility of commerce raiding to significantly alter a war-at-sea outcome. He became convinced of the wisdom and necessity of the War College teachings concerning the requisite to command the sea rather than focusing on *guerre de course* and coastal defense.

BATTLESHIPS AND POLITICS

Herbert's first report, submitted to Congress in late November, supported former secretary Tracy's focus on the need for large armored capital warships. Herbert counted only nineteen ships in service plus another nineteen in various states of construction and three more authorized but not yet contracted. He showed sixty-four wooden or iron ships as unserviceable. After listing the capability of other nations, he placed the U.S. Navy as number seven. Additionally, he stated that the difficulty in procuring steel armor was causing delays and that none of the armored vessels, including the *Texas* and the *Maine*, were complete. He also wrote that unarmored cruisers for commerce raiding were not practical war vessels and asked Congress for one battleship and six torpedo boats.[9]

A rejuvenated Cleveland sent his annual message to Congress in December. To his great delight, his second daughter Esther had entered the world in September and remains the only presidential baby born in the executive mansion. At the end of October a closely divided Senate had finally agreed with the Democratic House of Representatives and, in their special session, the legislature repealed the silver purchase act. Subsequently, Cleveland's report to Congress in December 1893 was upbeat and lengthy. He began by praising U.S. foreign policy concerning disputes across the world. Getting down to financial business, he detailed the status of the treasury and predicted that the recent repeal of the silver act "will be most salutary and far-reaching."[10] Cleveland also noted that in one year the pension rolls, because of newly qualified veterans and wives and children of deceased veterans, had increased by approximately ninety thousand. The payment on the new pensions alone was $33.7 million, while the annual sum expended on all pensions equaled $156.7 million. By comparison, Army expenditures stood at $51.9 million and the 1893 Navy budget, including new warship construction, was $22.5 million.

The president's section on the state of the Navy listed by name the ten new cruisers and other smaller warships that were currently in service. He reiterated Herbert's report of construction delays caused by the difficulty in procuring armor and incorrectly asserted that the problem had been overcome and progress was forthcoming. He also wrote that the first of four "first-class" battleships should be completed by February 1896, a little more than two years in the future. Cautioning fiscal prudence, he made only a passing endorsement of Herbert's request for new construction.

As the spring and summer regular congressional session of 1894 progressed, Herbert focused on Navy organization rather than lobbying for new warships. Early in the legislature, Senator Hale, in his eleventh year on the naval committee, introduced legislation once again "to reorganize and increase the efficiency of the personnel of the Navy."[11] The Fifty-third Congress had political party unity with Democrats in control of both the houses of Congress. However, it lacked the regional cohesiveness necessary to address radical changes in the Navy officer organization. In its earlier special session to repeal the silver act, Democrats from Maryland, Pennsylvania, and South Carolina had introduced bills to place Navy steam engineers on equal terms with line officers.[12] The resolutions carried over to the regular winter-spring session, but never made it past their respective naval committees. The best that the committees could accomplish was to form yet another joint subcommittee to study the entire problem of reorganizing personnel in the Navy.[13] However, the issue now had the attention of the Republican minority of new progressives, who were dissatisfied with the inefficient bureaucracy of the Navy.

Taking action, the Senate had the two-year-old Phythian Report of Secretary Tracy reprinted and sent to the recently established joint subcommittee to examine the problem. In March, Herbert appeared before that committee to review the current situation of Navy officer promotion stagnation. He proposed a range of solutions involving some level of merit promotions, increasing the number of admirals, and involuntary retirement. Ten years previously, while a member of Congress, Assistant Secretary of the Navy McAdoo had put forward similar solutions in his resolution of December 1884. Once again the legislature did not take action.

While Herbert labored on behalf of the Navy, Cleveland unsuccessfully wrestled with a great depression. Discounting the possible beneficial effect of inflationary money on the struggling agrarian and labor community, he remained stubbornly committed against any semblance of a silver standard and vetoed a silver coinage act passed by the Congress in March 1894. His larger, almost all-consuming task consisted of cleaning what to him was the Augean stable of tariff regulations. Southern and western agrarian interests could not abide with the president's financial policies. The developing congressional election campaigns witnessed the rise of Silverite and Populist third parties. Meanwhile, strikes by coal miners and railroad workers characterized spring activities across the country.

In late June, the Pullman railroad car manufacturing company reacted to depression-related loss of sales by lowering wages. The majority of its laborers lived in company-owned villages, where rents were already higher than comparable domiciles in nearby Chicago. When company owner George Pullman reduced jobs and pay but did not lower rent, the workers took strike action to shut down production. The Pullman company reacted by carrying out a lockout. In sympathy with the strikers, the newly formed American Railway Union (ARU) began a boycott of any railroads handling Pullman cars. As the situation escalated, ARU leader Eugene V. Debs instructed members to refrain from destructive activity. Nevertheless, sympathy strikes broke out on rail lines from Texas to California as disgruntled workers used force to stop the trains from operating. In response to the exaggerated press reports about violence among the Pullman strikers in Chicago, President Cleveland declared martial law and sent in U.S. Army troops to maintain order.

Cleveland was greatly influenced by Attorney General Richard Olney, who judged the strikes to be illegal acts against the government's ability to deliver mail. Without waiting for the mayor of Chicago or the governor of Illinois to request federal assistance, the president agreed with Olney that federal action was necessary. After the president's decision of July 3 to engage the Army, work stoppage involving over 100,000 participants spread across the country and federal troops clashed violently with the strikers in the Chicago area. Within a week, federal authorities arrested Debs and other ARU leaders. The strikes and boycotts soon ended. The public and the press mostly sided with the president against the so-called labor anarchists.

Meanwhile, throughout the turmoil, Herbert continued his efforts in Congress for Navy growth. On the floor of the House of Representatives,

naval affairs chairman Amos Cummings (D-NY) explained why his committee reduced the secretary's request by $2.3 million while also stating that his
"committee was unanimously in favor of continuing the policy of building
up the Navy as any committee's [*sic*] that preceded it." On the floor of Congress, Boutelle of Maine heatedly disagreed with Cummings' appraisal and
castigated the Democratic Party at length for its current and past lack of
commitment to the new Navy and growth of the nation. Several leading
Democrats then took issue with Boutelle's characterization impugning their
loyalty and also criticized the record of Republican-led shipbuilding decisions. Populist William Baker of Kansas sided with the Democrats and added
his own criticism of spending for naval increases. He argued that the current
Republican plan would commit the United States to sell more gold-bearing
bonds, which for him meant "more wealth to the classes and more poverty to
the masses of our people."[14]

Navy increases were now presented as an integral part of the ongoing
financial crisis. In spite of Herbert's pleas and the Republican Party endorsement, the Democratic-led Congress denied funds for additional shipbuilding.
The legislature also rejected efforts to approve a national naval reserve force
but continued to finance state naval militias. At the end of its session, Congress
reduced the Navy's appropriation request of $28 million to $25.5 million. The
annual Navy act passed at the end of July 1894 authorized only three torpedo boats to be funded from previous appropriations for a second dynamite
cruiser, now deemed impractical by the Navy.[15]

As an aside, Congress expanded the administration of the Navy Bureau of
Provisions and Clothing and changed its name to the Bureau of Supplies and
Accounts. Six years previously James Fulton, then paymaster general of the
Navy, was on record with Congress, explaining his need for two assistants.[16]
He wanted a legal deputy to be in charge of the audit of all fiscal accounts and
another deputy to be in charge of all supply purchasing. The paymaster corps
had limited seagoing billets that were restricted mostly to junior officers. As
usual, Congress showed little interest in increasing the number of shore duty
officers in any branch of the Navy. But finally, years after the popular Fulton
left his office, Navy supporters in Congress convinced their colleagues that for
sound business reasons it was now essential to create the position of assistant
chief of the Bureau of Supplies and Accounts, recognizing its increased responsibilities in both purchasing and payroll for all the bureaus. Accordingly, during

the turbulent summer session of 1894, the legislature created a second military assistant position a year after the previous Congress had authorized an assistant for the navigation bureau.[17] Change indeed came slowly.

The administration of a growing naval service posed a problem for successive Congresses that over the years showed a deep reluctance to either increase the number of military officers in staff positions ashore or to increase those officers' authority. Legislative action to simply provide a total of two officer assistants to the Navy bureau chiefs came four years after the 1890 appointment of a civilian Assistant Secretary of the Navy. At least one historian accurately contended, "Congress lost power to the executive" because its inaction allowed the Navy to organize its bureaucracy without congressional oversight.[18] Although late in coming, Congress stopped procrastinating and took charge of military bureaucratic growth by managing a slow path that in due time led to increasing Navy administration and, more importantly, reinforced congressional power over the process.

President Cleveland had bigger issues than Navy organization. The Pullman strike had engaged his energies virtually day and night from late June to mid-July. At the same time he continued to face congressional recalcitrance to reduce the highly protective Gilded Age tariff laws of the Republican Party. His fruitless tariff battle had begun in February and lasted until August when Congress passed a somewhat watered-down tariff act at the end of its session. Typically, Cleveland took an uncompromising position and insisted on significant tariff reductions and readjustments. In the process he alienated many of his own Democratic Party members, especially those in the South who depended on tariff protection in spite of the raging depression. With repugnance, he refused to sign the watered-down Wilson-Gorman Act. However, he allowed it to become law by not vetoing it. He reasoned that the long-fought-over measure was at least slightly less protective than the previous McKinley Tariff Act of President Harrison's administration.

After Congress adjourned, the Democratic Party, with Cleveland as its teetering titular head, faced insurmountable odds in retaining its legislative majority. Through the president's own unyielding dealings and unwillingness to compromise, he lost labor's vote over his actions against the Pullman strikers. He lost the support of the important swing state of Illinois as well as key Southern states because of his perceived disregard of states' rights in declaring martial law and sending troops to Chicago without the approval of state officials. He lost the votes of agrarian interests and western silver states because of his unbending stand against silver coinage in favor of gold.

As the mid-term election tempest ran its course, Herbert kept his focus on departmental issues, primarily associated with Navy organization. In October he approved a lengthy opinion piece written by McAdoo concerning "Reorganization of the Navy," which was published in the widely read *North American Review.*[19] McAdoo wrote of the very pressing need to reorganize the structure of naval personnel management, with an emphasis on revising the stagnant seniority system of officer distribution and promotion. He understood the regulation of the Navy Department to be a congressional function and proposed his solutions to a joint legislative commission as an essential requirement to invigorate the new Navy. McAdoo reiterated the remedies that he had introduced ten years ago when he was a freshmen member of the House of Representatives. His focused on the importance of selection rather than seniority for promotion, a process that would include early retirement for those not selected. He again charged Congress with the responsibility for naval reorganization. Because of the precedent and expense of retirement pensions, the issue was beyond the bounds of party politics. Bills to change the Navy's promotion and retirement regulations continued to fail in both houses.[20]

The November 1894 congressional elections brought an unprecedented shift in the House of Representatives majority not seen again until the total Republican Party takeover of 1994, exactly one hundred years later. Republican representatives of the Fifty-third Congress elected in 1892 had a 37 percent minority. The 1894 election of the Fifty-fourth Congress resulted in a 70 percent Republican Party majority. Navy issues were not high on the agenda of the outgoing Congress when it sat for its lame-duck session of December to March. Cleveland's Democratic presidency was stalemated.

In his second annual report, Herbert began by describing the status of ship construction in progress and emphasized the Navy's preference for fast defensive torpedo boats. He noted that seventeen countries had at least twenty-two vessels of that class, while the U.S. Navy had only six. Herbert again took up the problem of management. First, he explained that he recently gave the Bureau of Construction full responsibility for design, strength, and stability of new ships.[21] Then, he emphasized the need to fix the line officer promotion problem. In closing, Herbert announced that although the current new Navy was almost paid for, it would be unwise to stop the increases. In the present state of a national depression, lack of funds to American shipbuilders would be harmful, increasing unemployment and crippling the industry. Specifically, he asked for three battleships and twelve torpedo boats.[22]

In his December 1894 annual report to Congress, President Cleveland reiterated Herbert's request for battleships and torpedo boats and reaffirmed the necessity of keeping shipbuilders and armor manufacturers in business. He estimated that all armor necessary to complete the warships under construction would be delivered by June 1895. His optimistic presumption was again off by a few years. He also called attention to Herbert's concern in regard to line officers of the Navy and wrote that "the stagnation of promotion" was seriously impairing Navy efficiency.[23]

As the Democratic lame-duck Congress concluded its business over the next three months, naval issues remained on the back burner. Before the impending adjournment of the legislature on March 4, Cleveland, by necessity, faced the consequences of the deep-seated financial crisis that had been brewing for over a year. He asked Congress to approve long-term, low-interest bonds to shore up national banks, and also to redeem and cancel interchanged currencies such as greenbacks and Sherman Act notes. But the western Silver Party held out for an alternative switch to free silver legislation. Cleveland then decided to replenish the gold supply by using his executive authority to offer a private bond subscription with bank payments from European gold. Bankers John Pierpont Morgan and August Belmont Jr. formed a syndicate and purchased government bonds for $65 million in accordance with the president's terms. The immediate reaction was the successful cessation of gold exports to Europe. Unfortunately for Cleveland, the scramble for subscriptions from Morgan and Belmont greatly inflated their own profit. Many Americans, both Republicans and Silverites, claimed that the government had been cheated and that Cleveland was to blame.[24]

During the final session, House naval committee member Adolph Meyer (D-LA) introduced another bill "to reorganize and increase the efficiency of the personnel of the Navy and Marine Corps."[25] His resolution for Navy reorganization endorsed by both Herbert and the president died on the table as members of both houses crafted their final naval appropriations act. In

March 1895, the outgoing Congress approved $29.5 million for the Navy, which was a significant $7 million increase from the previous year in spite of the ongoing gold crisis. Not only would increased government spending provide employment, the appropriations would also continue to build a Navy fleet according to the vision of the legislature. The act authorized the construction of two coastline battleships, six light gunboats, and three torpedo boats.

CHALLENGES AND ACTION

Shortly after Congress adjourned, the fledgling Navy prepared to become involved in an escalating international affair with Great Britain over the boundary between British Guiana and Venezuela. At stake were British rights to the mouth of the Orinoco River, which were based on a rather casually drawn line by British explorer Sir Robert Schomburgk in the 1840s. Great Britain was obdurate about retaining the now-significant Schomburgk line, which demarked their control of considerable internal trade in the area. Cleveland saw British refusal of arbitration as a serious encroachment against the Monroe Doctrine and decided to take a stand against Great Britain.

As negotiations bogged down, Cleveland's close friend Secretary of State Walter Q. Gresham died in late May. After a funeral in the Executive Mansion, the grieving president and his entire cabinet accompanied the body on a train from Washington to Chicago. Upon his return to Washington, he recovered from his deep melancholy, resumed his executive duties, and appointed Attorney General Richard Olney to succeed Gresham at the State Department. Cleveland experienced some respite in July, with the celebration of the birth of his third daughter, Marion. Meanwhile, the Venezuelan–Monroe Doctrine crisis remained unresolved throughout the summer and fall.

During this period Herbert necessarily confronted escalating difficulties at home concerning the contracting of warship armor plating. A longstanding issue for the Navy involved the quality of ship armor. Since 1885, Congress had approved several classes of ships to be constructed with belts of protective hardened steel produced by U.S. companies. The technology for manufacturing suitable nickel-steel armor was relatively new and expensive. The Bethlehem Steel Company and the Carnegie Steel Company each received contracts, although their industrial development of armor plate was quite slow. Prior to the completion of deliveries, informants accused the Carnegie Steel

Company of malfeasance. They claimed that Carnegie had tested only specially treated plates, which met the specifications, and then sold the Navy untreated plates of inferior quality. As a result of investigations, Herbert found Carnegie guilty and levied a stiff fine against Carnegie Steel. Upon consultation, Cleveland reduced the fine with his determination that management was not aware of the deception. In spite of an extensive 980-page report by its House naval committee with findings of culpability prior to adjournment in March 1895, Congress decided to drop the matter entirely.[26]

As Herbert prepared new contracts, he continued to have considerable difficulty dealing with the Bethlehem and Carnegie companies. Because of price fixing at $600 per ton for armor plate by both companies, Herbert could not stay within his budget limitations. The most recent naval appropriations act had authorized slightly less than $5 million for warship armor and armament, but did not set a maximum price per ton for the required nickel-steel.[27] Herbert felt that the companies' start-up costs had already been covered and that they now colluded in setting a common price considerably higher than the international market rate. By law, he was required to accept the lowest domestic bid. Eventually, Bethlehem and Carnegie reduced their price to $550 per ton, causing cost overruns for the Navy and incomplete warship construction. As a result, Herbert decided to have the incoming Congress set the maximum contract price.

In his third annual report sent to the opening session of Congress in late November 1895, Herbert announced that construction of the *Maine* and the *Texas* was finished. Both second-class battleships had been authorized in August 1886 and laid down in the summer of 1889. After six years of delayed construction, they were finally commissioned. Meanwhile several other battleships and cruisers remained in their yards awaiting their turn for armor. As the armor-plate crisis continued, the legislature spent considerable time attempting to determine legitimate costs. In his report, Herbert also exhorted the new Congress to fix the line officer promotion system. Furthermore, he requested an increase of two battleships and twelve torpedo boats.[28]

A week later, President Cleveland sent his annual message to the legislature. In it, he broke from the tradition of outlining the state of the nation, department by department. In his opening paragraph he devoted but one sentence to the various reports of the heads of his administration as containing their accomplishments and recommendations. He then went on for fourteen pages explaining the state of foreign relations, and used another fourteen pages to explain the condition of national finances and the absolutely essential need to stay on the gold standard for the survival of the country.[29]

Two weeks later, Cleveland sent an urgent special message to Congress concerning escalation of the Venezuela border crisis. Great Britain had finally officially replied to the United States that the Monroe Doctrine had no application in settling the boundary and that arbitration was not appropriate. Cleveland asked Congress "to make adequate appropriations for the expenses of a commission, to be appointed by the Executive" to investigate and report on the matter.[30] The president expected the report to show the necessity for U.S. resistance to the actions of Great Britain. Congress immediately reacted with an allocation of $100,000 for the commission.[31] Leading Republicans such as Senators Lodge and Chandler, with warlike enthusiasm, spoke out strongly against Great Britain. Moderates were aghast at the real possibility of war and Herbert's Navy leaders expressed to him their concern over the unequal condition of the respective naval forces. Cooler heads prevailed as a new round of diplomacy convinced the British to soften their government's anti–Monroe Doctrine stance, thereby retaining status quo relations with the United States.

At the same time, European nations were facing serious saber rattling between Germany and Great Britain over the failed Jameson raid in South Africa in January 1896. Leander Jameson, an English colonial leader, had organized the raid hoping to create an uprising to overthrow the newly created Transvaal Republic, an area settled over the past century by Dutch farmers called Boers. Kaiser Wilhelm II of Germany sided with the Boer leaders, causing serious tensions to rise in Europe. The crisis settled down when Great Britain took swift action against Jameson. Historians have tended to downplay the relationship between the South African confrontation and the timing of the peaceful British arbitration of the Venezuelan crisis. However, Cleveland's strong Monroe Doctrine position and Britain's timely capitulation are a matter of record.

In its long session of 1896, Congress continued to debate Navy issues throughout the presidential election season. Herbert again advised the Senate against bills to raise the status of steam engineers who, many in Congress felt, were vital shipboard operators as the Navy left the age of sail.[32] He consistently protected the traditional military and command authority of line officers. Herbert especially objected to proposed Navy bureau consolidation that would raise the chief of the Bureau of Steam Engineering, a staff officer, to a position of authority higher than any of the other bureau chiefs. Although generally supportive of progressives in Congress, Herbert considered the proposals too radical. The legislature put off any consideration of reorganizing staff corps rank and status for yet another session.

In the debates over the price of warship armor plate, the Senate took a harsher view than the House of Representatives and at one point set a maximum price at $350 per ton. The House rejected such a low amount and would not agree on anything below $425 per ton. Finally, when the session ended in June, Congress directed the Secretary of the Navy to determine the actual cost of armor manufacturing and report to the outgoing legislature no later than January 1, 1897. In accordance with the directive, Herbert could not contract for any armored vessels authorized in the appropriations act until Congress received and debated the secretary's report. Notwithstanding its proscription, the legislature approved three armored coastline battleships, pending the price of armor, as well as three torpedo boats and ten smaller craft.[33]

As presidential election events came to a conclusion, Cleveland remained stubbornly committed to maintaining the gold standard. His Democratic Party, led by western Silverites and Southern farmers, coalesced against him by supporting some level of bimetallic currency. The growing third party Populist movement also opposed Cleveland's position. Additionally, Southern leaders who were not necessarily committed to silver also moved toward the Democratic bimetallic stand in fear of another Republican sweep. The Republican machine was better organized and more unified over tariff protection and currency issues than the Democratic Party. The leading Republican presidential candidate and ultimate victor, William McKinley Jr., had for the past few years been positioning himself as the people's choice for sound economic policy. His right-hand man and relentless organizer, wealthy Cleveland, Ohio, businessman Marcus Hanna, ran his campaign.

The Democratic convention was considerably wilder than the Republican meeting. President Cleveland did not honor rumors that he would run for a third term and held fast to maintaining the gold standard. He grossly misjudged the large groundswell of Populists, agrarian, and western Silverites that condemned his position. At the convention, thirty-six-year-old congressman William Jennings Bryan of Nebraska delivered his famous "Cross of Gold" speech, blaming the gold standard for all the financial ills of the working classes, and won the Democratic nomination on the fifth ballot. Cleveland and his cabinet were not part of the movement.

After the convention and prior to the general election in November, Secretary Herbert traveled to Europe to investigate the cost of manufacturing warship armor plate by European companies. Initially he intended his trip to be secret but a Carnegie company agent booked passage on the same ship with the intention of influencing the European estimates. Frustrated by the collusion, Herbert finally received good estimates through the minister of marine in Paris from a steel plant under construction for the French government.[34] A friend of Herbert acting undercover in England verified the French figures. Herbert returned home in September after spending a total of six weeks in Europe and began preparing his annual report, which would be forwarded to Congress. Meanwhile McKinley handily won the November election and a few months later, in early March, Cleveland and Herbert would be out of office.

Herbert's account sent to the outgoing Congress in early December stated that the Navy now had forty-one war ships in commission.[35] In the thirteen years since Congressman Thomas had reported a low of thirty-eight ships available for service, the Navy fleet had increased by only three warships. Although the growth of the new Navy was slow, the warships now in operation were larger and more capable, containing considerably more firepower than their early 1880s counterparts being decommissioned. Also, several additional ships not yet ready for sea were either under construction or authorized by Congress. In his report, Herbert declared that the number of junior officers was now insufficient to fill the requirements for shipboard duties. He proposed establishing a new clerical corps of staff officers to relieve the junior line officer shortage. Herbert did not ask for an increased level of officers; rather, he argued that low-ranking staff personnel could relieve line officers from routine shipboard administrative work, which had mushroomed beyond the capacity of the number of ensigns assigned.

The bulk of Cleveland's final annual message to Congress contained a summary of the American international and domestic state of affairs. As a portent of future American-Spanish antagonism, he devoted six pages to the "perplexities" of the insurrection in Cuba and expressed his support for its inhabitants to enjoy "the blessings of peace."[36] In his two-page summary of the state of the Navy, he noted the number of armored vessels in commission and praised the various domestic manufacturers. He also supported Herbert's opinion that the Navy now only needed an increase in battleships and torpedo boats, and reiterated the importance of naval militias as being equivalent to the Army National Guard of the states.

The outgoing Congress debated both the cost of armor plate and Navy personnel issues. Based on his European findings, Herbert asked the legislature to permit the Navy to purchase armor plate at $400 per ton. With leadership from Senator Chandler, the dominant obstructionist against large armored warships, the Senate set an impossibly low price of $300 per ton, causing work stoppage again. On the matter of personnel, in their earlier session members of the House of Representatives had introduced nine bills to reorganize the Navy, while members of the Senate had introduced four of their own. These bills varied only slightly in content. The real problem remained the lack of line officer vacancies and the expense of early retirements. Over the course of the winter, the House combined twenty-one separate proposals into yet another bill on reorganization and pay.[37] That latest attempt again remained in committee when Congress adjourned on March 4, 1897. As it ended its lame-duck session, Congress authorized only three torpedo boats.[38]

Nevertheless, the increases in the Navy throughout the second administration of Grover Cleveland were significant. During the fourth four-year period of naval expansion, from 1893 to 1897, Congress authorized a total of thirty-two new warships, which included five coastline battleships, nineteen torpedo boats, six light gunboats, and two submarines (the last were subsequently canceled). The growing new Navy of the 1880s and 1890s was under way as a consequence of congressional focus on defense.

8

WAR AND IMPERIALISM, 1897–99

President William McKinley Jr.'s ancestors were Presbyterian Scots-Irish colonists who came to Pennsylvania in the mid-1700s. His family later settled in the town of Niles, Ohio, where William was born in 1843. Nine years later, the McKinleys relocated to the small nearby village of Poland in order for the children to attend school at the Poland Academy. William's teachers were members of the Methodist congregation, and from them he developed a lifelong adherence to Methodism and the Protestant work ethic.[1] As he grew up, his environs of the Ohio Western Reserve continued to develop as a major hub for abolitionists, and the corresponding Underground Railroad for those escaping slavery in the South.

McKinley was barely eighteen years old when the Civil War began. He enlisted as a private in the Army in July 1861 and his unit began chasing Confederate guerrillas in Virginia. In keeping with his faith, he wrote in his diary that he was a soldier for his country and a soldier of Jesus.[2] The following year, he earned a battlefield promotion to lieutenant for bravery while delivering supplies under fire at the Battle of Antietam. For the remainder of the war, he continued to fight in the West Virginia and Virginia areas. His superior officer, friend, and patron, also from the Ohio Western Reserve, was the future president Rutherford B. Hayes. Twenty years older than McKinley, Hayes rose from company commander to regimental commander and to the rank of major general. McKinley mustered out in July 1865 with the rank of brevet major, having been closely involved in four years of combat.

After the war he studied law, became a member of a prosperous partnership, and began his political career as a twenty-seven-year-old prosecuting attorney. A year later he married Ida Saxton, the daughter of a prominent banker. Soon McKinley and Ida had two daughters. Unfortunately, the second girl died three weeks after childbirth and the oldest died two years later at the age of four. These tragedies, combined with the sudden death of her mother, were defining events for the already high-strung Ida, who spent the rest of her life fighting depression and epileptic seizures. In spite of his wife's condition, McKinley continued his political career while always showing compassion and attention toward her.

At the age of thirty-five, McKinley won election to Congress and served for seven terms from 1877 to 1891. Within a few years he made himself an authority in the legislature on the complex tariff issues of free lists versus protection duties. He stayed closed to sound money policy but was not an ardent gold-standard politician. In the 1888 presidential campaign, he had a strong hand in writing the Republican platform, disavowing his own dark-horse candidacy while supporting the loser Blaine over Harrison. During the next two years, McKinley drafted and made compromises to the complex, all-encompassing tariff act that Congress passed in 1890.

Opposing Democrats soundly discredited his bill as being disastrous to the working class and overwhelmingly defeated the Republicans in the emotionally charged 1890 congressional election. McKinley himself was a casualty of the Democratic sweep and lost his seat. A bit nonplussed but essentially unruffled, he left Congress in March 1891 and returned to his practice of law. His hiatus from politics was short-lived, since he ran for governor of Ohio, winning the 1891 and 1893 elections, and winning the Republican presidential primary on the first ballot in June 1896. Following his election to the presidency, he had four months to pick his cabinet.

As a former congressman and governor, McKinley knew many of the politicians then in office. His choices for cabinet positions needed to fit into his political power formation. First, he selected seventy-four-year-old senator John Sherman for secretary of state. This vacated a Senate seat for his home state of Ohio and, with considerable maneuvering, allowed McKinley's tireless supporter and close friend, Marcus Hanna, to receive the appointment. Because of his age and health, Sherman was not a vibrant choice and McKinley subsequently selected Judge William R. Day to be assistant secretary and de facto run the department.[3] For the important Treasury position, McKinley selected relatively unknown Chicago banker Lyman Gage, a tariff and sound-money moderate. Michigan politician and businessman Russell Alger received the appointment to head the War Department.

The laconic John D. Long of Massachusetts succeeded Hilary Herbert as Secretary of the Navy. Long was born in 1838 in Maine, and his prominent farming and trading family's ancestors were Massachusetts Bay Colony Puritans. He graduated from Harvard Law School and began to practice law in Boston in 1863. He launched his political career in the Massachusetts House of Representatives followed by a term as governor from 1880 to 1882. He then won election to the U.S. House of Representatives, served three terms from 1883 to 1889, and afterward returned to his Massachusetts law practice. During his years in Washington, he established a close personal friendship with his younger fellow congressman William McKinley, but did not actively participate in the raucous 1896 "Cross of Gold" presidential campaign.

Barely a month before his inauguration in March 1897, McKinley chose his friend John Long to fill the unspoken New England quota of his cabinet.[4] Long would be another last-minute Secretary of the Navy selection, appointed for political balance rather than for his naval acumen. Removed from national politics for the previous eight years, he approached his Navy secretariat position affably and with a managerial spirit that survived on delegation of authority. Once in office he confided in his journal: "My plan is to leave all such matters to the Bureau Chiefs, or other officers at naval stations, or on board ship, limiting myself to the general direction of affairs."[5]

In his inaugural address in early March, McKinley commended the progress in building the Navy and added that the United States sorely needed a comparable merchant marine. But his main focus was not on the naval service. In his speech, he announced his calling of an immediate special session of Congress to meet the critical demands of the U.S. Treasury. He summoned the legislature to assemble early in order to balance the budget and pass a new tariff law, which would ensure that expenditures would not exceed revenues.[6] Congress then met from March to July 1897 to resolve the financial crisis. Budget concerns far outweighed McKinley's attention to the Navy.

A month after his inauguration, McKinley settled on appointing Theodore Roosevelt to be the Assistant Secretary of the Navy. Several progressive politicians had already been scrutinizing him for the Navy position. Prior to the Republican victory in November, Roosevelt himself had expressed interest in the position and judged himself well qualified.[7] As a published historian and frequent lecturer at the Naval War College over the previous ten years, he had acquired an understanding of naval issues and nurtured close associations with Navy leaders. Roosevelt had served for six years as Civil Service commissioner under Presidents Harrison and Cleveland, and was then making his mark as police commissioner of New York City. The politically astute McKinley expressed his reservations concerning Roosevelt "getting into rows with everyone" and being "too pugnacious."[8] However, support from Vermont senator Redfield Proctor, Massachusetts senator Henry Cabot Lodge, and New York senator Thomas Collier Platt, who desired to remove Roosevelt from New York State politics, overcame McKinley's reluctance.[9]

Prior to his appointment, Roosevelt already had a reputation for disrupting the existing state of affairs. As a cautionary measure, Long chose to distance him from direct association with politically sensitive activities. As such, he issued special regulations removing Roosevelt from the general supervision of the Navy bureaus that regularly dealt with congressional patronage. The *Army and Navy Journal*, the unofficial magazine of the military, recognized that Secretary Long was curtailing Roosevelt.[10] As Long settled into his own new position, he instructed Roosevelt to conduct inspections of Navy shipyards. From Long's perspective, this task appeared to be a potentially fruitful and relatively safe assignment for the new assistant. He correctly assumed Roosevelt would serve as a troubleshooter for efficiency without interfering with the communications between the bureaus or Congress.

Calling on his experience with the Civil Service Commission, Roosevelt looked for abuse in Navy facilities and reported on compliance with Navy Department regulations. He relished his shipyard inspection work, meeting with many civilian laborers and union men to uncover favoritism.[11] In his initial inspection of the New York facility, he unexpectedly discovered that the majority of complaints concerning unjust layoffs had occurred after the recent inauguration of President McKinley. But he did not find evidence of unfair hiring practices or an active Republican Party spoils system associated with the changeover from Democratic Party control.[12]

The special session of the new Congress that met that spring had the single mandate from McKinley to create a new revenue tariff act. After months of spirited discussions, protectionist policies held sway over the Silverites and Congress approved the highest U.S. tariffs to date. A disappointed McKinley had hoped for moderation but settled on provisions that gave the executive branch a limited ability to negotiate individual reciprocity agreements with selected countries to lower some tariff schedules.[13] He signed the bill into law and it stood for the next twelve years.

By the summer of 1897, Roosevelt had performed reliably for a few months without causing political trouble for the Secretary of the Navy. To get away from the heat of Washington, Long chose to take a routine two-week vacation and left Roosevelt in charge. Long's laid-back management style and Roosevelt's satisfactory execution of his duties afforded the secretary an opportunity for another hiatus, this time for two months in August and September during the slow season in Washington. He no longer seemed to worry about Roosevelt's capacity for disrupting the relationships between congressmen, the Navy bureau chiefs, and the secretariat. In Long's absence, Roosevelt assumed the secretary's duties, which included ordering fleet commanders to conduct training maneuvers and deployments.

Under direct civilian control, the Navy's military command structure continued to remain problematic. In fact, the U.S. government shunned the very concept of centralized military staffs, which were emerging in Europe. In September, Ira Hollis, a Naval Academy graduate and Harvard professor of engineering, wrote a critical public review of Navy officer administration and presented recommendations for reorganization. Secretary Long reviewed the article, published in the widely read *Atlantic Monthly*, and forwarded it for deliberation to Roosevelt.[14] Prior to the beginning of the regular legislative session in December, Roosevelt and a board of Navy officers met to prepare reorganization proposals for Congress.

In his first annual report routinely forwarded to Congress, Long referred to the board's forthcoming findings. Rather than expounding on the anticipated reorganization recommendations, he focused on the need for fifty lieutenants, twenty-five junior grade lieutenants, and seventy-five engineers. Regarding the physical state of the Navy, Long wrote of "embarrassing delays" in battleship construction due to the impossibly low price Congress had set for armor plate, $330 per ton. The report also noted that the Navy had its first contract for manufacturing a torpedo boat with an engine using liquid fuel instead of coal. Finally, he asked for one battleship to be constructed on the Pacific coast and for a "few" additional torpedo boats.[15]

President McKinley's annual message, delivered to Congress two weeks later, reiterated that three battleships remained unfinished because the price of armor was set too low. He also repeated Long's request for a battleship on the Pacific coast and for several torpedo boats. His policy statements addressed the status of Cuba and the Hawaiian Islands. First, he expressed optimism concerning the liberal government of Práxedes Sagasta, the prime minister of Spain, who had taken over in October after the assassination of Antonio Cánovas del Castillo. Accordingly, McKinley hoped for a humanitarian settlement of the ongoing revolution in Cuba. Second, he wrote that he had sent a treaty to Congress, which he and the Hawaiian government had both signed, to incorporate the islands into the United States.[16] The treaty remained in the Senate awaiting final approval.

Roosevelt's recommendations for Navy reorganization, presented to the incoming Congress by Secretary Long, contained the perennial and contentious provision to retire some line officers in mid-grades to open the flow of promotions to junior officers. This was yet another variation of the early retirement solutions proposed since 1885. During the twelve years of debates that had ensued, the size of the officer corps had dropped considerably due to attrition. That reduction of officers did not totally solve the overmanning problem but did relieve the congestion at the top. The number of officers to be plucked from the mid-grades for early retirement now presented less of a problem in retirement costs.

Roosevelt's review board took up staff corps issues as well as officer promotion and retirement regulations. He was a staunch advocate of combining steam engineers and line officers as one and helped convince his Navy officer board to forward that recommendation to Congress. He pointed out that every officer on a modern warship needed to be an engineer as well as a seaman.[17] The subsequent personnel bills introduced in both houses of the Fifty-fifth Congress were later consolidated into a single bill that became known as the "Roosevelt Bill."[18] Among other things, the Navy Department recommendations provided for the full integration of steam engineers with line officers and equal rank for all other staff officers. The reorganization proposals did not include recommendations to establish a centralized military staff. In the event, more pressing issues concerning escalating tensions with Spain caused Congress to focus on real-time events rather than on Navy organization.

PRELUDE TO WAR

By early 1898, the new Spanish government had replaced the top leaders in Cuba, assuring the United States that they would halt the atrocities and the forced relocations on the island. However, their warrants proved to be nonbinding and insufficient to resolve the enormity of the situation. The revolution had been ongoing since early 1895 and very repressive on-scene Spanish officials had brutally relocated, imprisoned, and killed hundreds of thousands of Cuban subsistence farmers and revolutionary sympathizers.[19] But with an ever-optimistic eye on future possibilities, McKinley continued diplomatic relations with Spain and sent the second-class battleship *Maine* to Havana harbor as a part of an agreement to conduct friendly mutual port visits.

The *Maine* arrived on January 25, 1898, to serve the twofold purpose of showing goodwill to the new government in Spain and of projecting U.S. power, to ameliorate recent anti-American outbursts led by old regime forces. Cuban officials exchanged courtesies with the *Maine* and for the next three weeks the presence of the battleship seemed to have a salutary effect. As a precaution in order to avoid unfavorable incidents, enlisted men were not allowed to go ashore. On the night of February 15 an explosion blew up the bow of the anchored battleship, killing 262 U.S. seamen.

Many Americans reacted to the sinking of the *Maine* with anger followed by a call for revenge, even though neither the cause nor the culpability of the explosion had been determined. But those Americans strongly believed that the responsibility rested with Spain. In contrast, McKinley took a line of caution and patience. Having strong memories of his own combat experiences during the Civil War, he was not eager to start a war with Spain. He was mostly alone. Politicians and the public at large saw Spain as the enemy and clamored for action. Three days after the explosion Wallace Foot, a second-term representative from New York, introduced a resolution to purchase a battleship to replace the *Maine*.[20] His bill went to the House naval committee to be incorporated into the appropriations act of early May. Other members of Congress joined the outcry with proposals to increase the Navy as relations with Spain worsened.

On the afternoon of Friday, February 25, ten days after the explosion, in the absence of Secretary Long, Roosevelt telegraphed Commo. George Dewey in Japan to consolidate his forces in Hong Kong. (U.S. telegraph service went via undersea cable to Europe and then to Asia. The trans-Pacific cable was not completed until 1902.) Roosevelt instructed Dewey to keep a full supply of coal and prepare for offensive operations against the Spanish fleet in the Philippine Islands.[21] The order to Dewey transmitted a definite sense of immediacy for war against Spain. On March 9, a committed Congress gave the president $50 million for urgent defense preparations.[22] The Navy quickly used $18 million to buy ships from American, British, and German shipbuilders. The purchase included cruisers, gunboats, torpedo boats, ocean liners, and private yachts.[23]

The circumstances leading to a declaration of war against Spain coalesced rapidly from late March to mid-April. On March 28, McKinley sent a message to Congress transmitting the findings of the U.S. naval court of inquiry in Havana concerning the sinking of the *Maine*. The court of experts concluded that an external mine had destroyed the *Maine* but had no evidence to fix responsibility.[24] McKinley sent the findings and associated correspondence to Spain and hoped for a just and honorable course regarding the revolution in Cuba. As he waited for a response, an agitated Congress and the public in general expressed their desire for concrete action. The Spanish government reacted to McKinley's diplomatic endeavors with carefully worded responses that continued to promise a reduction in coercive military action and an increased level of Cuban autonomy. But Spain would not specify a time frame for easements or conduct further negotiations until the rebels stopped hostilities. Upon reaching this impasse, McKinley waited until U.S. citizens could be evacuated from Cuba and then in April addressed both houses of the legislature concerning the now grave and escalating crisis.

In his message to Congress, he outlined the history of the recent revolution in Cuba and the accompanying horrors inflicted by the occupying Spanish forces. McKinley wrote that if Spain did not make any progress toward relieving the suffering, the only remaining action would be intervention to end the strife.[25] On April 20, Congress passed a four-part joint resolution: first, recognizing the independence of Cuba; second, demanding the Spanish withdrawal of military forces; third, empowering the president to use the Army and Navy to carry out the resolution; and fourth, disclaiming any intention to exercise sovereignty over Cuba. Five days later, McKinley declared to Congress that due to Spanish inaction a state of war between the United States and Spain existed. As a result, Congress executed a declaration of war signed that day by the president; vice president; the president of the Senate, Garret Hobart; and Speaker of the House Thomas Reed.[26] At the same time, the aged John Sherman resigned as secretary of state, recognizing both his ineffectiveness and his growing animosity toward McKinley. Second Secretary William Day immediately assumed his duties.[27]

WAR WITH SPAIN

Upon the declaration of war, McKinley and his cabinet set up telegraph and telephone lines in the White House to communicate with Dewey in Hong Kong, mobilize the Navy's fleets, and direct Rear Adm. William Sampson's North Atlantic Squadron to blockade Cuba. At the end of April, Washington received news that a Spanish force consisting of armored cruisers, destroyers, and torpedo boats, under the command of Rear Admiral Pascual Cervera y Topete, had left Cape Verde in the eastern Atlantic and headed for the Caribbean. Over the course of the next week and a half, Sampson's ships maneuvered around the Puerto Rican area to intercept Cervera and also continued to blockade Cuban ports.

The Navy went into action on two fronts, while the Army labored over logistical planning to recruit and move soldiers into Cuba and the Philippine Islands. McKinley ordered Dewey in Hong Kong to engage the Spanish fleet and the commodore arrived in Manila Bay at dawn on May 1.[28] Although the area had reasonable defenses, Dewey's fleet mostly avoided detection by running into the bay at night and in spite of firepower from ashore engaged and sank the assembled Spanish warships. The next day, he cut the undersea telegraph cable to Hong Kong after the city of Manila refused him permission to report to the United States. Dewey then blockaded Manila and awaited further orders from the president via ship relays from Hong Kong.

Congress remained in session while McKinley and the rest of the country awaited news from the Philippines. On May 4, Congress passed the largest appropriations act for the Navy since the Civil War. The total of almost $63 million, more than double that of the previous year, was in addition to the emergency $50 million authorized in March for war preparations. The act contained funds for three coastline battleships (one to be named *Maine*), four monitors, an assortment of twenty-eight torpedo boats and torpedo boat destroyers, and one gunboat. With the war barely underway against a distant enemy, Congress continued to approve warship construction, a mix of coastline battleships to engage an enemy and shallow draft monitors, torpedo boats, and a gunboat for future coastal defenses. The legislature had no expectations that the three battleships could be constructed in a timely manner to participate in the immediate circumstances of war with Spain. The act also raised the authorized price of armor plate to $400 per ton.[29]

On May 6 Dewey's report of victory in Manila, sent by ship to Hong Kong for relay via telegraph to the United States, reached McKinley, who in turn instructed him not to cooperate with the rebels who were fighting the Spanish government and to await the arrival of the U.S. Army. Roosevelt notified the press of the news of Dewey's victory on the same day and then submitted his resignation from his Navy Department position to join the Army.[30] Congress had approved the formation of three voluntary cavalry regiments and Roosevelt accepted an appointment to be second-in-command of a unit under Col. Leonard Wood.[31] A week prior to the declaration of war, Roosevelt had written a public letter to the editor of the *New York Sun* asserting that the Navy was in "very good shape indeed."[32] Upon vacating his office, he reiterated that the Navy was in a state of excellent preparedness and was ready for war.

A few days after Roosevelt's resignation, the recently retired Captain Mahan declared that the Navy was not properly organized to fight. Without impugning Roosevelt, Mahan remonstrated that the Navy's administration was not structured for combat. Secretary Long had recalled Mahan from Europe to serve on a temporary Naval War Board consisting of senior Navy officers and headed by Assistant Secretary Roosevelt, who would forward recommendations to the president concerning the course of wartime naval operations. Upon arrival in Washington, Mahan solicited Long to eliminate the board on the grounds of ineffectiveness. He suggested that military responsibility be vested in a single officer who had his own staff of military advisers.[33] Commenting on the board just a few weeks later, Roosevelt's friend Senator Lodge wrote to Rear Admiral Luce at the Naval War College that "there ought to be a chief of staff" and that the Navy was "entirely unprepared when the war began."[34] McKinley ignored Mahan's and Lodge's judgments and, as commander in chief, personally directed Navy and Army war maneuvers through his civilian cabinet gathered at the White House.

In his year in office with the Navy Department, Roosevelt had seriously measured the importance of sea power for use by heads of government. Through his association with the Naval War College, he had become a friend of its second president, Captain Mahan. By the 1890s, Roosevelt, Mahan, and Lodge regularly discussed the need for a dynamic modern Navy. But the three friends disagreed, in different venues, on the state of the Navy when war broke out. As the naval service grew and became more powerful, corresponding changes in the Navy's organization did not occur. In spite of his exuberance, Roosevelt did not involve himself in a process to centralize military control in the Navy he so diligently promoted as an instrument of statecraft. With no military command authority, the Naval War Board, originally led by Roosevelt, continued to give strategic advice to the president throughout the conduct of the war via Roosevelt's uninitiated civilian successor as Assistant Navy Secretary, Charles Allen.

When he exited the cabinet to join the Army, Roosevelt had no voice in the selection of his replacement. Midwestern congressmen and senior naval officers rallied around recently retired Rear Adm. John Walker, then president of the Nicaraguan Canal Commission.[35] Former secretary Tracy and leading northeasterners pushed for Tracy's former private secretary Henry W. Raymond.[36] Philadelphia politicians sought the appointment of former congressman John Robinson, who had close ties to the League Island Navy Yard.[37] McKinley did not have a consensus and sought a compromise candidate. Ignoring nominees who would favor a particular faction in Congress, Secretary Long acted as a conciliator by suggesting the appointment of his friend Charles Allen, a Massachusetts businessman.[38] Allen had served two terms in Congress with McKinley and Long from 1885 to 1889. The president agreed with Long and appointed Allen, making an exception to his policy of not allowing both the secretary and his assistant to be from the same state. The naval neophyte Allen took office on May 11, and immediately chaired the Naval War Board as the Navy proceeded with its war against Spain.

Unbeknownst to the Navy, Cervera's vanguard had arrived at the French Island of Martinique the day before but was not permitted by the local government to purchase coal. He then took his squadron southwesterly to the

Antilles, to continue evading the American fleet and get much-needed fuel from a Spanish collier at Curaçao. When he arrived, the collier was not in port and the Dutch government allowed him to purchase only a token amount of coal. This enabled his squadron to steam to Cuba, where he arrived undetected at the southeast port of Santiago de Cuba on May 19.[39]

Not knowing Cervera's whereabouts, McKinley cabled Rear Admiral Sampson to leave Puerto Rican waters and rendezvous at Key West with his Flying Squadron, commanded by Commo. Winfield Scott Schley, en route from South Carolina. When the White House received intelligence that the Spanish flotilla had reached Cuba, McKinley ordered Schley to confirm the sighting and blockade the port. Sampson's group remained in Key West while Schley's squadron slowly steamed in and around Cuba's southern coast, finally establishing Cevera's presence in Santiago on May 29. Upon receiving the news, Sampson immediately departed Key West and arrived off the coast of Santiago to take command of the blockade and await the arrival of the U.S. Army.

Throughout the latter part of April and the entire month of May, the Army scrambled to organize itself for deployments to the Philippines, Cuba, and Puerto Rico as directed by McKinley. Similar to the Navy, the Army administration consisted of bureau chiefs with no central command organization. Spread out in forts across the United States, its troops and leaders were considerably less prepared for a foreign war than the Navy. After the United States declared that a state of war existed in April, Congress followed the time-honored American tradition of depending on volunteers for defense of the nation rather than establishing a large standing army. In spite of plans to engage the Spanish in offensive operations on distant shores, the legislature as well as McKinley saw no contradiction in filling out state militias rather than building regular federal Army units for overseas operations. At the time, the Army consisted of just more than 28,000 troops. By the summer, it reached its wartime limit of 65,700, while state militia numbers swelled to 216,500.[40] In spite of this glut of state volunteers, McKinley and his cabinet chose to send mostly filled-out regular Army units abroad while a large number of militia remained in inadequate training camps with inadequate equipment.

The first order of business for Secretary of War Russell Alger and Maj. Gen. Nelson Miles involved groundwork to send troops to Cuba and the Philippines. Miles was the most senior officer in the Army and as such bore the title of "Commanding General." However, he did not have chief of staff authority. Command of the Cuban invasion went to Maj. Gen. William Shafter, grossly overweight but generally responsible and competent, who proceeded to Tampa at the end of April to organize his force.[41] At the same time, Maj. Gen. Wesley Merritt received command of the invasion of the Philippines. His task was to secure Manila and establish a modicum of peaceful negotiations while not turning the colony over to the rebels until the formation of a legitimate government. After a month of preparations, in late May Merritt began the movement of the first wave of soldiers from San Francisco to the Philippines.[42] With the confirmation of Cervera's presence in Cuba at the same time, McKinley directed Shafter to depart Tampa as soon as possible to assist the Navy in Santiago de Cuba, join forces with the Cuban insurgents, and subdue the Spanish army at that location.

The situation in Tampa was chaotic. The single-track railroad leading to the port became jammed with soldiers and supplies. Aggressive commanders, including Roosevelt with his "Rough Rider" cavalry regiment, literally ran to the transports to claim berthing for their men. Unfortunately, the cavalry found no room for their horses. McKinley anxiously sent repeated messages prodding Shafter to get underway. The disorganized Fifth Army Corps managed to finally leave port on June 8, only to be delayed at sea for several more days because of false rumors of Spanish warships in the vicinity. The U.S. troop transports eventually arrived off the southern coast of Cuba on June 20, two and a half weeks after Schley sighted and blockaded Cervera's ships in Santiago.[43]

The land battle of July 1 in Cuba was a serious and difficult engagement conducted in debilitating summer heat and rain over barely passable, sodden trails. Shafter's principal objective was the San Juan Heights, which overlooked the city of Santiago. With élan Roosevelt played his part well in gaining the high ground by leading his unmounted cavalry up Kettle Hill. A combination of white and black infantry units took neighboring San Juan Hill. With 244 killed and 1,381 wounded, the Army succeeded in closing down the city while the Navy blocked the port.[44] Two days later in a bold move, Cervera led his squadron out of the confined harbor. In the ensuing seven-hour battle at sea, Sampson's flotilla chased down and either sunk or grounded every one of the Spanish warships.[45] Shafter then chose to lay siege to the city rather than re-attack and on July 15 the Spanish commander surrendered all the forces in eastern Cuba.

The aftermath of this theater of the war brought additional challenges to the Army and Navy. According to the terms of surrender, the Navy found itself tasked with managing the repatriation and transportation of over 23,000 Spanish troops back to Spain. Disease ran rampant throughout the U.S. occupying Army, and McKinley decided to evacuate the Fifth Army Corps from Cuba to a quarantine camp set up on Montauk, Long Island.[46] Malaria was common, with a real threat of the more serious yellow fever taking hold. As the course of battle, siege, occupation, and quarantine played out, the U.S. Army suffered approximately 2,500 deaths due to disease—more than seven times the total casualties due to fighting the entire war on all fronts.[47]

After the success in eastern Cuba, McKinley continued to direct U.S. war efforts against Spain in other theaters while seeking peace negotiations. Prior to the war, Congress had passed a resolution that the United States disavowed any intention to annex Cuba. Without such a mandate for the Philippines, Guam, or Puerto Rico, McKinley mulled over the possibilities of annexation rather than turning those colonies over to the local insurgents. Events worked in favor of McKinley's deliberate approach as he opened negotiations in July with Spain through the French ambassador in Washington. McKinley took the lead on the path to U.S. expansion by declaring Puerto Rico as an "indemnity" and holding the area of Manila for subsequent disposition in the proposed peace conference.[48]

Earlier in the month, the United States had completed its annexation of Hawaii. The treaty approval process, on the Senate agenda since the beginning of its session in December 1897, had bogged down, with supporters unable to get the necessary two-thirds of the vote for concurrence. The war with Spain bolstered American interest in the strategic location of the Hawaiian Islands and on July 7 Congress chose the annexation method of a joint resolution, with a simple majority vote of both houses rather than with a treaty approved by the Senate. This had been done once in the past with a joint resolution for the annexation of Texas in 1845.

Shortly after the congressional settlement with Hawaii, Commanding General Miles proceeded to Puerto Rico with reinforcements from Cuba. Transports from the East Coast delivered additional soldiers, to begin operations in early August. The Army's complex campaign to totally invest the island from the south to the north met only sporadic resistance as Miles advanced.

On August 12, the United States and Spain reached an agreement to cease all military operations, leaving Miles short of his objective of the San Juan stronghold. The U.S. Army had lost seven killed and thirty-six wounded over the course of four days.[49] Suffering considerably fewer casualties than experienced in Cuba, both the U.S. and Spanish armies in Puerto Rico then disbanded.

The distant war in the Philippines had begun with Dewey's victory. Shortly thereafter, insurgents led by Emilio Aguinaldo presented a united force-in-waiting against the defenses of the occupying Spanish army. McKinley chose not to give recognition to the rebels and directed the U.S. Army to subdue the Spanish without Aguinaldo's help. Because the long trip across the Pacific took more than a month, transports carrying the advance party, escorted by the cruiser *Charleston* (C 2) did not arrive until late June. While en route, the ships called on the Spanish island of Guam, arranged a friendly surrender on June 20, and proceeded to Manila.[50]

Merritt and his complement of troops arrived in Manila on July 25 and conducted preparatory skirmishes against the city until July 31. Finally, in mid-August Merritt gathered his force of almost 11,000 soldiers for a coordinated assault. Neither side in the Philippines was aware of the already negotiated agreement between Spain and the United States to stop fighting. However, the Spanish leaders in Manila recognized their untenable position and secretly negotiated with Merritt to put up only token resistance. News of the cease-fire finally reached Manila a few days later and both sides stood down. The total American casualties in the Philippine battles included fifteen killed and seventy-nine wounded.[51] This distant engagement was a far cry from the bloody fight in Cuba. The war was now over and Aguinaldo's status, as well as the subject of U.S. annexation, would await settlement at a peace conference to take place in Paris in October.

POSTWAR

By the end of August, all war fronts were quiet, while U.S. election-year politics heated up. The responsibility for fleet movements, which had temporarily been in the hands of the Naval War Board, reverted back to the Bureau of Navigation.[52] Assistant Secretary of the Navy Allen reoriented his office away from fleet activities and toward Navy business and management. Wartime activities had confirmed that McKinley was clearly the commander in chief of the country and in charge of his armed forces, his cabinet, and his party. Although generally not in line to be known as one of the fathers of the new Navy, he clearly was one of the fathers of the modern strong presidency. He emerged from the Spanish-American War as a leading expansionist while allowing his appointees to manage the resultant Treaty of Paris to his liking.

In October he decided to take a campaign tour of the Midwest states to further his agenda. He generally chose not to back specific candidates for the off-year elections and instead promoted the accomplishments of the Republican Party itself. During his tour, he learned that popular opinion strongly favored U.S. control of the Philippine Islands, reaffirming his position favoring annexation. Typically, the majority party loses significant seats in congressional midterm elections. But in November 1898 the House Republicans lost only nineteen places, maintaining a solid sixteen-member margin. The Senate Republicans gained nine seats, adding to their majority.[53] Peace treaty negotiations continued in Paris throughout November after the elections.

In mid-November, Secretary Long forwarded his annual report to the outgoing lame-duck Congress. For the record, he presented a separate long and detailed account of all Navy activity during the recent war. Then in a second section, he commented favorably on the July legislation, which had raised the authorized price of armor plate to $400, and wrote that the Navy was making good progress with all contracts. He also claimed that the recent war experience showed the need for a naval reserve force. Once again, he asked for passage of the pending "Roosevelt Bill" for Navy reorganization and recommended an increase of three battleships and twelve cruisers of various sizes and capabilities.[54]

In his forty-one-page annual message sent to Congress in December 1898, President McKinley began by highlighting the prosperity of the people of the United States. He recounted events of the year leading to the declaration of war with Spain and the ensuing successful campaigns. He wrote that military commanders now supervised the Spanish evacuations of Cuba, Puerto Rico, and the Philippines, and hoped soon to lay a treaty before the Senate. Considering the expansion of the United States, he wrote of the pressing need for congressional action regarding a canal committee to establish the construction of a maritime highway between the Atlantic and Pacific Oceans. In his short section on the Navy, he "earnestly" approved Long's recommendation for battleships and cruisers without listing specific numbers.[55]

As Congress convened its December session, McKinley's first priority was to complete peace talks with Spain and get a treaty accord to the Senate. At the same time, he instructed his delegation in Paris to be unyielding on holding the Philippines. Five days after sending his annual message to Congress, McKinley learned by cable that Spain had signed a treaty of peace ending the war and accepted $20 million for granting the Philippines, Guam, Puerto Rico, and part of the Spanish West Indies Islands to the United States. Next, McKinley needed to convince two-thirds of the outgoing Senate to approve the treaty.

Several anti-imperialist senators, led by the venerable George Hoar of Massachusetts in his twenty-ninth year in Congress, bitterly opposed the agreement on constitutional grounds arguing that the United States could not acquire territory not intended to be states.[56] Also, influential journalist and political leader Carl Schurz joined Senator Hoar and the powerful Speaker of the House Thomas Reed in contesting the accord. Undaunted, President McKinley carried out a successful tour of the South, gaining patriotic support. Ultimately, under the leadership of Lodge, Hale, and Orville Platt, the Senate ratified the treaty with Spain on February 10, 1899.

9

REORGANIZATION AND GROWTH,
1899–1901

Continuing its lame-duck session in January 1899, the House naval committee of the outgoing Fifty-fifth Congress presented its latest version of the Roosevelt Navy personnel bill for approval. Chairman Boutelle of Maine, a zealous leader for the development of the Navy, had the respect of both the legislative and executive branches for his knowledge of naval organization. His committee presented to the House a reworked Roosevelt bill with no minority report. At the same time, Capt. Arent Crowninshield, chief of the Bureau of Navigation, strenuously objected to the provisions for staff officers to receive the actual rank of line officers. Secretary Long duly forwarded the protest to Congress, where it did not alter the committee's decision.[1] At the time, Crowninshield was purportedly one of the most powerful officers in the Navy. He enjoyed the personal support of Thomas Platt of New York who had returned to the Senate in 1897, but lacked the power to affect the recommendations to overhaul the Navy rank and retirement system.[2]

The lengthy Navy reorganization debate in the full House of Representatives during the months of January and February took place along neither party nor regional lines. In general, a number of members objected to the provisions for early retirement as being too generous, questioned the amalgamation of the steam engineer staff corps with officers of the line, and disagreed with various aspects of revised midshipmen training.[3] However, the majority supported the proposals as necessary to reduce the number of lesser qualified officers, agreed with its naval committee that the line officers of the modern Navy needed both engineering and ship-handling skills, and accepted the considerable overhaul of training requirements.

Without further input from the Navy, the House sent the bill to the Senate, where a minority also questioned the amalgamation of engineers and the retirement requisites as well as a myriad of lesser reorganizational issues.[4] After review, the Senate sent its revisions to a joint Senate-House committee, which agreed on various modifications and extended the timelines for full implementation of various measures. Both bodies of the legislature approved the amended bill at the end of the session. With newfound harmony, Congress showed itself acquiescent to very significant Navy organizational changes. The process had occurred slowly and deliberately over time. The markedly consequential act of March 3, 1899, "To reorganize and increase the efficiency of the personnel of the Navy and Marine Corps," provided watershed changes to enlisted, midshipmen, and officer precedent, promotion, pay, and retirement of both the Navy and Marine Corps.[5] The legislation ultimately provided an officer selection process partially based on merit by establishing a new Navy retirement system that thinned the ranks of mid-grade and senior officers, making room for higher qualified leaders. However, this process also increased the rolls of retirees and carried the military pension program beyond its post–Civil War munificence. Congress seemed to have at least partially overcome its deep-seated fear of merit selection in the military and its dread of expanding a welfare state of retired military pensioners. The Navy retirement program now included officers who were not part of "the deserving core of a special generation," that had fought in the Civil War.[6]

One of the most significant articles of the 1899 personnel act abolished the Navy staff corps of steam engineers, transferring all current engineer officers to the line. Additionally, it established increased quotas for all Navy ranks, created a commissioned warrant officer class for enlisted men, and spelled out the rank requirements and allocations of Marine Corps officers. Congress took these actions after almost twenty years of deliberations. With the exception of steam engineering, separate staff corps classifications still existed, but all commissioned officers now had equal titles, status, and pay. Navy staff corps bureau chiefs retained their specialties and their relationships with Congress. The legislative process of the 1880s and 1890s leading to this act was neither swift nor inevitable. It was part of a much larger whole that involved Congress preserving its long-standing constitutional mandate "to provide and maintain a Navy." As the twentieth century was about to open, Congress steadfastly retained the upper hand in determining Navy organization. Secretary Long supported the Roosevelt Bill, while McKinley did not play a significant role in its passage.

In spite of the advances of the personnel act, the post–Spanish War deliberations concerning the necessity for a centralized Navy staff remained unsettled. The personnel act did not address any reorganization of the Navy bureau system or change the Navy's warfighting administration. Progressive officers of the growing Navy, led by retired Rear Admiral Luce and Capt. Henry Taylor, continued to plead for the formation of a Navy general staff. Ira Hollis' reorganization plan of 1897 included the need for unified military command.[7] However, Congress would not consider creating a permanent military organization that even remotely resembled the Bismarckian staff arrangements developing in European nations. In spite of the military coordination problems encountered during the war with Spain, neither McKinley nor Long showed interest in creating a general staff for the Navy.[8] The president expressed his satisfaction in using the White House as a crowded wartime command center run by himself and his advisers. Also, legislators insisted on retaining the status quo of the Navy's eight independent administrative bureaus without a single military head.

While Congress developed a new Navy organization, Senator Hale introduced an unsuccessful complementary bill to provide for naval reserves. His proposal was a reaction to the Navy's difficulty in getting qualified recruits to man ships in the recent war against Spain. Sailors in the modern Navy needed mechanical skills that required long periods of training. Hale's bill provided for a reserve force of four thousand men, trained on a part-time basis, to man the regular Navy's newest ships in a few years' time. This naval reserve component would furnish temporary enlistments and training without the expense of large numbers of officers and men on the active list inefficiently waiting for ships to be completed. Naval volunteers were to come from the growing civilian U.S. merchant marine.[9] Hale's bill died in committee, in spite of the Navy Department's strong endorsement, because advocates could not attract sufficient regional or partisan interest in Congress.

In addition to approving personnel reorganization, at the end of its session in early March 1899 the outgoing Fifty-fifth Congress authorized three coastline battleships, three armored cruisers, and six unarmored cruisers. The coastline designation and the approval of unarmored cruisers reflected the legislature's continued focus on a defensive Navy. The naval appropriations act also reduced the authorized price of armor plate to $300 per ton.[10] Opposition to profit making by the Bethlehem and Carnegie steel companies came from the obstreperous, patronage-driven senator Benjamin Tillman of South Carolina and, of course, from Senator Chandler, who vociferously accused the manufacturers of collusion and convinced the majority of the Senate to hold out for the $300 mandate.[11] Chandler persisted as an opponent of battleships and an offensive Navy. Unable to get bids for constructing the six authorized armored ships, the Navy Department again suffered a serious setback and would not get the possibility of relief for more than a year, until the next Congress passed its appropriations act in the summer of 1900.

During the spring of 1899 McKinley mistakenly remained optimistic concerning the escalating uprising in the Philippines. The newly appointed military governor, Maj. Gen. Elwell Otis, was the on-scene commander against the Filipino insurgents led by Aguinaldo, who demanded self-government. While the Senate finalized the treaty of peace with Spain, new hostilities erupted. McKinley maintained that the Philippines as well as Guam and Puerto Rico were dependencies, rather than territories under the Constitution, and that the native inhabitants were not yet ready for self-government. Dissatisfied with the performance of Secretary of War Alger during the war with Spain, McKinley awaited an opportunity to replace him with a more decisive leader. When Alger decided to run for Senate that summer, McKinley accepted his resignation and appointed Elihu Root to the Army secretariat. Root, a well-placed New York lawyer noted for his no-nonsense administrative ability, took over the conduct of the Philippine War and the overhaul of Army organization.

Although neither the U.S. Army nor Navy could compete with the European empires, the United States was a growing force as a result of its successful foreign war with Spain and its ongoing military venture in Asia. In May 1899, the United States and twenty-three other nations sent representatives to a peace conference called for by Tsar Nicholas II of Russia to be held at The Hague. The enlightened purpose of the convention was to establish international protocols for the conduct of war and arbitration. Andrew White, the

U.S. ambassador at Berlin, led the American delegation. Captain Mahan, now retired, participated as the U.S. spokesman on naval matters. With prescient cynicism, Sen. Thomas Platt summed up the conference as "visionary and beautiful, but impractical."[12] As predicted, the meetings ended in late July with only a handful of minor agreements concerning arms limitations and the treatment of civilians and property at sea, which would have major implications when world war broke out in 1914.

On the international scene closer to home, McKinley and Secretary of State John Hay continued to labor over relations with Great Britain regarding the boundaries of the Alaskan peninsula. The growing gold rush necessitated clearer agreement on the jurisdiction over important harbors. The 1825 treaty between Russia and Great Britain only roughly defined the areas in question. As the gold rush continued, British negotiators generally were amenable to settle the Alaskan borders in favor of the United States, with the caveat that they must first resolve U.S. plans for building a canal through Central America. According to the Clayton-Bulwer Treaty of 1850, Great Britain and the United States agreed not to build such a canal unilaterally. Now in 1899, the British seemed willing to accept that the United States could perhaps build a canal by itself that would be unfortified and open to all.

Secretary Long's annual report of late November 1899 focused on the state of the Navy, rather than international affairs. He began by writing that operations in the Philippine Islands were arduous and that, due to grounding on an uncharted reef near Luzon, the Navy had lost the *Charleston*, the cruiser that had joined Dewey's fleet supporting the U.S. Army. At the urging of his assistant secretary, Long also included another appeal for the formation of a naval reserve force. He continued his account with the status of the several ships under construction. Due to the $300 fixed price per ton for armor plate, the Navy did not receive any bids for the three armored battleships and three cruisers authorized by the previous Congress in March. Long asked for relief from the price restriction as well as appropriations for three additional armored cruisers, three smaller unarmored cruisers, and twelve gunboats.[13]

The day before Long signed his report Vice President Garret Hobart, McKinley's close friend and confidant, died after a brief illness caused by a heart attack. A few weeks after the vice president's funeral, McKinley began his annual message to Congress by extolling Hobart's character and integrity.

Following the somber eulogy, his remaining fifty-page message was mostly upbeat. Highlighting the country's prosperity, McKinley again called attention to the importance of building up the merchant marine for international commerce. In accordance with the desires of the previous Congress, he noted the establishment of the Isthmian Canal Commission and his appointment of retired Rear Admiral Walker as its head. The president hoped for a report as soon as practical regarding a feasible canal route and probable cost. In his section concerning international relations, he wrote that the *Boston* landed a guard of Marines in China to protect the U.S. legation at Peking. Continuing his tome, he pointed out American preparations for the World's Exposition to be held in Paris during the upcoming year and expected over seven thousand U.S. exhibitors to participate. In a one-page segment about the Navy, he endorsed Long's recommendations and specifically reiterated the need to remove the $300 per ton armor plate restriction.

McKinley's section on the war in the Philippines began with a strong condemnation of "the sinister ambition of a few leaders of the Filipinos."[14] The president presented the Army intervention as unavoidable and stated that the rebellion must be put down. He reported that 65,000 U.S. soldiers were currently deployed to the Philippines and that war would continue until the insurgents ceased their operations. Only then could civil government under the United States be inaugurated, followed by a path toward self-government. Unfortunately, the insurrection festered at various levels until 1916 and involved hundreds of thousands of Filipino casualties inflicted by U.S. forces.

EXPANSION

While the incoming Fifty-sixth Congress met for its regular long session of the winter and spring of 1900, Secretary Long decided to create a General Board of the Navy. Even though Navy officers had been urging the creation of a general staff with a military head for the Navy, he insisted that the board would not be put above civilian control. In later years he reiterated the wisdom of his decision and criticized the congressional act of 1903 that created an Army Chief of Staff of the War Department.[15] The Navy's General Board remained separate from the Navy bureaus and acted in an advisory capacity to the Secretary of the Navy.

To no avail, Navy officers had persistently advocated the establishment of a general staff rather than an advisory board. Captain Taylor, a past president of the Naval War College and well-known naval philosopher and administrative reformer, led the movement.[16] Another Naval War College leader, Capt. French Chadwick, offered his authoritative voice to the discourse. He had served as chief of staff of the North Atlantic Squadron during the war with Spain and was a major participant in wartime strategic decisions. As expected, retired Rear Admiral Luce remained at the forefront of the Navy's position. Nevertheless, Long created a permanent General Board of the Navy rather than a general staff and appointed Admiral Dewey as its head. Dewey had been promoted to Admiral of the Navy by a grateful Congress and subsequently headed the board from 1900 to 1917.

The first order of Navy business for the Fifty-sixth Congress, which convened its first session in December 1899, concerned the notion of national reserve forces. Specifically, Rep. Melville Bull of Rhode Island reopened the subject by sponsoring a House of Representatives bill to organize a naval reserve.[17] With Navy facilities in his district, he and his constituents would benefit from legislation that established a larger shore component. At the end of the session, George Foss of Illinois introduced another version of a bill to provide for naval reserves.[18] His home state had already established two naval militia battalions and he desired Congress to fund permanent reserve naval training sites. Ascending in power and taking the place of Charles Boutelle a few months later as chairman of the House naval committee, Foss was in a position to guide Navy legislation. But neither Bull nor Foss could round up sufficient support for a Navy reserve force. The majority of legislators opposed subsidizing a national naval volunteer program.

Instead, whenever they could, Congressmen directed naval appropriations to benefit industries and government-owned Navy yards in their districts. Improvement of the government facilities in Pennsylvania and California kept those states in competition with New York and New Hampshire to dock large battleships. Spreading the wealth, Congress also specified that warships would be built by Pacific Coast contractors.[19] The only spoilsports were isolationist Republicans and Populists from non-coastal and non-industrial states, who resisted government spending on the Navy. They balked against any naval expansion on the grounds that it unnecessarily took national treasure from the people.

Southern Democrats, led by Oscar Underwood of Alabama, resolutely insisted on the use of government facilities for both shipbuilding and armor manufacturing. His bloc of fellow representatives pushed to shift battleship construction from private shipyards to government facilities and to establish a government steel plant in the South.[20] Although several Navy harbors were located in the South, only the Norfolk yard had sufficient water depth and extensive shipbuilding capabilities. Nevertheless, the Southern bloc continued to oppose profit taking by Northern capitalists and desired to accelerate regional economic advances by direct government involvement in military manufacturing in their areas.

However, Secretary Long, supporting private enterprise, advised the House naval committee that warship construction in government Navy yards "costs twice as much and takes twice as long." He preferred the steady employment of ship repair in Navy yards to experiencing the irregular highs and lows of new ship construction work. The secretary gravely predicted that shipbuilding by the government would bring back wasteful pre–civil service patronage struggles. He testified that the Navy Department would be pressured to spread the work among various shipyards regardless of efficiency. For him, competition between government yards would increase the demand for redundant buildings, machinery, and business staffs.[21] Congress compromised by mandating both government and private shipbuilding.

The president had a tough spring because the new Congress did not agree with his foremost concerns. First, the Senate rejected the Hay-Pauncefote Treaty signed by Great Britain in December 1899. Secretary of State Hay and British ambassador Julian Pauncefote had worked out an agreement for the United States to construct an unfortified Isthmian canal open to all. To McKinley's disappointment, the Senate and the U.S. public objected to restrictions prohibiting security for such a major U.S. enterprise and investment. The treaty abrogating the old Clayton–Bulwer restrictions needed to be reexamined again by both governments in another round of negotiations. Second, the House of Representatives rejected his protective tariff proposal covering the newly obtained commercial activities of the territory of Puerto Rico. The rejection of the president's Puerto Rican tariff schedule in the House forced McKinley to change his economic plan, which reduced tariff income, in order to save party unity and his own pending reelection. The legislature adjourned in early June and congressmen dispersed to participate in the presidential campaign season.

Congress' Naval Appropriations Act of June 1900 included funds for two seagoing battleships, two armored cruisers, three small unarmed cruisers, and five submarines.[22] The inclusion of the battleships and submarines went considerably beyond Long's request at the beginning of the session. Congress had previously been authorizing seagoing coastline battleships even though the Navy's battleships in fact had worldwide capabilities. Deleting the word coastline in the latest authorization reflected a significant change in outlook. For several years, the legislature had insisted on the defensive coastline description, at least on paper. Now at the beginning of the twentieth century, for the first time in U.S. history the Fifty-sixth Congress conceptualized the U.S. Navy as a worldwide force capable of *guerre d'escadre*. The next Congress would drop the designation "seagoing" and instead simply authorize first-class battleships. Thomas Reed, a powerful opponent of an offensive Navy, had resigned from the House of Representatives in the fall of 1899 in a fit of pique over U.S. imperialism and could no longer influence wording to artificially limit the role of the Navy's principal warships. The appropriations act also included a critical provision lifting the $300 per ton restriction for the purchase of armor plate.

When the Republican National Convention met in Philadelphia in mid-June, McKinley had virtually no opposition. However, selection of a vice presidential nominee remained somewhat open, with a groundswell favoring popular New York governor Theodore Roosevelt. The colorful Rough Rider held out as a reluctant candidate and tried to move attention away from himself and focus on McKinley's success. Behind the scenes, Senator Platt of New York and Sen. Matthew Quay of Pennsylvania saw Governor Roosevelt as a destructive force to their Republican Party organization and maneuvered to isolate him into the vice presidency. Delegates unanimously nominated McKinley on the first ballot and Roosevelt received all of the convention votes for vice president—except his own.

Meanwhile, events in China took a nasty turn. The United States, being a new power in the Far East since its acquisition of the Philippines, was in the process of seeking equal access to important Chinese commerce. However, China was in such a state of warlord internecine disarray that partitioning of the declining empire by the established trading nations seemed imminent. Secretary Hay attempted to create an "Open Door" agreement with all parties. But Great Britain, France, Germany, Italy, Austria-Hungary, Russia, and Japan would not commit to free trade as the local fragmented governments lost authority. Amidst the commercial turmoil in the summer of 1900, a rebellious group of Chinese nationalists called Boxers, taking the image of hard-hitting pugilists, sought to expel all foreigners from China. Internal fighting ensued between anti-foreigner and pro-foreigner Chinese factions as the Boxers laid siege to the legations of eleven nations in Peking. To protect the embassies, the United States sent four thousand soldiers to China to augment the troops of foreign navies that were already on scene. Meanwhile, the U.S. Army also continued to maintain its significant operations in the Philippines. The Boxers lifted their fifty-five-day siege in August after the opposing Chinese coalitions inflicted considerable casualties on each other, and the area settled down for a while.[23]

Back in the United States, the Democratic Party had held its national convention and continued to focus on attacking the gold standard. With only token opposition, William Jennings Bryan won the nomination again. In addition to supporting free silver, the Democratic Party condemned both the recent war with Spain and the administration's current imperialism in the Philippines. Neither Bryan nor his platform resonated with the majority of the American public, gathering only 45.5 percent of the popular vote. McKinley, instead, carried the day with his promise of prosperity. Democrats did manage to pick up a few seats in the Senate while Republicans had some gains in the House. Overall, the Republican Party maintained its comfortable margin in both houses of the legislature.

Looking forward to four more years of naval progress, Long completed his postelection annual report for the outgoing Congress in November. In his opening section he described in detail the Navy and Marine Corps participation in the siege in China. He then noted a growing shortage of sea-duty officers and also requested raising the quota of enlisted men by five thousand. Long continued with the news that he had received a good price for armor plate from Bethlehem and Carnegie at $455 per ton. Additionally, he claimed to need a reserve force run by the Navy Department as well as militias run by the states. For warship increases, he asked for two battleships, two armored cruisers, at least six light-draft gunboats, and a few other auxiliaries.[24]

President McKinley sent his annual message to Congress a few weeks later. In three short paragraphs concerning the Navy, McKinley forwarded "the recommendations of the secretary for new vessels and for additional officers" and commended "the establishment of a national naval reserve."[25] Although presidents in the past two decades had often used their annual messages to Congress to personally push detailed naval priorities, McKinley chose to let the Navy Department speak for itself. He acted with an assuredness that the combination of national prosperity, recent naval victories, and U.S. territorial acquisitions would keep Congress on a path of fleet increases.

Early in the following short, lame-duck session of Congress, Amos Cummings of New York, a former chairman of the House naval committee, introduced yet another bill to establish a Navy reserve. He again emphasized the concept of a federal, rather than a state, standby Navy. Secretary Long agreed that a national naval reserve force should be an entity separate from the existing naval militia of the states. He recommended organizing a reserve force into districts across state lines, with a regular Navy officer in charge of each district, and reiterated the national character of a naval reserve contingent.[26] However, seafarers' unions did not share the enthusiasm of maritime industry owners and shipmasters for a naval reserve. They expressed concern that seamen would sign up as naval volunteers in the merchant marine to gain preferential employment, thereby negating the unions' role in labor-management relations.[27] The majority in Congress also opposed granting federal subsidies to ship owners participating in a reserve program and again tabled the reserve bill.

Participating coastal and Great Lakes states preferred to receive appropriations for their own naval militia units rather than establish national reserves run by the Navy Department.[28] According to enthusiasts, state units satisfactorily augmented the federal Navy by performing a variety of local maritime tasks. Naval militia manned coastal signal stations, patrolled coastal areas in private vessels, and assisted in laying defensive torpedoes and mines. But unlike the Army's citizen soldiers, Navy citizen sailors did not have a long-embedded tradition. The Army militia dated from the days of the American Revolution's minutemen, and served state governors. The fledging Navy militia had no comparable history with the majority of governors and was not a significant element of a loosely defined spirit of American navalism.

The outgoing Fifty-sixth Congress passed its annual Army appropriations act on March 3, 1901, a day prior to its Navy act. The Platt Amendment, a rider on the Army act, indicated congressional interests to remain closely involved in Cuba and the Caribbean area. It established a permanent U.S. naval base at Guantanamo Bay and stipulated that the United States had the right to re-intervene in Cuban affairs. The associated Navy appropriations act of $78 million, passed a day later, amounted to a significant increase over the previous year and was considerably above the $56 million wartime funding of 1898. In fact, the last two annual authorizations during McKinley's first term represent the highest increases since the buildup of the new Navy began in the 1880s. As it ended its March session, Congress authorized two battleships and two armored cruisers.[29] By leaving out gunboats and auxiliaries, the legislature was guiding Navy strategy by choosing a force structure emphasizing large combatants. The Navy now had nineteen battleships either commissioned, under construction, or awaiting a contract.

In the early afternoon of March 4, McKinley was in good spirits for his second presidential inauguration. After taking his oath of office, he spoke to the crowd gathered outside the capital building. Heavy rain did not dampen his mood. In his relatively brief address, he spoke of the well-being of the nation, the disappearance of sectionalism, the encouraging progress in Cuba, and the hope for lasting peace in the Philippine Islands.[30] McKinley looked forward to four more fruitful years. All but one of his cabinet members had returned for a second term. Philander Knox replaced Attorney General John Griggs, who left for private practice and joined former President Benjamin Harrison as a member of the newly established Permanent Court of Arbitration at The Hague. Soon after he began his second term, McKinley finalized his plans for a six-week tour of the country between April and June with his wife and members of his cabinet.

McKinley was very upbeat concerning his trip throughout the South and West. He intended to spread goodwill as well as enjoy a vacation while Congress was not in session. Four of his cabinet members accompanied him and his wife on the train when it departed Washington.[31] Others, including Secretary Long, planned to join the party in San Francisco. McKinley's trip through the South was a rousing success. Hundreds of well-wishers met his train at every stop. He understood the importance of continually cultivating Southern support. Unfortunately, McKinley's wife Ida took sick in mid-May while the entourage was spending a restful weekend in Del Monte, California. McKinley immediately rushed her to nearby San Francisco where her condition worsened. A few days later, he sadly began to make preparations for an anticipated funereal return trip to Washington. But to the amazement of her attending physicians, Ida rallied to recovery. The presidential party waited until Ida's condition permitted further travel and then during the third week of May they all decamped for Washington.[32]

Shortly after his return to the capital, McKinley emphatically declared to his cabinet and the country that he definitely would not be a candidate for a third term. Due to his wife's condition, he decided not to participate in a major ceremony to be held in his honor in June at the Pan-American Exposition in Buffalo, New York. Instead, he sent Secretary of State Hay and Secretary of War Root on his behalf, but promised to speak at the event later in September. In early July, he and Ida departed Washington to spend the remainder of the summer in their home in Canton, Ohio.

ANOTHER ASSASSINATION

As promised, McKinley and his recovered wife traveled to Buffalo where he delivered a speech to tens of thousands of spectators a day prior to his fatal encounter. The next day, Friday, September 6, 1901, a crazed anarchist named Leon Czolgosz felt it was his duty to bring down the government, and he shot the president. Ida was not with McKinley as he shook hands with the many people waiting in line. Czolgosz waited his turn with a pistol bandaged to his right hand. Upon greeting the president, he fired twice and then made no attempt to escape. Agents quickly disarmed and apprehended the assassin while the wounded McKinley watched. Within several minutes an ambulance arrived to carry the president to the local Exposition hospital. Surgeons on the scene decided to cleanse the wound and determine the extent of damage. They first administered ether to the still-conscious president and proceeded with their probes. They recovered one bullet, which had grazed his ribs, but could not find the other bullet, which had gone through his stomach and lodged somewhere in his back. Attendants then carried McKinley to the house of Exposition director John Milburn, where they expected him to recover.

Within hours government officials and the public learned of the assassination attempt via telegraph. A deeply shocked Roosevelt immediately left his speaking engagement in Vermont and traveled by train to Buffalo.[33] The vice president and all but two cabinet members found their way to the president's side by Saturday afternoon. After their arrival, news from the Milburn house remained optimistic. Anticipating that the president would survive, some of the cabinet members dispersed in order to publicly downplay the crisis. Roosevelt proceeded to his remote vacation camp in the Adirondack Mountains of New York. But soon McKinley's prognosis changed for the worse. By the end of the week, it was obvious to the doctors and people around him that he was not recovering. In response to urgent telegrams delivered by hand to his mountain retreat stating that the president was dying, Roosevelt rushed back to Buffalo. He arrived at the railroad station in North Creek, New York, during the early morning hours of September 14, following a grueling five-hour nighttime trip by horse and wagon down the mountains, to learn that McKinley had died at 2:15 that morning.[34]

Roosevelt reached Buffalo again by fast train early that afternoon. Rather than intrude on the melancholy aura at the Milburn House, Roosevelt chose to stay in the nearby residence of Ansley Wilcox, a longtime friend. After dressing in mourning clothes, some borrowed, Roosevelt made his way to the nearby Milburn House to pay his respects. Instead of officially meeting with the present members of his inherited cabinet, he chose to have everyone move to the Wilcox house for the swearing-in and the conduct of necessary immediate business. In Roosevelt's short but famous inaugural speech to his small audience he said that he aimed "to continue absolutely the unbroken policy of President McKinley for the peace, the prosperity, and the honor of our beloved country."[35] He was then officially sworn in by federal judge John R. Hazel. The new president's words were repeated around the country by the press and had the calming effect of assuring that Roosevelt would stay the course of the popular fallen leader.

A NEW PRESIDENT

Roosevelt, raised as a child of privilege, had dissociated himself from robber-baron capitalism and became a leader of regulatory progressivism, caring for the so-called common man. His American roots began with the Dutch settlers of New York City in the mid-1600s. His grandfather and father maintained the family's fortunes through real estate and import businesses. Born in 1858, he particularly admired his father's altruistic work for the welfare of others. Unfortunately, Theodore developed asthma at an early age, which slowed down the advancement of his physical abilities. With the help of his father, he overcame his handicap through exercise and determination. As a youngster and then as an adult, he traveled several times to Europe and was schooled in Germany for a year, where he learned German and French. At eighteen, he entered Harvard and a year later endured the death of his much-loved father and the gradual loss of his father's subvention.

Shortly after graduating from Harvard, Theodore married his first wife Alice Hathaway Lee, honeymooned in Europe, and then entered Columbia Law School. After less than a year he left school and entered politics, having been elected to the New York State Assembly. As a first-time representative of the people, his energetic enthusiasm for public life and an unabated hostility toward corruption made him both political enemies and friends. One of his new acquaintances was recently resigned Lt. Cdr. Henry Gorringe, who had written about the scandalous spoils system in the Navy Department's eight bureaus. Navy Secretary Chandler unsuccessfully tried to use the article as testimony that the bureau system indeed needed serious revamping. At that time, in 1883, Gorringe ran hunts for the dwindling number of buffalo in the West and easily convinced the young Roosevelt to participate. Roosevelt took a short vacation away from his pregnant wife to shoot buffalo and purchase land.

After his exuberant return from the western lands, a second major sorrow struck Roosevelt in February 1884. Just two days after his daughter Alice was born, his widowed mother died of typhoid and his wife Alice died of kidney disease in the same house on the same day. Within a year of his personal losses, he decided to leave New York and seek a new life on his recently acquired ranch in Dakota Territory. Leaving his daughter with his sister Anna, he spent three years as a ranching cowboy and added to his successful authorship of history books by writing adventure stories about the West. According to his own autobiography, Roosevelt credited his western experiences with shaping his future and his path to the presidency.[36] In the West he observed and befriended a wide range of people, and there his background as a tutored easterner did not matter.

A year after his return to New York he married his childhood chum, Edith Kermit Carow, and returned to the world of government. With his record as an outspoken politician against corruption, he was a natural to be selected by President Harrison as the first Civil Service commissioner and took on the spoils system in Washington, D.C. Six years later he returned to New York

City and assumed the post of police commissioner, where he again rattled the cages of the establishment until his Republican Party kicked him upstairs to the position of Assistant Secretary of the Navy. Following his military success during the Spanish-American War, he easily won the governorship of New York State. Again, as governor, he followed his own counsel—to the dismay of Republican kingmakers, who successfully maneuvered him into the benign office of the vice president. Now, by accident and to their concern, he was the president.

Roosevelt made use of the long, mournful train ride from Buffalo to Washington to craft the structure of his new office. On the train, he met privately with cabinet members, members of the press, and the powerful Senator Hanna, McKinley's closest friend and confidant. Roosevelt assured them all that he would both listen and lead, but also began to develop his own plans for governance. First on his personal list was the replacement of certain members of his administration. He waited for that to occur in due time rather than announcing radical changes at once. Funeral and burial arrangements dominated the immediate attention of the government in the capital. Rather than immediately move into the White House, Roosevelt stayed in Washington with his sister Anna, who had married Lt. Cdr. William Cowles and cared for Roosevelt's daughter Alice. McKinley's coffin rested in the President's House for the multitude of mourners to pay their last respects to the popular president. The final program involved a train trip to Canton, Ohio, for interment.

Roosevelt's first days in the White House office were routine, but he got himself involved in a very noisy controversy within a month. Previously, as vice president, he had intended to visit the Tuskegee Institute in Alabama and had known its founder, Booker T. Washington, for some time. As president, he met with Washington to discuss federal appointments of blacks and sympathetic whites in the south and decided to invite Washington to the White House for dinner. This was intended to be a simple, private affair, rather than a civil rights statement. Unfortunately it did not play out that way. News of the dinner made headlines in the press and the response from the South was especially disheartening. Roosevelt was absolutely stunned by the angry and vicious response, especially the hateful rhetoric of Sen. Ben Tillman of South Carolina who wrote: "The action of President Roosevelt in entertaining that nigger will necessitate our killing a thousand niggers in the South before they learn their place again."[37] Tillman had been on the Senate naval committee since 1895 and would be its Democratic chairman from 1913 to 1917. Roosevelt was abashed and in the future kept a low profile concerning race relations, although he continued to campaign in the South cognizant that white Democrats would never vote for him.

Prior to sending his first annual message to the new Congress, Roosevelt scrutinized the formation of a huge railroad business combination called the Northern Securities Company. Competing corporate titans James J. Hill, E. H. Harriman, and John Pierpont Morgan hatched a scheme to unite rather than compete with each other. In November, they announced the creation of a huge railroad holding company embracing services covering more than one-third of the United States. The company was an anti-competition instrument most likely well beyond the provision of the relatively weak Sherman Antitrust Act of 1890. Roosevelt decided to take executive action. He charged Attorney General Knox to prepare a government position against such combinations, with Northern Securities as the target. The government offensive began with Roosevelt's annual report of December 1901.

His long tome was somewhat shorter than some of McKinley's but was typically comprehensive.[38] Roosevelt devoted the first several pages to the calamity of anarchism versus democracy, resulting in assassinations, and then got down to business. He praised the prosperity of the United States and wrote that it was noble to form great industries that benefited mankind, but also insisted that the private sector be honest and just. He stated that the federal government held a legal position to regulate corporate combinations. Roosevelt then summarized other areas of internal and international affairs, including military, political, and commercial developments in Hawaii, Puerto Rico, Cuba, and the Philippines. He also introduced his interest in forestry and conservation.

Roosevelt began his four-page section on naval affairs with the statement: "The work of the Navy must be steadily continued. No one point of our policy, foreign or domestic, is more important."[39] For the specific amount of necessary increases in warships and manpower, he referred to the Navy's annual report forwarded to Congress in November. Secretary Long had recommended a formidable increase of three battleships, two cruisers, eighteen gunboats, and seventeen miscellaneous auxiliary ships, and again wrote of "the pressing need of a national naval reserve force from which to draw for sea service immediately upon an outbreak of war."[40] Referring to Long's official testimony, Roosevelt reiterated the necessity of building up state naval militias and requested the immediate creation of a separate national naval reserve organization under the direction of the Navy Department.

Congress had more immediate concerns and, to Roosevelt's delight, in mid-December 1901 the Senate passed a reworked Hay-Pauncefote Treaty with Great Britain granting the United States unrestricted rights to build a canal between the Atlantic and Pacific Oceans. Roosevelt could now work on other priorities and prepared for a federal antitrust suit against the Northern Securities Company. He also made a few cabinet changes. Establishing himself as a patron of the old Republican guard, Roosevelt replaced financier Lyman Gage at the Treasury Department with conservative banker Leslie Shaw, then governor of Iowa. In a similar move, businessman and Republican Party committee chairman Henry Payne relieved Postmaster General Charles Smith.

In their opening regular session, legislators in both houses of the Fifty-seventh Congress submitted bills to define the existing naval militias and to establish a national naval reserve.[41] This was the fourth Congress in succession to put these issues to its members. Militia supporters argued that the militias had a unique role and should not simply be a "preschool" for the seagoing Navy. Although the naval militias had been in existence for only ten years, they had in fact served in the Spanish-American War. But militia advocates legitimately complained that many of these men, trained for coastal defense duties, had been misused and treated as second-class sailors when they were assigned to deep-water billets on regular Navy ships. To rectify this abuse, legislation could specifically delineate the role of the militias, thus ensuring their exclusive use as a coastal (i.e., state) defensive force.[42] Supporters of a national reserve force disagreed with the concept of exclusive duties for naval militias. They held the view that the commander-in-chief had wartime authority to place militias and reserves wherever he saw fit. Ultimately the reserves bill and the militia bill again died in committee.

10

AN OFFENSIVE NAVY,
1902–5

While the Fifty-seventh Congress was in its regular session in January 1902, Senator Hanna, in agreement with the president, issued a press release proclaiming the canal route through Panama as being superior to any other course. With international constraints removed by the newly agreed Hay-Pauncefote Treaty, the United States executive department brokered a significantly low offer from the French Panama Canal company, which was anxious to cut its losses. Endorsing the $40 million asking price, Roosevelt sent the bid to the Senate canal commission for immediate consideration.[1] In spite of strong support from Hanna, the White House, and a stream of lobbyists, the obdurate senator John T. Morgan of Alabama, now in his twenty-fifth year in Congress and chairman of the committee on interoceanic canals, managed to temporarily delay a decision. However, Roosevelt finally got his way in the summer and received congressional authority to choose the Panama route.

During the springtime, Roosevelt also faced an ugly series of events in the Philippine Islands. The campaign against the insurgents was essentially over, with their surrender close at hand. However, reports of U.S. Army troops brutalizing Filipino guerrillas found their way into the press and onto the floor of Congress, strengthening the position of anti-imperialists against Roosevelt. An on-scene account revealed that Brig. Gen. Jacob H. Smith had approved the torture and killing of Philippine natives, including boys as young as ten years old. During congressional hearings, administration supporters attempted to justify the Army's behavior by exposing the utter savagery of the rebels and the atrocities carried out against American soldiers, who unfortunately responded in kind.[2] The crisis subsided after the court-martial of General Smith and a few others, plus the subsequent surrender of the rebels. Smith was found guilty of conduct prejudicial to good order and military discipline and ordered to retire from the Army.

In April, Roosevelt chose a new leader for the Navy Department. John Long, who had agreed to stay on for a while after McKinley's assassination, amicably left office. William Moody, a fourth-term congressman from Massachusetts, took over the position in May. Moody was five years older than Roosevelt; his successful family came to New England from Wales in the 1630s. He was educated at Phillips Academy and Harvard. After college, he studied law under Richard Dana, a famous author and lawyer, and became a member of the Massachusetts bar. Moody had an excellent reputation for his thoroughness and had previously gained positive notice as the junior prosecutor in the famous Lizzy Borden case in Fall River. He was serving as an influential member of the House appropriations committee when he accepted the Navy Department portfolio. Roosevelt chose him for his mastery of detail, pugnacity, and performance, as well as his ability to help with political campaigns. Moody proved to be a good choice because of his harmonious relations with Congress.[3]

The Naval Act of July 1902, which was passed a month after Moody took office, authorized two battleships, two cruisers, and two gunboats. This was considerably fewer than the combination of forty warships and auxiliaries recommended by Secretary Long at the opening of the session in December. The act also required that at least one battleship be built by the government.[4] The new naval patronage system in Congress favored broad regional applications rather than personal beneficence. This regionalism gained potency as the civil service structure became permanently entrenched in the civilian side of Navy Department business. Instead of pre–civil service conditions, where masses of individual workmen received government jobs as a reward for voting for a candidate, early twentieth-century patronage focused on improving the general economy of a specific locale. Under civil service rules congressmen could no longer guarantee the direct hiring of party faithful but could claim credit for funding decisions that brought jobs to an area. Congressmen received thousands of petitions to authorize government shipbuilding in their districts. Workers and "concerned citizens" appealed to the legislature for new construction contracts in addition to repair work for Navy yards. Supporters of government work railed against private industry, which they claimed used nonunion labor and did not abide by the government-mandated eight-hour workday for government contracts.

As secretary, Moody held the responsibility of selecting the first government facility to build a modern battleship. In the House of Representatives, naval committee member Ernest Roberts (R–MA) had voted with his colleague John Rixey (D-VA) in support of the legislation for government shipbuilding. They represented their committee's minority view against private contractors in the prolonged floor fights of the spring session. Congress as a whole agreed with the naval committee minority and subsequently mandated the use of government facilities. The *New York Times* presented the vote as a Democratic victory with Republican support.[5] As the new Navy Secretary, barely two months removed from his own congressional debates, Moody rejected using either the Boston or Norfolk Navy Yards of Roberts and Rixey respectively. Instead he selected the more expensive Brooklyn Navy Yard for the first battleship construction by the government. Preserving his important connections to the legislative branch, he claimed he based his decision on the needs of the labor market. The Brooklyn area, incorporated as part of New York City since 1898, had a key political power base as well as large numbers of unemployed shipbuilders.

A few months after Congress adjourned in July, a group of men in New York City organized themselves along the lines of other special interest groups of the period and fashioned a Navy League to advance an undefined American navalism. Members drafted the incorporation of the league with the objective to spread "information as to the condition of the naval forces and equipment of the United States" and to develop public cooperation in all matters tending to improve those forces.[6] Contemplating the successes in Great Britain and Germany, the league leaders optimistically anticipated playing a role in congressional decisions by promoting public awareness rather than by direct lobbying. Initially the league helped advance a certain degree of naval awareness, but its long-term effect on Congress was problematic at best.

The founders of the Navy League saw themselves as important personages but were not especially powerful on the national scene. Generally, members might have served in the Navy during the Civil War or the Spanish-American War, or were retired naval officers. They knew each other through association in the New York Yacht Club, the Army-Navy Club, U.S. Naval Academy alumni clubs, and various veteran's organizations. Herbert Satterlee, an energetic thirty-nine-year-old lawyer and yachtsman, was a founder and prime mover of the league. He had served as a Navy lieutenant during the Spanish-American War and was a leading figure in supporting the New York State naval militia. As the son-in-law of financier J. Pierpont Morgan, he was also well connected to New York City entrepreneurs.[7] Satterlee would later become the Assistant Secretary of the Navy in late 1908 for the final three months of Roosevelt's presidency. The new league enlisted Benjamin Tracy and his former Assistant Secretary of the Navy, William McAdoo, to serve as its president and vice president respectively. Tracy, by then a prominent New York lawyer, had national name recognition with the Navy but was no longer a force in national politics. The press accompanied the initial notice of the league's formation with a confirmation of promise for the future.[8]

As the Fifty-seventh Congress gathered on schedule in December for its short lame-duck session, both Moody and Roosevelt sent their respective annual correspondence to the legislature. In his first report as Secretary of the Navy, Moody presented the need for coaling stations and additional officers. His minimum recommendations for new warship construction included two battleships, two hospital ships, and other types of vessels at the discretion of Congress.[9] Roosevelt followed with his own official message and wrote: "There should be no halt in the work of building up the Navy, providing every year additional fighting craft."[10] He then asked for one thousand additional officers, but did not request specific types of ships and did not mention the Navy League, naval militias, or a need to create a national Navy reserve force.

Shortly after Congress convened, Roosevelt faced an increasingly dangerous naval confrontation with the navies of Great Britain, Germany, and Italy in Venezuela. The crisis had been brewing for a few years and involved Venezuela's inability to pay its foreign debts due to a series of revolutions. By the late summer of 1902, the European allies had announced the prepara-tion of a naval blockade of Venezuela to force payment. Prior to initiating a blockade, British and German warships began at-sea skirmishes with the Ven-ezuelan Navy. At first Roosevelt did not object to the European action. He saw the situation as one of legitimate debt collection rather than an attempt to take over territory in violation of the Monroe Doctrine. However, as a precautionary display of U.S. interests, Roosevelt ordered Moody to organize a large fleet under Admiral Dewey to patrol the waters of the southern Car-ibbean Sea.

In a subsequent flurry of confidential meetings with British and German diplomats during the month of November, Roosevelt attempted to prevent escalation while putting into practice his soon-to-be famous pronouncement: "Speak softly and carry a big stick." He had casually written this African prov-erb in correspondence when he was governor of New York and later used it in a speech when he was vice president.[11] Without consulting Congress, he now acted. When the Europeans established their blockade in December and annihilated the small Venezuelan navy, Roosevelt threatened that the United States would take naval action against any attempt to gain Venezuelan terri-tory. Although the total U.S. Navy order of battle force did not compare favor-ably with the worldwide forces of Great Britain or Germany, its on-scene fleet of fifty-four combatants, under the command of Admiral Dewey, out-numbered the European allies almost two to one. Under these circumstances, a timely concession from Venezuela allowed Great Britain to execute a face-saving withdrawal. Germany and Italy soon followed, lifting the blockade in mid-February 1903. This Navy victory for Roosevelt resonated positively in the legislature as well as with many U.S. citizens.[12]

Congress adjourned in early March after passing bills supporting Roo-sevelt's top priorities. His handling of the crisis in Venezuela stimulated the legislature to expand the breadth of U.S. offensive naval power beyond the recommendations of the president and the Navy by authorizing the construc-tion of five battleships and an increase in the numbers of officers.[13] Unlike the European powers that had multi-year building programs, the U.S. Congress could only affect naval growth within the restrictions of annual appropria-tions. It could not obligate future congresses to finance a shipbuilding plan for multi-year authorizations.

Although Congress added almost four hundred officers to the Navy, the total was well short of the one thousand recommended by Roosevelt and did not address either the militias or the Navy reserve. Representative Foss of Illinois, in his second term as House naval committee chairman, had acted on behalf of Navy supporters of the Great Lakes area by introducing bills "to establish a Naval Militia and define its relations to the General Government" and "to provide for the enrollment and organization of a United States Naval Reserve."[14] However, neither of his proposals moved out of committee.

Even though it stalemated on naval militia and Navy reserve proposals, Congress passed an act reorganizing the Army militia.[15] This action caused Secretary of War Root to put aside his plan for a national Army reserve force, as the legislature redefined the relations between the National Guard of the states and the regular Army of the federal government. The Army Militia Act of January 1903 increased federal supervision of the state forces while governors maintained appointment powers. This compromise was acceptable to both the states and the executive branch. As a result, plans for a national volunteer Army reserve organization lost relevance. A few years later, Congress approved the formation of an Army Medical Reserve Corps but did not authorize a national reserve fighting force until after the outbreak of the First World War.

In the spring of 1903 the fledging U.S. Navy League began its quest to advance positive public opinion toward naval affairs. Its goal would be accomplished through lectures, conferences, development of naval militias, and the commemoration of important naval events. But unlike its European counterparts, the U.S. league did not thrive at their level. The British League had more than 12,000 members of high status and supported global imperialism as well as a conservative remaking of English nationalism. This was visible to many interested Americans and presumably played an important role in the politics of determining the "naval estimates" in the British parliament.[16] The German Navy League of more than 700,000 members—founded by Alfred Krupp and William V, Prince of Wied, in 1898 and publicly supported by Kaiser Wilhelm II—was directly associated with the government and functioned as an unofficial arm of its Navy.[17]

The U.S. league did not evolve in a similar fashion. Writers in the magazines and journals that favorably noticed the presence of the new U.S. Navy

League in 1903 speculated that it would create positive public opinion toward naval affairs. A letter to the *Scientific American* cited the creation of the Navy League as being "of considerable importance to the nation" and of "interest to naval folks and citizens in general."[18] The author expressed concern about insufficient naval construction, inadequate naval training, and potentially weak enforcement of the Monroe Doctrine. But over time the league directors failed to establish a significant number of subsidiaries throughout the country. Resting on their social base of coastal men, boat owners, businessmen committed to the naval service, and retired naval officers, they did not attract significant interest or a large membership from the general population.

The summer season of 1903 was quiet for both Roosevelt and Moody. Approaching his third year in office, Roosevelt was not only clearly in charge of the presidency, he also had established a strong base of public support. With the new legislature elected in the fall of 1902 not scheduled to meet until December, he chose to take an eight-week tour and vacation across the country, which had become a biennial presidential routine when Congress was not in session. As a close adviser, Moody accompanied him on his western holiday. When they returned, Moody worked with senior Navy officers to continue developing specifications for ship propulsion and gunnery systems, while Roosevelt began to consider him to replace Attorney General Knox, who desired to return to private practice. That move occurred the following summer.

In the fall Roosevelt involved himself in political events in Colombia and Panama. Much to his distress, the Colombian government did not accept the U.S. treaty to build a canal across their Department of Panama. As a result, through diplomatic channels and intentionally leaked press speculations, he strongly encouraged Panama's independence movement to secede from Colombia.[19] It had been a department of Columbia since the 1840s and over the years had made several attempts to form its own government. In November, with strong U.S. backing and no bloodshed, it created itself as the Republic of Panama. Under Roosevelt's guidance, Secretary of State Hay immediately prepared a treaty, signed by the United States and Panama on November 18, establishing a U.S. Panama Canal Zone within Panamanian territory.

A few days later and not directly related to Panama, Roosevelt called a special session of both houses of the incoming Congress to settle the trading status of Cuba.[20] The Platt Amendment, approved by the government of Cuba in early 1903, had given the United States the right to interfere in Cuban affairs and develop naval bases in exchange for certain protections and accommodations. Because Roosevelt felt that Congress was avoiding its obligations, he called the session to establish reciprocity, which would allow the free trade of Cuban sugar. The House of Representatives quickly accepted reciprocity arrangements, but the Senate, under the influence of powerful sugar beet growers, stubbornly held up approval for a month before relenting.

In his third annual report to the regular session of Congress that convened in December 1903, Roosevelt briefly extolled the nation's prosperity and then covered the status of the various government departments. His short section on the Navy echoed Moody's annual report, requesting a general staff similar to the Army's and a continuation of new warship construction without listing any specific type or number of vessels desired at the time. Roosevelt also expressed the need for a naval base in the Philippines.[21]

PROGRESS

The new Fifty-eighth Congress was a body in transition from long-entrenched senior leaders to a bevy of mostly progressive newcomers. Reapportionment from the 1900 census added twenty-nine members to the House of Representatives. The Republican Party maintained its majority but the addition of new seats due to normal turnover resulted in a freshmen class of 120. Speaker of the House Joseph Cannon of Illinois, in his twenty-ninth year in Congress, headed the all-important rules committee, which decided whether or not a bill could come to the floor for debate. He was a member of the old guard that in general supported Roosevelt but did not back the developing progressive movement.[22] On the other hand, naval committee chairman Foss was a progressive committed to Navy development. But Cannon, not Foss, chose which bills would go forward.

The more static Senate also maintained its Republican margin, but some of the older members expressed concern regarding Roosevelt's bullish international positioning and his bellicose treatment of so-called robber barons. William P. Frye of Maine, elder statesman and experienced president pro tempore of the Senate, had joined the House in 1871 and the Senate in 1881 as a replacement for James C. Blaine. Frye was a conservative who led the Senate for two years in the absence of a vice president after Hobart died and again for three years after McKinley was assassinated. Frye supported territorial expansion and the growth of the U.S. Merchant Marine. However, he did not blindly approve Roosevelt's progressive proposals and set the Senate agenda according to his conservative bent.[23] His old-guard Maine colleague, Eugene Hale, chaired the Senate naval committee. Hale, occasionally at loggerheads with Frye, initially supported the development of the Navy but became an ardent anti-imperialist, opposing the war with Spain and the subsequent acquisition of territory. By the early 1900s Hale resisted increasing appropriations to the military, including the construction of battleships.[24] Although both chambers of Congress held Republican majorities, the members had disparate agendas that generally did not promote further Navy increases.

In January 1904, when Elihu Root left the War Department on schedule in favor of a private law practice, Roosevelt selected William Howard Taft to take his position as secretary of war. As governor general of the Philippines appointed by McKinley, Taft had established a workable civilian government and brought some stability to the war-torn islands. Roosevelt chose Taft for the Army position as a forward-looking venture, to possibly groom him for the higher office of president in the future.

A month later in early February, Japan broke relations with Russia and began a series of attacks against Russian naval forces in order to cover the movement of their army into Korea and Manchuria. A few days later, Roosevelt announced the neutrality of the United States, although he privately favored the up-and-coming naval power of the Japanese empire over the decaying government of Tsar Nicholas II.[25] Over the next few months, the Japanese unexpectedly defeated the Russian fleet in the vicinity of Port Arthur, Manchuria.[26] Seemingly out of nowhere, the Japanese suddenly proved to be a viable force in world events. The U.S. Congress chose not to become involved in a distant foreign war. Meanwhile, Russia unsuccessfully sought allies as it prepared to counterattack.

Both houses of Congress ended their sessions relatively early in late April, and the members dispersed to take care of presidential election year business. Although the annual Navy appropriation of April 1904 was considerably higher than the previous year at $97.5 million compared to $81.9 million, the increase in warships included only one battleship, two armored cruisers, and a few auxiliaries.[27] The extra funding reflected significant increases in operational expenses and the buildup of the shore establishment infrastructure, rather than new ship construction. In spite of the deployment of the Navy to extend the Monroe Doctrine in the Caribbean and executive branch concerns about the rise of Japanese naval power in Asia, Congress was generally satisfied with the current number and type of U.S. naval vessels. House bills perennially presented by Foss to define the relations of the naval militias to the Navy and to establish a national naval reserve force continued to languish in committee.[28] As usual, Speaker Cannon chose not to put those proposals on the calendar.

When Congress adjourned, it passed an act giving the president authority to establish a government for the Panama Canal Zone.[29] Roosevelt expressed delight that plans to build an interocean canal had come to fruition. As previously arranged, he gave Secretary Taft the responsibility to directly oversee the Isthmian Canal Commission. Taft had proven himself, under difficult circumstances in the Philippines, to be an excellent colonial administrator who understood both his role and the interests of the people involved. In the process of establishing this new and important American venture, and recalling his own experience in Cuba, Roosevelt also wrote of the importance of improving "the health conditions on the Isthmus" to protect everyone from the ravages of the prevalent diseases.[30]

The presidential election season of 1904 began with Roosevelt selecting George Cortelyou over the heads of the old bosses for the national chairmanship of the Republican Party. The forty-two-year-old lawyer, stenographer, and secretary had served as Cleveland's chief clerk and stayed on as McKinley's and then Roosevelt's personal secretary. As part of his duties, Cortelyou quietly established highly professional administrative and protocol practices for the office of the president. More importantly, he strengthened important lines of communication with the press and with young progressives. In 1903 Roosevelt had appointed him as, first, secretary of commerce and labor, and now confirmed that after the election Cortelyou would take over as postmaster general. Moving Cortelyou to the most patronage-laden cabinet position could not be ignored by the party faithful, who sought visibility during the election season.

The people of the United States, as well as leading politicians, generally approved of Roosevelt's administration. But to continue in office, he needed to be reelected in the fall. Although the selection of Roosevelt at the Republican convention in Chicago was a fait accompli, he took control of the assembly with typical vigor and micromanaged events to ensure his nomination. Roosevelt easily carried the day by receiving the convention's unanimous vote. His running mate was Sen. John Fairbanks of Indiana.

A few days prior to the convention, long-term senator Matthew Quay, powerful but often reviled, had died, and the governor of Pennsylvania appointed Attorney General Knox to his seat. After the convention adjourned, Roosevelt transferred Secretary of the Navy Moody to the vacant attorney general position and chose Paul Morton, another naval novice, to take over the Navy Department. His selection was not made at the spur of the moment. Morton was a self-made man whose pioneering parents had settled in Nebraska Territory prior to the Civil War. His deceased father J. Sterling Morton had served as secretary of agriculture in President Cleveland's cabinet and had befriended Roosevelt, who at the time headed the Civil Service Commission.

Meanwhile, Paul Morton had worked his way up to the third vice presidency of the Atchison, Topeka, & Santa Fe Railroad.[31] When he was governor of New York, Roosevelt rode in Morton's private railroad car on trips to the West in 1899 and 1900, becoming impressed with his business acumen and political sensibility. Over the next few years, Roosevelt kept in contact with Morton and decided that he was the right man for a cabinet position. Roosevelt confidently charged him not only to run the industrial activities of the Navy but also "to give full force to the military efforts of the Navy and to establish a high standard of efficiency of the fleet."[32] In his brief term as Secretary of the Navy, Morton tried to develop a workable general staff arrangement to ensure preeminent operational readiness.

Roosevelt's run for a second term was not a completely one-sided affair. His Democratic opponent, Judge Alton Parker of New York, ran a crusade against Roosevelt's caprices and his close association with big money and big business. At first it appeared to the candidates and the press that the Democratic Party charges might sway the people away from the president. But the actions of the better organized and financed Republican Party, plus Roosevelt's energetic refutation of all charges, led to a solid victory. Ultimately, Roosevelt received more than 56 percent of the vote while Parker drew less than 38 percent, with third-party candidates accounting for the remaining 6 percent. For the first time in U.S. history, an accidental standing president gained election on his own.

Preparatory to Roosevelt's fourth annual message to be given to the outgoing Congress, Morton's annual report reached Congress as it gathered in December.[33] He explained that his enclosed naval estimates were the largest ever because of the expenses to keep the fleet moving and maintained. He also wrote of the Navy's continued need for officers and battleships. Rather than recommend specific increases, he referred to the separate schedules submitted by Admiral Dewey's General Board and by the bureau chiefs' Board of Construction. These purported schedules were actually long-range paper timelines for constructing new warships and auxiliaries. The boards differed both in composition and in their long-range strategic views. Neither had authority to approve increases and neither deferred to the other. By submitting the schedules of both boards, Morton conceded to Congress its own examination of priorities without a unified recommendation by the Navy Department.

In his message sent to Congress a few weeks later, Roosevelt first pointed out the prosperity of the nation and the enlargement of government for permanent improvement. He then expressed concern over the casualty lists of the railroads and called for safety legislation. He also took a hard stand against the railroad practice of giving rebates to preferred customers. As he continued, Roosevelt praised the "great corporations" for their accomplishments while maintaining that the government needed to act directly with them. On international matters, he noted that he asked other nations to join with the United State in a second conference at The Hague. At the same time, he stated that adherence to the Monroe Doctrine in cases of flagrant wrongdoing might force the United States to reluctantly exercise an international police power. For him, that power rested in the Navy and so he recommended that there be no halt in building up naval forces, especially battleships.[34] After he delivered his message, Roosevelt approved Morton's consolidation of the General Board and the Board of Construction schedules in the form of a request for three battleships, five cruisers, six destroyers, six torpedo boats, and two colliers.[35] This went beyond a program to maintain the status quo.

Above
Steam screw frigate *Colorado* at anchor in the Han River, Korea, during the Korean expedition of May–June 1871. *Naval History and Heritage Command, NHHC-NH 66304*

Left
Rear Adm. John Rodgers, in photograph circa 1870, headed Secretary of the Navy William Hunt's Naval Advisory Board, 1881–82. *Naval History and Heritage Command, NHHC-NH 46930*

Above
Protected cruiser *Atlanta*,
commissioned with full sail
rigging in 1886, was one of
the ABCDs of the new steel
Navy that cruised in the
Atlantic and Mediterranean
for many years. *Naval History
and Heritage Command,
NHHC-NH 67502*

Right
Rear Adm. Stephen B. Luce,
portrait photograph taken
circa 1888, a founder of the
U.S. Naval Institute in 1873,
first president of the Naval
War College at Newport,
Rhode Island, 1884–86, and
president of the Naval Institute
from 1889 to 1898. *Naval
History and Heritage Command,
NHHC-NH 2323*

L-Class submarines at Bantry Bay, Ireland, in 1918.
From left to right: unidentified, *L-1* (SS 40), *L-10* (SS 50),
L-4 (SS 43), *L-49* (SS 49), laid down 1914–15.
Naval History and Heritage Command, NHHC-NH 51171

Left
Adm. William Benson,
first chief of naval
operations, portrait taken
during his term in office,
1916–19, selected by
Secretary of the Navy
Daniels over thirty-one
more senior officers.
*Naval History and
Heritage Command,
NHHC-NH 366*

Below
Wooden Submarine
Chaser SC-324, laid down
in 1917, within one year
after the United States
entered World War I;
355 of the 110-foot long
SC-1–class sub chasers were
constructed. *Naval History
and Heritage Command,
NHHC-NH 391*

Throughout the life of the short outgoing congressional session from December 2, 1904 to March 3, 1905, Roosevelt focused on the need for tariff review, the possibility of mediating a peace between Russia and Japan, and the continuing increase of the Navy. First, he felt that the entire tariff schedule should be revised. He looked to Congress to take charge by increasing free lists and making reciprocity arrangements more transparent. But he also recognized the split in political support within the Republican Party, with the majority showing no interest in change. Roosevelt ultimately decided not to call a special session of the recently elected Congress to make any adjustments to the existing sacrosanct tariff schedule, which had been drawn up during McKinley's administration.[36]

Second, Roosevelt began to make concrete, but quiet, plans to act as a self-appointed mediator between Russia and Japan. By now tens of thousands of soldiers on both sides had been killed and hundreds of thousands more continued to face each other on various battlefield areas in Manchuria. He did not trust either the inscrutable Japanese or the perennially dishonest and troublesome empire of the tsar. To begin setting the stage, he assigned trusted diplomat George von Lengerke Meyer (future Secretary of the Navy for President Taft) as the U.S. ambassador to Russia. In a confidential letter to Meyer, he wrote of the importance of the position and of conferring with Cecil Arthur Spring-Rice, England's chargé d'affaires in St. Petersburg and close correspondent of Roosevelt.[37] Soon after the appointment, Japan defeated the Russian ground forces at Port Arthur, while the Russian Baltic fleet steamed to the China seas for a showdown that would come later that spring.

Third, Roosevelt personally lobbied Congress to continue increasing the Navy. He obligingly wrote to Foss, whom he considered to be an ineffective chairman of the House naval committee, that the United States needed heavy battleships now because any halt in authorizations for new construction would be a serious mistake and a violation of the faith of the Republican Party. At the same time, he wrote to Speaker Cannon in a softer tone to express his appreciation of Cannon's efforts to continue with Navy increases.[38] Roosevelt confirmed to him that the most important thing was to "keep going," and that he would be satisfied to have less than he wanted as long as building continued. The Fifty-eighth Congress obliged by funding two battleships, leaving the remainder of Morton's shopping list on the table.[39]

Not surprisingly, the Congresses of the sixth four-year period of new Navy development, which occurred under Roosevelt's first presidency, were almost as generous as the previous wartime legislature, focusing on battleships at the expense of smaller and defensive combatants. In the course of the first four years of the new century, they authorized thirty-one vessels: ten battleships, four cruisers, four submarines, two colliers, and eleven smaller combat and support ships. By comparison, the congresses of McKinley's four-year presidency, which included the war with Spain, had authorized sixty-seven vessels: ten battleships, seventeen cruisers, sixteen torpedo boat destroyers, seven submarines, and seventeen various coastal support ships.[40]

As was its prevailing pattern, the outgoing Congress also chose not to change the status of the naval militias. The latest House militia bill introduced by Foss simplistically proposed that the provisions of the 1903 Militia Act for the Army National Guard apply to the Navy. The bill had originated with Adm. George Dewey's General Board of the Navy and had the endorsements of secretaries Moody and Morton as earnestly desired and needed.[41] However, time ran out in the lame-duck session ending on March 3, 1905, as Congress wrestled with the higher priority of granting record appropriations for warship operations and for Navy public works. The militia bill did not have provisions important enough to gather support from the regional blocks of congressmen directing Navy growth and administration. Also, gubernatorial appointments of a few naval militia officers did not add to state power. By contrast, the Army National Guard involved significant patronage-laden selections of officers, who led local armed forces in times of state emergencies, especially during labor strikes. Funds to arm and equip the navy militias remained at the 1899 level of $60,000 to be shared among participating states, while appropriations for the Army National Guard militias stood at more than $2 million.[42]

After his celebratory inauguration in early March, Roosevelt took a brief respite to New York City to give away his orphaned niece, Eleanor, in marriage to his fifth cousin, Franklin D. Roosevelt. Promptly returning to Washington, the president faced the fact that John Hay, his beloved secretary of state, was not well enough for the rigors of dealing with the conflicting agendas of the European powers and Japan. Hay departed on a convalescent cruise to Europe while Roosevelt himself assumed the duties of secretary of state for the next several months.

ROOSEVELT

Exercising a "wait and see" international policy, Roosevelt departed in early April for a six-week southern tour and a hunting trip in Colorado. He left Taft in charge of the White House rather than Vice President Fairbanks, and kept track of world events by telegraph.[43] From his Colorado camp, Roosevelt continued to discreetly communicate with well-placed diplomats and, because of increasing tension between the powers, decided to return to Washington earlier than planned. Most importantly, the Japanese ambassador to the United States had confidentially indicated the possible acceptance of Roosevelt's offer to arrange mediation while the tsar held out and the war raged on. Although in agreement with Japan's quiet entreaty, Roosevelt outwardly gave the appearance of American neutrality.[44] The press, and those not in his small inner circle, associated his early return with his Monroe Doctrine interest in Santo Domingo foreign debt payments, instead of with the larger events unfolding in Europe and Asia. Once back home, he intensified his closed-door efforts to settle the fighting in Asia.

With the war now in its fifteenth month, it appeared to Roosevelt and others that Russia was involved in a lost cause. Events came to a head during the last days of May at the Battle of the Tsushima Strait, when the Japanese smashed the Russian Baltic fleet that had traveled 18,000 miles to take on the Japanese. The war had begun in February 1904 with the Japanese victory over the Russian Pacific fleet at Port Arthur and now, fifteen months later, Japan annihilated the Russian naval forces in the waters between Korea and Japan.[45] In spite of the bad news from the strait of Japan, the tsar considered holding out and continuing the ground war in Manchuria. With crippling strikes and unrest at home, the tsar needed to win but could not. His situation in the Orient was simply untenable.

Roosevelt orchestrated a masterful diplomatic denouement. Ambassador Meyer, a polished aristocrat and experienced diplomat with direct access to the tsar, confronted the latter with the harsh truths, forcing him to make a move. Roosevelt personally dealt with Japanese foreign minister Komura Jutarō through Ambassador Takahira Kogorō. Unknown to the public, both Russia and Japan accepted Roosevelt's matchmaker role only if he himself openly pretended to initiate the invitation for them to meet with each other on neutral ground without intermediaries. According to the plan, once Roosevelt's offer was public, Russia and Japan would agree on his proposal to solve their differences together. Both protagonists, therefore, saved face in their respective homelands by accepting an invitation that they had already secretly approved.[46]

As the war in the Pacific moved toward a conclusion, the civilian leadership of the U.S. Navy changed hands again over issues unrelated to the complex international state of affairs. Secretary Morton faced accusations of authorizing illegal rebates to preferred customers while he was a railroad vice president. The issue had come up in the winter after Roosevelt, in his annual message to Congress, absolutely condemned the railroad rebate practice as unfair to the American people and insisted that it must be eliminated. During the ensuing spring season of 1905, both Roosevelt and Attorney General Moody found no evidence implicating Morton. However, members of the press and opposition politicians saw collusion in an executive decision to shield Morton. In early June, when Roosevelt was fully engaged with international power diplomacy, Morton decided that for the sake of the cabinet he should resign. Upon his resignation, Roosevelt praised him with hyperbole, in spite of his brief one-year term, as being the best Secretary of the Navy that "we have ever had."[47] Morton accepted a lucrative position as chairman of the board of the Equitable Life Insurance Association and submitted his official resignation to the president effective July 1, 1905.

Roosevelt selected Charles Bonaparte to succeed Morton as his fourth Secretary of the Navy in four years. Charles' grandfather Jérôme, Napoleon's youngest brother, had married into a very wealthy Maryland family while on a cruise with the French navy in 1803. Jérôme was forced by his emperor brother to return to France and abandon his American wife and son. He received a French absentee divorce, remarried, and became the unpopular king of Westphalia. His American son, born in Maryland and also named Jerome, grew up as a child of privilege, received his education at Harvard, and married a Baltimore woman also of considerable financial means. Jerome Bonaparte's son Charles, seven years older than Roosevelt, graduated from Harvard Law School in 1874 and began practicing law in Baltimore.

Roosevelt and Charles Bonaparte first met as members of the National Civil Service Reform League, formed in 1881. Ten years later, when Roosevelt was Civil Service commissioner, Bonaparte provided invaluable help in investigating federal corruption in Baltimore. He became a well-known law-yer throughout Maryland and a strong supporter of the Catholic Church. In 1899 he delivered the graduation speech at the College of Notre Dame in Maryland, the first four-year college for Catholic women in the United States, on the occasion of its awarding its first bachelor degrees. In 1902 Roosevelt appointed him a member of the Board of Indian Commissioners. Bonaparte was simultaneously acting as a special counsel for the White House in the prosecution of fraud in the postal service.[48] On the same day that Bonaparte joined the president's cabinet, Roosevelt's longtime confidant and friend John Hay died.

Hay's death was not a surprise as he had been ill for months. However, with international tensions brewing, Roosevelt certainly needed a strong and trusted ally in the State Department. He convinced former Secretary of War Elihu Root to leave his law firm and return to government service as secre-tary of state. In Europe, to the dismay of Great Britain and France, Germany appeared to be embarking on a belligerent path toward expansion. Meanwhile, Japan had clearly emerged as the power in the Orient, potentially destabiliz-ing Western trade with China and U.S. interests in the Philippines. Russia was in the process of losing a major war in Asia and undergoing a revolution at home. Furthermore, the Russian-Japanese peace negotiations planned for August had not begun. Root's immediate tasks concerned strengthening the internal leadership of the department and dealing with Venezuela, the Domin-ican Republic, and Panama. Roosevelt would monitor the European situa-tion himself and continue his role as arbitrator to end the war in Asia.

New to the inner sanctum of national politics, Bonaparte immersed him-self in day-to-day Navy issues and did not engage in international affairs. In spite of his well-known advocacy of civil service, business as usual for his Navy Department involved a barrage of patronage requests from influential con-gressmen. His first serious challenge occurred in mid-July when a boiler on board the gunboat *Bennington* (PG 4) in San Diego exploded, killing sixty-six crew members. Because the ship was in poor material condition Bonaparte took a hard line against those in authority and, with Roosevelt's approval, ordered courts-martial for both the captain and the chief engineer.[49] But in spite of Bonaparte's rectitude, he could not influence the courts and both men were acquitted six months later. For the remainder of the summer and fall season, while Congress was not in session, Bonaparte met with Navy leaders to deliberate the department's collective position on new ship construction. He sought a thorough examination of both the strategic and congressional interest of outfitting battleships primarily with big guns rather than a multi-purpose variety of calibers.[50]

The two battleships authorized the following March eventually became the Navy's first big-gun ships, each with a main battery of eight 12-inch guns. Meanwhile, the major international naval powers also continued the process of evaluating the effectiveness of torpedoes, secondary batteries, and primary batteries during the Japanese's great victory at Tsushima.

By the end of July, Roosevelt readied himself to meet the Russian and Japanese peace delegates at his summer residence in Oyster Bay, New York. Each emperor sent a senior and a junior plenipotentiary and four aides to New York City, in preparation for negotiations at the Kittery naval station in Maine. With suitable hotel lodging for the delegations across the bay in Portsmouth, New Hampshire, Roosevelt chose the location as a secure and reasonably cool site distant from the crush and heat of Washington. Foreign Minister Komura Jutarō represented Japan and Secretary of State Sergei Witte represented Russia. The principals and aides first met informally in Roosevelt's residence on separate days and then formally together on August 5 on board the converted yacht *Mayflower* (PY 1) anchored in Long Island Sound. After their first official meeting, Roosevelt returned to his residence and the two parties embarked on separate U.S. Navy vessels for the trip to Portsmouth.

For the next three weeks Roosevelt tracked the conference from his home and sent a stream of notes to various Russian, German, English, and Japanese diplomats, ambassadors, and heads of states to break the deadlock and bring on a peace settlement. Japan was adamant about holding Sakhalin Island and demanded payments from Russia for war expenses. The Russians were unbending on the same two issues: no territory exchange and no payment of war indemnities. Roosevelt constructed a Solomon-like compromise acceptable to both parties who, recognizing the war's tremendous cost in men and matériel, needed a face-saving middle ground. Japan would return half of Sakhalin Island to Russia, who would in turn pay for that return. This would not be a territory exchange for Russia because Japan already occupied it and the money would simply be payment for Russia to reoccupy the land. Japan in turn would get legal possession of territory that it won by war and would in fact receive money from Russia. The emperors of Japan and Russia agreed to the compromise terms. The Treaty of Portsmouth of September 5, 1905, was a great achievement for Roosevelt as well as for the peace of the world.

After only five months in office, Bonaparte sent his first annual report to the new Fifty-ninth Congress prior to its opening session in December. Noting the inefficiency of the Navy's bureaus, he suggested yet another scheme to reduce them from eight to four and proposed reorganizing the bureaus according to the functions of ships (shipbuilding and maintenance), men (manpower direction and management), ordnance (guns and ammunition), and supply (provisions and accounts).[51] For increasing the Navy, he recommended building two additional big-gun battleships, two small cruisers, four destroyers, and three gunboats. His list was smaller than the schedule of the General Board. He also wrote of the Navy's need for a large states' militia as a reserve force rather than developing a separate national reserve organization. Finally, to the disappointment of Congress, he disapproved of making any further repairs to the *Constitution*, the historic "Old Ironsides" of the Revolutionary War. For him it would be a waste of funds rebuilding an old ship that by this time did not contain much original material anyway.

Roosevelt's annual message to Congress of December 1905, the longest and most important for him to date, covered the mandates that would define his presidency. The solidly Republican incoming Congress had been swept in with him in 1904 and now, when it met for the first time thirteen months later, Roosevelt was prepared to establish his mark. He would be the outgoing president during the next congressional election cycle and the members would not be as beholden to his priorities as was the present assemblage.[52] He began his message by extolling national prosperity and followed up by reiterating the great need for the ICC (Interstate Commerce Commission) to supervise railroad rates. Then he recapped Russia's request for a second peace conference to be held at a future date at The Hague.[53] And finally, he told Congress again about the importance of husbanding national forest resources and the work of the National Forest Commission.

In his relatively short section on the Navy, Roosevelt wrote that there was no need to increase naval units beyond the present level.[54] However, outdated vessels should be replaced by bigger, heavily armored, and heavily gunned capital warships, at a replacement rate of one battleship per year. While stating that the Navy only needed substitutes rather than additional ships, he endorsed Bonaparte's recommendations, which called for two battleships and an assortment of small escorts. It was up to the presumably friendly Congress to respond.

11

POWER PROJECTED,
1905–9

The Fifty-ninth Congress held its first session from December 1905 to June 1906. Foss and Senator Hale continued to head their individual naval committees, while Cannon and Senator Frye respectively remained Speaker of the House and president pro tempore of the Senate. Although solidly Republican, this Congress consisted of a mix of old-line conservatives and new progressives not committed to further Navy expansion.

As the U.S. Congress sat, Roosevelt spent considerable energy in order to influence the legislative debates concerning railroad regulation. A unified House of Representatives passed to the Senate a resolution that became known as the Hepburn Act. A key section of the bill gave the ICC authority to set railroad rates. The senior and entrenched conservative senator Nelson Aldrich of Rhode Island led the opposition, vehemently opposing both ICC control of all railroads (including private lines) and the requirement for open and standardized bookkeeping. According to the conservative old guard, the act was a socialistic takeover attempt supported by the shippers to increase their profits at the expense of the railroad industry. Newer, progressive members of the Senate eventually sided with the president and overruled the old guard. However, the ensuing vitriolic fights were wearying for the president until passage of the Hepburn Act in May prior to the end of the session in June.

Despite his enervating labors with Congress, Roosevelt found time in February 1906 to give away his daughter Alice in marriage to Nicholas

Longworth III, a congressman from Ohio. Fourteen years older than Alice, Longworth played the role of an eligible bachelor in Washington society and successfully wooed the president's daughter. In the summer and fall of 1905 Longworth, along with twenty-two other congressmen and seven senators, had accompanied Alice and Secretary of War Taft on a three-month goodwill cruise and diplomatic mission across the Pacific to visit Japan, China, and Korea. Roosevelt had selected Taft to quietly negotiate with Japan and show U.S. success in the Philippines. Five months after their return, Alice and Nicholas were married in a packed White House ceremony.

Beyond that happy occasion, throughout the spring the president deeply involved himself in pure food and drug legislation. *The Jungle*, Upton Sinclair's recently published exposé of the horrors of the meatpacking industry, significantly raised public awareness of the need for regulation. Roosevelt disagreed with the degree of Sinclair's negative approach but certainly understood that the people of the United States should be protected from harmful products. Choosing lines from John Bunyan's *Pilgrim's Progress*, he impugned the messenger by comparing those journalists who mired themselves in scandalous reporting to the muckrakers in Bunyan's story who only looked down to rake muck. Roosevelt chose to look up and lead the public with an optimistic agenda against the ills that could be alleviated by government action. In late June, Congress complied by passing the landmark Pure Food Act, which gave the government authority to examine and regulate the manufacture and sale of food and drugs.

The most important business for the Navy during the session as usual concerned the annual appropriations act. Early in the Congress and unrelated to ship construction, Foss reopened the issues of defining the role of naval militias and establishing a separate Navy reserve force.[1] Routinely, neither of these perennial resolutions moved to completion through the House and Senate. A more immediate concern for the Navy was the critical shortfall of funds for current operating expenses, especially for the purchase of coal. Assistant Secretary of the Navy Truman Newberry notified commanders of both ships and shore facilities that the Navy had insufficient funds to operate unless Congress provided additional appropriations.[2]

While the legislature prepared an emergency allotment for the remainder of the year, several members of Congress took issue with Navy leadership for allowing the shortcomings to occur in the first place. Some representatives on the House appropriations committee considered that Navy management officials were legally culpable for the troubling deficit. They argued that the appropriations act for that fiscal year had allotted funds to be spread over the entire period and had the force of law. Therefore, Navy leaders could be prosecuted for violating the statute. Cooler heads prevailed and, one day after passing its annual Navy appropriations act in June for the next fiscal year, Congress approved a bill to fund the current deficiencies.[3] However, the fall-out placed extra scrutiny on all naval expenditures.

Embracing the philosophy of his leading Navy advisers, Roosevelt initially advocated building heavily armed battleships, all with large-caliber guns at the expense of smaller secondary armament. Theoretically, ships armed with big guns could destroy an enemy fleet at great distances. However, upon receiving the Russian account of their recent defeat by Japan, both Roosevelt and Navy leaders such as Alfred Thayer Mahan expressed doubts about the effectiveness of an all-big-gun configuration. In a note to Secretary Bonaparte regarding Russia's claim "that the Japanese superiority in secondary battery fire was one of the main causes of their defeat," Roosevelt cautioned against taking a path toward all-big-gun battleships until the Navy had all the facts.[4]

After the British launched their big-gun super battleship HMS *Dreadnought* in the spring of 1906, Roosevelt decided to approve the Navy Department plan to configure the two previously funded battleships with large-caliber guns as their primary armament. In its June 1906 appropriations Congress acted conservatively by authorizing only one additional first-class battleship with the proviso that, prior to issuing proposals for bidding, the Secretary of the Navy shall report full specification details to the legislature at its final session to meet in December.[5] The result was the battleship *Delaware* (BB 28), launched three years later, which matched the British *Dreadnought's* displacement and firepower. The 20,000-ton *Delaware* carried five twin mounts of 12-inch caliber main battery guns and fourteen 5-inch caliber guns for secondary fire. This was a congressional decision concerning the gun configuration for the Navy's first "super" battleship. The act also approved funding for three destroyers and seven small submarines, while lowering the previous fiscal year's spending allotment by $8 million. To no avail Roosevelt and Bonaparte had expressed a need for additional escort cruisers, increased operating allowances for all departments, and an expanded militia to act as a standing reserve force. Congress instead chose to fund only the one super battleship, small destroyers, and submarines while reducing operating allotments, leaving the other issues to die in conference or committee at adjournment.

In mid-August, the president faced an immediate challenge from Cuba. After protesting the results of its recent elections as being rigged, the liberal party rebelled. Both the government in power and the rebels looked to the United States for help. According to the Platt Amendment, the United States had protectorate authority over the country, with the responsibility to intervene in order to prevent a foreign takeover. Roosevelt sent Taft and Assistant Secretary of State Robert Bacon to Cuba to negotiate between the factions. Unable to get direct assistance for his cause, Cuban president Estrada Palma resigned at the end of September, forcing Roosevelt to send the U.S. Army to the island to protect American citizens and their economic interests. Shortly thereafter, the rebels laid down their arms and Roosevelt assigned Taft to head again a provisional government as he had done in the Philippines. The U.S. Army remained as a peacekeeper in Cuba for the next three years before a functioning local government could be established.

Two weeks before the November congressional elections, Roosevelt announced another major reconstruction of his cabinet to take effect on March 4, 1907, in synchrony with the adjournment of the Fifty-ninth Congress. First, he appointed Attorney General Moody to the Supreme Court to replace retiring associate justice Henry B. Brown. Second, Roosevelt moved Bonaparte to replace Moody as the attorney general. Third, Victor Metcalf, at the time the secretary of commerce and labor, would then take over as Roosevelt's fifth Secretary of the Navy in five and a half years. Originally from western New York State, Metcalf had relocated to California after graduating from both Yale Law School and the law department at Hamilton College. He had been a member of the House of Representatives from 1898 to 1904 when he resigned to join the president's cabinet. Roosevelt made the changes to place Moody and Bonaparte in positions appropriate to their judicial talents rather than to have Metcalf provide fresh leadership to the Navy Department.

Following his cabinet announcements in October, Roosevelt faced a messy international crisis regarding the segregation of Japanese school children in San Francisco. As a result of a devastating earthquake in the spring of 1906, many schools had been destroyed. In the rebuilding process San Francisco decided to establish a separate Oriental public school system. The city was motivated by a growing West Coast contingent of nativists who expressed their strong concern over the influx of Japanese workers as threatening American enterprise. San Francisco acted by empowering its school board to exclude children of "Mongolian" descent from attending local schools being rebuilt. The Japanese government immediately reacted by telegramming its indignation to Roosevelt. In his prompt reply to Japan, Roosevelt claimed that prior to receiving their telegram the California problem was so local "that we never heard of it here in Washington."[6] He expressed his "greatest concern" to Kentarō Kaneko, who had participated with Roosevelt in the Treaty of Portsmouth ending the Russo-Japanese War and was now a member of Japan's Privy Council. Roosevelt assured Kaneko that the measure did not represent American sentiment as a whole and promised action to remedy the matter.

A day after his note to Japan, Roosevelt wrote in a different tone to Senator Hale concerning the potential for increased Japanese belligerency and the real possibility of war. He appealed to Hale, as an influential senator and chairman of the Senate naval committee, to continue building up the Navy with battleships carrying large-caliber guns.[7] Roosevelt certainly had a long-range view of preparedness, since the lame-duck Congress would not meet until December and would not pass its next Navy appropriations act until early March. Even if it decided to increase the rate of Navy construction, it would take a few years for new ships to become operational. The developing California–Japanese situation continued to deteriorate as the president endeavored to work out a solution agreeable to both sides.

Roosevelt kept himself relatively disengaged from campaign politics during the proximate November congressional elections and chose to not spend time or capital stumping for favorite candidates. Typically in a non-presidential election year, the majority party takes some losses, as was the case in November 1906. The Republicans lost thirty-two seats in the House of Representatives but still maintained a comfortable majority of fifty-six. In the Senate, Republicans gained two seats for a solid majority of thirty-one. The leadership in both houses remained essentially the same. Unless he called a special session, Roosevelt would not face this Congress until December 1907, thirteen months in the future.

At the end of November, soon-to-depart Secretary Bonaparte presented his normal lengthy report to the outgoing Congress. Reiterating his well-known contentions, he criticized the management of the entire Navy bureau system, which had been an issue for every Navy secretary since Chandler's complaints twenty-four years earlier. This time, rather than recommending reorganization by the legislature, Bonaparte asked it to establish a commission of at least three former secretaries and two or more members of the naval committees to give its recommendations to the first session of the next Congress. He also requested appropriations for two battleships and a few other smaller classes of vessels and again argued that the Navy needed a militia analogous to the recently created Army National Guard.[8] A month later, Bonaparte turned over his office to Metcalf.

Fresh from a trip to Panama in early December on board the battleship *Louisiana* (BB 19), Roosevelt delivered his annual message to Congress. He began by noting that he considered several of his projects to be highly important unfinished business and concentrated on the need for continued government supervision of a wide range of commercial and industrial endeavors. In his brief section on the Navy, he disagreed with Bonaparte's report to Congress and stated that the Navy did not need any increases. Rather, he again asked Congress to maintain the Navy at its current level by replacing old ships with new models, including one first-class battleship equal to the largest in the world.[9] He did not mention a need for an increased naval militia or reserve force.

One week after delivering his annual message, Roosevelt received official notification that he was awarded the Nobel Peace Prize for his work in settling the Russo-Japanese war. He later announced that he would donate the approximately $40,000 in prize money to the establishment in Washington of a permanent industrial peace committee.[10]

As the lame-duck Congress proceeded with its business, a minority of influential Republicans in the Senate, led by Frye, continued to extol the virtues of authorizing Navy reserves in the merchant marine, while Democrats strongly denounced proposals that they said would favor rich ship owners. States with little to be gained from commercial maritime growth filibustered against subsidizing merchant ships, claiming that government support of inefficient shipbuilders would tip the scales against legitimate market forces. The arguments covered many pages in the Congressional Record of the winter of 1906–7.[11] Senators from New England saw a pressing need for U.S. merchant marine expansion and concluded the stormy debate with an emphatic contention that a merchant marine with a naval reserve was unequivocally in the future. In the long run, they were as correct as they were loud, but the proposal failed that year. It would be a Democratic Congress that in 1915 finally established a U.S. Naval Reserve force separate from the coastal service of the naval militias. Nothing short of immediate war preparations finally convinced the legislature of the need for Navy Reserves.

The outgoing Fifty-ninth Congress did not treat Roosevelt well on naval issues and continued to build a Navy to its own liking. As it adjourned in March, it authorized one "super battleship" similar to the one approved the previous year and added only two torpedo boat destroyers. It also reduced the Navy budget for the second year in a row, as it optimistically waited for the commencement of the Second Peace Conference at The Hague that summer. Navy militia funding remained at a mere $60,000 to be shared by eighteen states.[12]

Congressmen showed more interest in raising the employment levels in local naval facilities than in spending for warships that purportedly contributed to peace by intimidation. With the exception of West Coast residents, who continued to voice concern over Japanese immigration, most U.S. citizens did not worry about a foreign invasion. However, laborers expressed great interest in the level of employment in government shipyards. This attention extended well beyond those who could actually be employed in the yards, as labor unions throughout the country gave strong support to government rather that private warship construction. For example, seemingly unaffected ironmonger and cigar-maker unions in the Midwest petitioned Congress to build battleships in the Brooklyn Navy Yard.[13] Their concerns involved high-stakes labor issues such as the government's policy of an eight-hour workday and paid holidays for employees in government facilities. By citing the labor gains of government workers, unions demanded similar performance from government contractors and strengthened their bargaining position with private industry.

In the years immediately following the Spanish-American War, U.S. warship repair activities had increased greatly. This development provided steady work as Congress appropriated funds to revitalize moribund Navy facilities at

Portsmouth, Pensacola, and Key West. Additionally, naval acts directed significant growth in the already active major Navy yards in New York and Norfolk, as well as in the smaller yards in Boston and Philadelphia. Congress also authorized locating new government facilities in South Carolina, Louisiana, California, and Washington, which all joined the burgeoning naval shore establishment.

ACTION AND REACTION

As the Fifty-ninth Congress concluded its business in March 1907, Roosevelt faced the increasingly serious crisis and genuine war scare with Japan over the treatment of its citizens in San Francisco. While acknowledging the claims of Hawaii and the Pacific Coast residents concerning the undesirable effects of Japanese cheap labor, Roosevelt took pains to avoid a casus belli for Japan. Through diplomacy, he calmed the state of affairs with a "Gentleman's Agreement," whereby the school board canceled its exclusion policy and Japan agreed to limit the immigration of certain categories of workers. Although his actions defused the situation, Roosevelt decided to demonstrate his resolve to maintain peace by a show of naval force.

In June 1907, he announced his plan to send a battleship fleet from the Atlantic to the Pacific Coast via South America on a public and visible show-of-force training cruise. Roosevelt's action dealt with both the worldwide naval expansions of other nations and the petitions of western states for increased naval protection. In a corresponding development a few months later, the peace conference at The Hague ended and failed to provide relief from the rapidly developing international naval arms race. Similar to the first round of talks in 1899, members of the second assembly could not reach an agreement on arms limitations, especially for new warship construction.[14]

Roosevelt delivered his annual message on December 3, 1907 to the first session of the Sixtieth Congress and asked for four battleships along with auxiliaries, docks, coaling stations, and colliers to support the growth.[15] The nineteen-member House of Representatives naval committee kept its majority of twelve Republicans, with Foss remaining as its chairman. However, Roosevelt candidly considered Foss, now entering his ninth year on the committee, as simply a "nuisance" and generally dealt directly with Speaker Cannon on substantial Navy issues.[16] Roosevelt the progressive and Cannon the old-time traditionalist continued to maintain a wary but workable relationship with each other.

In the Senate, Hale kept the chairmanship of its Republican naval committee and remained on reasonably friendly terms with Roosevelt. However, conservative opposition leader Sen. Joseph Foraker of Ohio aligned with big business against government regulations.[17] In addition, Sen. Nelson Aldrich of Rhode Island continued to chair the important finance committee and held the purse strings tightly against further Navy expansion. President pro tem Frye, an avowed expansionist interested in international commerce and strengthening the merchant marine, supported the general concept of an offensive Navy within a reduced budget. Two weeks after delivering his annual report, Roosevelt's grand fleet departed on its first leg around South America.

Roosevelt's request for significant increases had come on the heels of overseas warship construction programs. Britain, France, Germany, and Japan continued building fast and heavily armed dreadnoughts. As he pressed for additional warship construction, Congress took up the debate. Two historians called it the "bitterest legislative struggle in American naval history."[18] The year 1908 had the potential to be a watershed period for new U.S. naval development as American battleships and escorts steamed around South America into the Pacific Ocean. However, Congress acted with restraint and instead directed its attention to Navy infrastructure, forfeiting the opportunity to strengthen the ability of the Navy to command the seas.

Roosevelt's hands–on management of the naval service did not extend to reform of the Navy organization itself. As commander in chief, he actively employed the fleet but showed no inclination to consolidate the authority of military officers under his authority. In the absence of a Navy chief of staff, the bureau chiefs continued to appear before Congress in their own right without presenting a unified Navy position. Roosevelt also unwittingly helped Congress maintain the Navy bureaus' collective leadership role by favoring the staff corps officers over line officers, as other presidents had done.

A significant case of the president acting on behalf of the staff corps involved his approval of a medical officer taking command of a Navy hospital ship to accompany the battleship fleet in Pacific waters. Presley Rixey, surgeon general of the Navy, chief of the Bureau of Medicine and Surgery, and Roosevelt's longtime friend and personal physician asked the president to make that decision. Roosevelt's consent to the senior medical officer's request to have a doctor in command of a Navy ship precipitated Rear Adm. Willard Brownson to resign as chief of the Bureau of Navigation.[19] Brownson had considerable at-sea experience, which included recent command of a new battleship and command of a division of ships in the North Atlantic fleet. He and his fellow line officers unsuccessfully tried to convince the president that sound military principles required a line officer to command a Navy ship.

The controversy over the precedence of line officers was hotly debated within the Navy Department, in Congress, and in the press. When Brownson resigned from his position as bureau chief in protest, Roosevelt relieved him of all other duties rather than reassign him, and placed him on the retired list. While line officers quietly applauded Brownson's act of protest, Roosevelt castigated Brownson for being disloyal by choosing resignation rather than obeying the commander in chief.[20] The events drew the attention of Congress because the case involved both the president's position as commander in chief and the authority of Navy bureau chiefs, which affected Congress. The legislature upheld the president's determination to have a medical officer command the hospital ship as long as the crewmen and navigation master were civilians.[21] The ship-based medical staff could be composed of Navy men.

The ship in question was a passenger liner converted to a hospital ship for the Army during the war with Spain. The Army had transferred the ship to the Navy in November 1902, and it had remained in the Mare Island Navy Yard in San Francisco until it was commissioned in February 1908 as the *Relief* with Surgeon General Charles Stoker as its commander. It steamed with the battleship fleet in the Pacific from March 1908 until November when it was crippled by a typhoon, declared unseaworthy, and forced to remain in the Philippines as a floating hospital until decommissioned in June 1910.[22]

Although the hospital ship incident seemed a victory for executive authority, Roosevelt's decision strengthened the bureau chiefs' independent relationships with the legislature. Congress agreed that the chief of the Bureau of Navigation did not have authority over the chief of the Bureau of Medicine and Surgery. The episode was a stirring endorsement of the existing Navy bureau system. Wary of militarism, members of both the legislature and the executive branches firmly agreed on civilian control of the Navy. The Brownson case reinforced congressional resolve to keep line officers from gaining ascendancy and disrupting the bureaus. Congressmen preferred doing business with individual officers rather than face a centralized military front that might disturb their prerogatives.

Meanwhile, leading line officers continued to call for the creation of a streamlined organization under the Secretary of the Navy. They blamed warship construction defects on the "bureau system" acting in concert with Congress, and sought a reordering of responsibilities that would give increased voice to seagoing officers.[23] A contentious issue involved protective armor being improperly located below the waterline when a battleship was combat loaded. Another serious allegation concerned battleship gun turrets that had uninterrupted openings to powder magazines below decks, creating conditions for potential explosions. Emboldened by U.S. Naval Academy alumni, journalists sympathetic to line officers censured the Navy bureaus for their role in constructing poorly designed and unsafe battleships. Reports blaming the uncoordinated bureaus for the construction deficiencies raised public consciousness and precipitated yet another round of congressional hearings.[24]

In January 1908 *McClure's Magazine* published a scathing thirteen-page indictment of the Navy's shipbuilding program, placing the culpability squarely on the legislature and the bureau system for their failure in heeding the advice and warnings of seagoing officers. *McClure's*, a popular literary magazine edited by radical investigative journalist Lincoln Steffens, had joined the "muckraker" press of the early 1900s. In response, the *Scientific American*, an established forum of science and technology, defended both Congress and the bureau system, reproaching *McClure's* for invalid critiques. *McClure's* then reiterated its lamentations against the bureaus, and the *Scientific American* again came to the rescue of the existing organization by rebutting all criticism of the Navy organization.[25]

Congress did not remain passively on the sidelines. During congressional hearings, Senators Hale and Tillman formed an unlikely alliance, restricting the shipbuilding inquiry to the technical aspects of armor-belt placement and gun-turret safety. These old-timers prevented discussions on the essence of the problem by not allowing testimony concerning how the structure of independent bureaus at the time related to shipbuilding decision-making. As a result, the hearings did not address the underlying and more critical organizational questions.[26] The legislature again acted by default and the bureau oligarchy remained intact with business as usual.

Politicians were keenly aware of the local benefits of building up Navy facilities. To ensure future work, a government shipyard needed to have waterfront facilities that could accommodate the large battleships being approved by Congress. Shipyard overhaul and repair work had reached a peak in late 1907 as the Great White Fleet prepared for its two-ocean training cruise.[27] After the ships embarked on their journey, Congress produced eight separate bills for the location of new government dry docks.[28] Districts from Rhode Island to Hawaii vied for appropriations to make them capable of performing future overhaul and repair work. In February 1908, as an unprecedented continuation of its deployment, Roosevelt announced that the fleet would return to its Atlantic home ports via the Western Pacific and the Suez Canal.[29] Japan and the world would get a firsthand view of sixteen powerful battleships of the U.S. Navy as they steamed around the globe.

At the same time, the legislature accused the Navy Department of acting contrarily to the wishes of Congress by reducing the labor force in government yards. The Navy responded that the shipyards were still employing 7 percent more skilled workers than the year before in spite of the fact that a substantial portion of the Navy's fleet was now at sea. However, Metcalf did warn of impending drawdowns. After a barely a year in his new office with the Navy, he reported to Congress that his department had insufficient funds to maintain the government's Navy work force at its present level.[30] Congressmen opposing growth of the fleet charged that the Navy's threat to lay off workers due to a lack of funds was a leverage ploy to generate backing for the president's grand warship plan.

Francis Lassiter (D-VA), a third-term member of the House, and fellow anti-imperialists claimed they were not against providing a Navy but held that the number of ships was adequate and government funds would be better spent elsewhere. Alexander Gregg (D-TX) argued that more should be spent on local facilities and less on expanding the fleet. A second-term member on the House naval committee, Gregg opposed increased shipbuilding while introducing a bill for construction of a dry dock in his Galveston district. Likewise, Lassiter preferred to direct funds to his Navy yard in Norfolk and charged the Navy with improper management.[31]

ROOSEVELT'S FINAL YEAR

Neither the House nor the Senate naval committees advanced Roosevelt's latest charge for building four dreadnoughts. Instead they presented a naval program for two battleships and fewer other warships than recommended by the president. Traditional supporters of the Navy rallied on behalf of Roosevelt. In the House, Richmond Hobson of Alabama, former Navy constructor and hero of the Spanish-American War blockade of Cuba, introduced legislation accommodating the president's bid for four battleships. Hobson's colleagues on the issue were first- and second-term congressmen from both parties, with backing from defense-minded West Coast representatives. Albert Beveridge of Indiana and Samuel Piles of Washington introduced similar legislation supporting the president in the Senate. The naval debates on the floors of Congress were long and boisterous.[32] In the long run, Congress lacked partisan or regional unity to support the president and his shipbuilding program suffered defeat.

Even though Roosevelt sent a forceful special message to Congress in April 1908 urging increased warship construction, he did not have enough political capital in Congress to get the naval legislation he wanted. Roosevelt called for the new dreadnoughts because of the failure at The Hague peace conference and the ensuing increase of foreign naval construction. He advocated "that the United States build a navy commensurate with its powers and its needs."[33] Roosevelt also applied pressure by threatening to block appropriations for public buildings, a $20 million measure containing considerable "pork" for many legislators. He created a minor furor when he reportedly said: "Unless you give me my four battleships, I will veto your public buildings bill."[34] Opponents condemned his arrogance, while supporters downplayed his remark as being casually made in the heat of the moment without spiteful intent. Congress held its course and funded only two battleships. With sixteen battleships steaming in the Pacific at that time, the president unsuccessfully contended that four more were essential to gain equality with the world powers.

Congress was reacting to the local needs of its members, as the naval coalitions remained in a state of flux and disarray. The Navy's fleet, traveling in Pacific waters, appeared very powerful to the legislature and certainly not in great need of additional ships. Also, anticipated completion of the Panama Canal in a few years would allow the fleet to easily move from ocean to ocean. This analysis alleviated the requirement for building a two-fleet Navy. Without unified congressional advocacy, a grander long-term national policy of naval development could not compete with local issues. Congress served its constituencies by financing local naval projects rather than allocating extra sums for additional battleships. The president demanded one policy and Congress decided on another.[35]

The Naval Appropriations Act of May 13, 1908, provided approximately 23 percent higher funding than the previous year. But the increase applied to the maintenance and improvement of government shipyards rather than to warship construction, thereby maintaining the status quo of the force structure.[36] Although the House of Representatives originated all money bills, the Senate dominated the final details. The most powerful senators were experienced Republicans who for years had controlled both the Republican Party policy and the legislative agenda. For the past decade, the conservative senator Hale of Maine had guided naval bills through Congress. He consistently resisted the progressive wing of the Republican Party and contested appropriations for large warships, which he viewed as unnecessary weapons. With only minority opposition, he ensured that funds for naval shore establishments were distributed throughout a wide area. The $47 million approved for Navy shore activities was considerably higher than the much-criticized $25 million allocated in the omnibus bill for new public buildings in the states.[37]

Once Congress adjourned, Roosevelt prepared himself for the Republican Party convention to be held in Chicago in mid-June. As president he would not attend but needed to convince his many ardent supporters that he really and truly was not running for a third term and would not accept the nomination. His chosen successor William Taft was the heavy favorite at the convention and, with little effort, overwhelmingly won the nomination on the first ballot. Soon after the convention, Taft resigned from his cabinet position as secretary of war to conduct his campaign. He was replaced by Luke Wright, who had previously replaced Taft as civil governor of the Philippines. For the next three months Roosevelt took up his summer residence in his Oyster Bay home.

A few weeks after he settled into his routine on Long Island, his Great White Fleet headed westward from San Francisco on July 7, 1908, to show the power of the United States Navy to the world. Meanwhile a few days later, for the third time, William Jennings Bryan won the nomination for president at the Democratic convention held in Denver. To distance himself from election politics, Roosevelt remained at his Oyster Bay home until late September. Finally, at the end of the month, he returned to Washington to participate in the canvass and victory run for Taft. The Republican Party easily won the presidency in November and kept its solid majority in both houses of Congress. Taft chose to spend the wintertime away from Washington as he gathered his team for his new office, while Roosevelt readied himself to face a quarrelsome lame-duck legislative session in December.

Secretary Metcalf's annual report is dated November 30, 1908. However, he had resigned earlier in the month due to ill health. Roosevelt appointed Assistant Secretary Newberry to fill the office and selected New York lawyer Herbert Satterlee to the assistant position until Taft formed his own cabinet in early March. Metcalf's report lauded the success of the Great White Fleet, which was scheduled to return to the east coast via the Suez Canal in late February. He also noted that the Navy now had two submarines operating in the Philippines, two on the Pacific coast, and two on the Atlantic coast. In his section on foreign navies, he wrote that they continued to construct high-speed battleships of large displacement with large-caliber guns, and were also building submarines of increased size and speed. Metcalf rated the U.S. Navy as being number three behind England and France and ahead of Germany and Japan.

Rather than submit his own request for naval increases, Metcalf approved and forwarded the recommendations of the Navy's General Board. With Roosevelt's hands-on guidance, Admiral Dewey's board again asked for appropriations for four battleships and a minimum of four scout cruisers in order to eventually have one scout cruiser per battleship. The building schedule also included an assortment of destroyers, submarines, and auxiliary service vessels, including three colliers. The total list contained a significant increase of twenty-nine ships.[38]

Roosevelt sent his annual message to the opening session of the outgoing Congress a week later in December. He approved the recommendations of the General Board, calling "especial attention" to the need for four battle-ships, destroyers, and colliers. Roosevelt also recommended that the General Board be turned into a general staff and that there was "no excuse whatever for continuing the present bureau organization of the Navy." However, he did not support establishing an autonomous chief of staff of the Navy, as was developing in Europe. In spite of the fact that he had successively appointed six novice Secretaries of the Navy, Roosevelt wrote that the civilian secretary was supreme and should be advised by line officers assigned to coordinate the work of the bureaus. Finally, with typical upbeat prose, he gave high praise to the men of the battleship fleet, which was then in the vicinity of the Phil-ippines after having visited New Zealand, Australia, Japan, and China.[39]

As Roosevelt prepared to leave office, Taft separately and with minimum coordination prepared to move in. In late January, Secretary of State Root left the cabinet for the second time to accept a seat in the U.S. Senate offered by the New York State legislature. Similar to the Metcalf situation a month pre-vious, he was relieved by his assistant, Robert Bacon, who would serve as sec-retary of state for the remaining two months of the administration. Soon Taft would choose his own cabinet.

During the same period, Roosevelt attempted to lay the groundwork for Navy reorganization by forming a special commission to make recommen-dations for changes, charging it to report for the record prior to his depar-ture from the presidency in early March.[40] He chose U.S. Supreme Court Justice and former Secretary of the Navy William Moody to head the inquiry. Other civilians on the "Moody Board" were former Secretary of the Navy Paul Morton and Justice Alston Dayton. The four military members were all line officer admirals on the retired list: Alfred Thayer Mahan, lecturer at the Naval War College; Robley Evans, then serving on the Navy's General Board; William Folger, former chief of the Bureau of Ordnance; and William Cowles, former chief of the Bureau of Equipment and Roosevelt's brother-in-law.

Prior to the end of its session, Roosevelt forwarded the final report of the commission to Congress. The board recommended reducing the independent sovereignty of the eight bureaus by creating five superior divisions answer-ing to the secretary. One division, headed by a civilian Assistant Secretary of the Navy, would be in charge of all business and manufacturing. The other four divisions, headed by Navy officers appointed by the president with the consent of Congress, would respectively be in charge of operations, personnel, inspection, and material. The existing eight bureaus would remain intact but under the supervision of division chiefs. The Moody Board further advised that the responsibilities of the secretary needed to be separated into the civil and military divisions under the force of law.[41] Under the Moody plan, Congress would face a Navy hierarchy with the critical business and manufacturing functions led by a civilian appointee.

The proposed division of civilian and military responsibilities for the Navy was comparable to the Army staff composition tenuously in place since 1903.[42] But in spite of passing similar legislation for the Army, Congress and the executive branch were still at odds over the issue of Army organization pecking order and its military staff structure. The Army's reorganization was a work in progress headed backward.[43] The newly established office of the chief of staff of the Army did not develop into an authoritative body; indeed, it had been pushed aside as Congress revitalized the moribund position of adjutant general to its former premier status. As the Army situation came to a temporary close, Roosevelt's Navy had to settle for an executive report of words for future resolution rather than congressional action.

Leadership in Roosevelt's Navy Department lacked unity and was no match for congressional power. Following President Arthur's appointment of William Chandler in 1882, each succeeding president had the service of one Secretary of the Navy who remained in the cabinet during the president's entire term. Roosevelt had six Secretaries and five Assistant Secretaries of the Navy during his slightly abbreviated two terms in office. With such a destabilizing turnover, the civilian leadership of the Navy Department barely had time to contemplate the immediate tasks at hand. The lack of a long-term Secretary of the Navy weakened the authority of the Navy Department and allowed Congress to retrench as the final arbiter.

Roosevelt's crowning naval achievement, his Great White Fleet of sixteen battleships and escorts, returned to Hampton Roads on February 22, 1909. This was probably the proudest day of his presidency. Just eleven days later, he turned over his job to Taft. As Roosevelt left office, a fractious outgoing Congress passed its naval appropriations act, continuing its policy of providing only two battleships as replacements for older ships going out of service.[44] The president had been unable to get sufficient backing for a final burst that would add four battleships to his Navy fleet. Experienced senators led by California Republican George Perkins had drawn the line and voted for shore facility increases rather than for warships, directing tens of millions of dollars of naval appropriations to build up the Navy yard at Mare Island in San Francisco. Roosevelt angrily accused Perkins of continually hampering his eight-year effort to upgrade the Navy.[45]

During Roosevelt's second term in office, the seventh four-year presidential period of new Navy increases, Congress approved a total of six battleships, twenty destroyers, five colliers, and twenty-six submarines of various capabilities.[46] The authorizations represented reductions in the capital ship appropriations of the previous four-year period. Eleven of the sixteen battleships of Roosevelt's great White Fleet had been authorized by Congress before he took office in 1901. It would now be up to President Taft to continue shaping the U.S. Navy.

12

STEADY AS SHE GOES, 1909–13

William Howard Taft was a physically large man from an esteemed family. He descended, both paternally and maternally, from Massachusetts colonists of the mid-1600s. Born in Ohio in 1857, he grew up in an atmosphere of privilege, education, and politics. His father Alonso had been attorney general and secretary of war in the administration of President Grant, U.S. ambassador to Austria-Hungary for President Garfield, and U.S. ambassador to Russia for President Arthur. Following in his father's footsteps, William graduated from Yale University and returned to the Midwest to work at his father's law firm while studying at Cincinnati Law School. After earning a law degree, he courted Ohio-born Nellie Herron, who had similar New England ties and whose father was a law partner of former president Rutherford B. Hayes. At the age of twenty-five Taft held his first political appointment as collector of internal revenue for the city of Cincinnati. Disappointed with the unsavory necessities of patronage, Taft resigned after a few months. Following a brief trip to Europe to visit his parents in Vienna, he established his own law practice, worked for the presidential campaign of James Blaine, married Nellie in 1886, and returned to Europe for a brief honeymoon.[1]

Prior to his thirtieth birthday, Taft resumed his political career as a judge of the Superior Court of Ohio. With his law firm and judgeship doing well, he and his wife returned to Europe for the summer of 1888. Two years later, he moved to Washington, D.C., to become solicitor general and then a U.S.

Court of Appeals judge. During this period he befriended Theodore Roosevelt, who was then the Civil Service commissioner and later the Assistant Secretary of the Navy. Taft remained in Washington for ten years until 1900 when President McKinley sent him to the Philippines to establish a government; he became the first U.S. civilian governor-general of the islands a year later.

Although he was primarily a skilled judge, newly elevated President Roosevelt kept him as the territorial governor because of his administrative skills. In late 1901, Taft returned to Washington in a state of ill health and testified before the Senate regarding the Army's treatment of Filipinos. Barely recovered, he then traveled to Rome to successfully negotiate with Pope Leo XIII regarding compensation for the American sale of 400,000 acres of former church land in the Philippines. He then returned to the Pacific islands, via the United States, remaining for another year until Roosevelt appointed him in 1903 to succeed Elihu Root as secretary of war.

Taft was by far the most traveled president prior to the advent of air travel. He crisscrossed the Atlantic three times for personal travel and a fourth time to visit Pope Leo XIII. After his two trips back and forth to the Philippines as governor, he made a third round-trip across the Pacific Ocean as secretary of war leading a diplomatic delegation in 1905, with Roosevelt's daughter one of the luminaries accompanying him. He again traveled across the Pacific during the winter of 1907–8, on a mission to Japan that included a 5,700-mile return trip from Vladivostok to Moscow across the frozen lands of Imperial Russia via the transcontinental railroad, followed by travel across Europe and the Atlantic Ocean.

On March 4, 1909, Taft was inaugurated as president of the United States. Selecting his cabinet, Taft settled on progressive Republican George von Lengerke Meyer to be his Secretary of the Navy.[2] A wealthy Bostonian aristocrat, Meyer had ably dealt with heads of state as Roosevelt's ambassador to Italy and then as ambassador to Russia during the Russo-Japanese War. He had then assumed the patronage-laden position of postmaster general during the final two years of the Roosevelt administration. Meyer had worked diligently for Taft's election and was part of the inner circle of progressive decision-makers in the executive branch.[3] Similar to the majority of his predecessors in the office of the Secretary of the Navy, Meyer had no qualification or interest in the Navy. Nonetheless, he was an experienced leader of the Republican Party who understood the power and patronage hierarchy of Congress.

The Sixty-first Congress elected with Taft retained its solid Republican majority, as did its naval affairs committees. However, in order to move up to head the more powerful appropriations committee following the death of senior senator William Allison, Senator Hale turned over his chairmanship of naval affairs to George Perkins of California, who had been a member of the naval committee since 1895. Perkins had occasionally acted at loggerheads with President Roosevelt over Japanese immigration and also had influenced the previous Congress to limit battleship increases to two per year in spite of Roosevelt's plea for four each year.[4]

Upon taking office, Taft's immediate attention turned to the economy and the tariff schedules rather than toward the Navy. In his inauguration speech, given in the midst of an early March snowstorm, he announced the calling of a special session of Congress to meet within a few weeks to revise the tariffs. Taft noted that the current tariffs did not generate sufficient funds to run the government and were unfair to labor. He recommended reducing the tariff schedules and establishing a graduated inheritance tax to cover national financial obligations.[5] Over the course of the next five months, both houses of Congress—with considerable acrimony—hammered out proposals and revisions to House and Senate tariff and tax resolutions.

Meanwhile Meyer labored during his first months in the cabinet to streamline duties in the Navy yards by combining certain duties. Following the precedent of Secretary Tracy more than twenty years in the past, Meyer justified his actions as being properly within the control of a cabinet department head. Prior to the first regular session of Congress scheduled to meet in December 1909, he created a new level of military hierarchy by structuring an aide system of four officers, whom he positioned between the eight bureau chiefs and the civilian secretariat.[6]

The aides were senior line officers who functioned as Meyer's primary advisers. Following the recommendations of the recent Moody Board, they headed new divisions of Material, Personnel, Operations, and Inspection. The divisions crossed bureau lines according to functions. Meyer rationalized that aides would have a broader view than the bureau chiefs who were "intensely occupied with their executive duties" and were not "available for advisory matters except for the details of their bureaus."[7] Under this new arrangement, line officers with advisory authority over bureau chiefs were in a position to possibly undercut Congress in managing the details of the Navy establishment.

As congressmen argued about tariffs and taxes in their special session throughout the spring of 1909, Taft gave Meyer the job of reducing naval estimates by $10 million for the next fiscal year without specifying the areas to be reduced. This meant that for the first time in decades, the president himself called for meaningful reductions in the Navy budget. In spite of the known congressional focus on facilities, Meyer proposed to reduce the shore budget by almost 50 percent through economies in shipyard administration. The savings in the shore budget would allow $14 million for new ship construction while meeting the president's reduction demands.[8] Not until later in the month of December would Congress meet in its regular session to address Meyer's proposed appropriation details.

Taft had the considerably larger issue of tariff and tax revision to negotiate, with a majority of entrenched conservative congressman whose lifeblood depended on industrial and business support. By contrast, the minority, consisting of insurgents of the Roosevelt progressive mode, looked to get relief for the working class by using reduced tariffs as instruments of revenue rather than for commercial protection. Taft found himself supporting conservative Speaker of the House Joe Cannon, who believed in protective tariffs, rather than supporting the progressives. He knew that Cannon was a critical linchpin necessary to accomplish any tariff changes, and let the legislature take the lead.

By mid-spring the House had passed a bill authored by Ways and Means Committee chairman Sereno Payne of New York, lowering some duties and raising others. However, Nelson Aldrich of Rhode Island, chairman of the Senate finance committee, held a less compromising stance and made significant changes that raised protective tariffs. In July, the legislature as a whole recognized that the country needed new sources of income and approved a constitutional amendment to give Congress the power to lay and collect taxes on incomes.[9] Afterward, joint committees hammered out new tariff schedules and agreed on what became known as the Payne-Aldrich Tariff Act of August 1909. Taft decided that the act was the best he could get at the time. He not only signed it, he decided to take a trip across the country to bolster his actions and appease his opposition. However, he greatly misjudged the depth of negative reactions from the Midwest and from the western agrarian and progressive population.

Taft departed on his trip around the country in September, giving speech after speech while being feted by obsequious dignitaries and playing golf at almost every stop. Over the course of several weeks, he traveled for almost 13,000 miles. His train first took him across the northern states via Chicago and Milwaukee and then to Winona, Minnesota, where he unfortunately delivered a poorly prepared speech praising the new tariff as the "best ever" to an unreceptive audience.[10] In spite of his gaffe and its negative press coverage, he continued somewhat obliviously to the West Coast, supporting the new tariff. He then headed to south Texas where he rested at his brother's ranch for three days before proceeding home in early November.

Prior to the opening of the regular session of Congress in December, Meyer submitted his first annual report on the Navy, which pushed two interconnected components to achieve his naval plans.[11] First, he pressed the legislature to approve two big-gun battleships and one repair ship as being essential for maintaining the U.S. Navy as number three behind England and Germany. Second, in a move apparently insensible to congressional priorities, he offered to offset the cost of new construction with savings in shore facilities. However, to appease the voting bloc of Southern Democrats he also rescinded previously reported plans to close South Atlantic and Gulf Coast Navy yards. Additionally, Meyer called for construction of a new, large dry dock without specifying a location in order to allow Congress to make the selection, and proposed to introduce money-saving management practices in government ship repair operations. The changes purportedly would significantly reduce the cost of business as the Navy gained efficiency. Essentially, Meyer was asking Congress to authorize new ship construction while saving money by somewhat reducing congressional largesse to its constituencies. He also described his aide system consisting of four flag officers overseeing the eight bureau chiefs.

A few days later, Taft delivered his first annual message to the legislature. In his short section on the Navy, he repeated Meyer's limited request for two battleships and one repair ship, under a proposed lower budget than the previous year.[12] The president also approved Meyer's aide plan for Navy management and separately urged the passage of a ship subsidy bill to improve the independence and profit of the merchant marine. This was a political nod to President Pro Tem Frye of the Senate, an avowed expansionist interested in building up a profitable civilian shipping industry rather than expanding the Navy. Additionally, Taft called attention to the departments (including the Navy) that by law submitted their own reports and noted that it was unnecessary for him to elucidate further.

Within a month Taft found it necessary to confront Gifford Pinchot, head of the Forestry Service and arch-conservationist protégé of Roosevelt. Pinchot was fervently supporting unproven charges concerning supposed illegal land deals by the secretary of the interior. Ignoring Taft, Pinchot went over his head and appealed to the progressive senator Jonathan Dolliver of Iowa, an occasional contender for the vice presidency who was at that time chairman of the Agriculture and Forestry Committee, to conduct a congressional investigation. Pinchot then criticized the president in the Congressional Record for not taking action. Taft knew that his response would cause a serious blow to his relationship with Roosevelt but he had suffered enough duplicity and fired Pinchot. Taft also wrote to Roosevelt explaining Pinchot's disloyalty. The former president, still in Africa, deliberately chose not to intervene.[13]

While Congress continued to meet in its regular, long winter-spring session of 1909–10, Taft involved himself in East Asian and Caribbean foreign affairs. Unlike Roosevelt, he did not believe in the use of the "speak softly, big stick" method of arbitration. Rather, he chose a narrower path of non-negotiable action by fiat, which resulted in downgrading the diplomacy of U.S. foreign policy. He gave the lead to Secretary of State Philander Knox, former U.S. attorney general and senator from Pennsylvania. In early spring, Taft considered China to be an emerging economic entity and, through Knox, he unilaterally sought to increase U.S. trade without consulting the major powers, which earned the enmity of both Russia and Japan. Closer to home, Knox attempted to intervene in relations with Mexico, Honduras, and Nicaragua by orchestrating a U.S. takeover of debt collection and revenues to ensure the solvency of U.S. banking interests in the area. Unfortunately Knox did not display the tactful skill of former secretary Root. His authoritative opening rounds of State Department negotiations were not well received by either the U.S. Congress or by the Latin Americans.[14]

Meyer continued to run the Navy Department mostly independent of Taft, who chose to absent himself from Washington for long periods of time.

The secretary's efforts to increase efficiency and save money for the government received popular support. The *Outlook*, a New York magazine that often took a progressive line, agreed that a rearrangement of Navy yards would "absorb less of the people's funds than at present."[15] Meyer did not offer the legislature a role in planning the details of his economic restructuring. Rather, he kept his project for increased Navy yard efficiency within the confines of the Navy Department. As he continued to put his aide organization plan into action, Meyer met with opposition from both Representative Foss and Senator Hale. Other members of the legislature also expressed displeasure, arguing that the present Navy management system was the successful product of the effective bureau system reorganized during the Civil War. Supporters of the long-standing naval establishment held that bureau responsibilities covered areas of technical complexity requiring many years of experience.[16] Nevertheless, Meyer managed to persuade the majority of the legislature to at least allow the use of aides as a one-year experiment without statutory sanction.[17]

Congressmen who resisted Meyer's plans to alter Navy management infrastructure also demanded more business for their facilities. The members were responding to continued constituent petitions for capital ship construction in government shipyards rather than by private enterprise.[18] As the annual Navy appropriations bill slowly wound its way through Congress, the Senate added amendments to the House bill, increasing appropriations for Puget Sound, Key West, and Pensacola, which, according to the Navy Department, were marginal operations.[19] As part of the debates, both houses of Congress ultimately agreed that the government should remain in the shipbuilding business in various locations and continued the policy of having at least one battleship built in a government shipyard. Congress also tabled Foss' perennial resolution "to promote the efficiency of the Navy Militia" making it equivalent to the recently established Army National Guard.[20]

The Naval Appropriations Act of June 1910 had little of the infrastructure savings originally presented by both Meyer and Taft. Although it did not pass Foss' Navy Militia resolution, Congress increased the militia budget by a relatively small amount to $125,000 from its $100,000 allotment of the previous year. However, total Navy appropriations fell from $137 million to $133 million.[21] The reductions came primarily from decreases in shipbuilding rather than from facilities. Congress chose its own Navy order of battle by authorizing two battleships as well as two colliers, defensive submarines, and torpedo boats, but not Meyer's requested repair ship.[22] The members of the legislature then adjourned to conduct their campaigns for the November congressional elections.

After an absence of fifteen months, Roosevelt returned to the states in mid-June 1910 to a tumultuous reception by crowds of well-wishers in New York City. He took up residence in his home in Oyster Bay, Long Island, and waited until the end of the month to pay his respects to Taft at the president's summer home in Beverly, Massachusetts. During Roosevelt's travels to Africa and Europe over the past year he had chosen not to give Taft advice and Taft in turn generally wrote only occasional notes. However, on completion of his African safari, Roosevelt's letters from Europe to his close confidants showed his dissatisfaction with Taft's overall performance. In a long letter to Lodge, he referred to Taft's blunders with the tariff and with Pinchot, noting that Taft had "gone wrong on certain points." A short time later Roosevelt softened his position somewhat and wrote to his recently out-of-office friend Pinchot that Taft had reached his nadir and showed signs of improving. More importantly, Roosevelt considered that Taft remained the best candidate for the next presidential election and decided to help him by helping the Republican Party.[23]

However, during the off-year election season, Roosevelt and Taft found themselves with considerably different outlooks for the future. Taft stayed committed to the conservative old guard and put his efforts into overcoming upstart members of the progressive wing that Roosevelt supported. Subsequently, both men interjected themselves in opposing party politics, to the delight of the Democrats who correctly sensed that the Republican Party's internal differences were serious enough to result in a Republican loss. Taft consistently defended the conservatives' protection record. Conversely, Roosevelt toured the West to promote his progressive creed of "New Nationalism," stressing the need for government regulations and conservation activities.[24]

INTERACTIONS

Choosing not to participate in the congressional campaign, Meyer used the pre-election period to travel throughout the United States and Cuba on an inspection tour of Navy facilities. He left Washington in early October and traveled to South Carolina then to Maine and across the continent to Seattle. Once on the West Coast he faced the anxiety of people worried about a Japanese attack. Meyer recognized their concerns as being similar to those of East Coast residents who had feared attacks by the Spanish cruisers during the war with Spain. Officials in California clamored for a Pacific Ocean battleship fleet. Meyer pointed out to them the lack of deep-water approaches to the current naval bases and the dredging planned for the future. He seemed to satisfy his hosts by explaining that a battle fleet could possibly come to the Pacific after completion of the Panama Canal. Returning to the east, his entourage visited the shipyards that he planned to close at New Orleans and Pensacola. Meyer then boarded the *Dolphin* at Miami for a round-trip to the Key West and Guantanamo facilities.[25] He returned to Washington by train from Miami in time to vote in the November 8 congressional elections. The press noted his findings of a need for increased facilities on the Pacific and decreases on the Gulf Coast, as well as his complete satisfaction with the facilities at Guantanamo, Cuba.[26]

The Democratic Party won a significant majority in the elections, which resulted in their takeover of the House of Representatives, to occur after the adjournment of the lame-duck session of the Sixty-first Congress in March 1911. However, the Republican Party managed to remain in control of the Senate. On the day after the elections a disappointed Taft boarded the armored cruiser USS *Tennessee* (ACR 10) at Charleston, South Carolina, for a scheduled inspection tour of Panama Canal construction. The two-week trip would provide a respite from the tensions of the recent canvass and give the president a chance to relax a little in friendly territory. Upon his return to Hampton Roads, Virginia, Taft prepared his annual message for the opening session of Congress.

On November 30 Meyer forwarded his second annual report to the legislature and began by crediting his aide system for its effectiveness in preventing costly construction delays. Consequently he recommended permanently establishing the aide system by legislation. He then related that he had visited all the continental yards and the one in Cuba. Meyer emphasized to Congress the strategic necessity for maintaining the base at Key West while building up the facility at Guantanamo. He also acknowledged Eugene Ely's recent flight from the USS *Birmingham* (CL 2) and concluded that airplanes would be limited to scouting in the future. Meyer again repeated the Navy's long-standing interest in increasing its militia and establishing a naval reserve force. In closing, he requested an increase in the Navy of two battleships, one collier, submarines, small gunboats, and torpedo boats.[27]

Taft sent his second annual message to Congress with a statement of appropriation estimates that showed the Army at $148 million, a reduction of $23 million, primarily from the budget for rivers and harbors. The Navy estimate was $129 million, a reduction of $4 million due to construction and shipyard efficiencies. His key points about the Navy echoed Meyer's report concerning the need to approve the aide organization, the building plan—which included two battleships—and the abolishment of redundant and inefficient shipyards.[28]

Meyer's recommendation to close the Navy yards at New Orleans, Pensacola, and Port Royal immediately brought the expected sharp protests from Southern Democrats. In the Senate, Benjamin Tillman, Roosevelt's nemesis, spoke as a leader of the new South.[29] This agrarian reactionary from South Carolina demanded more, not less, Navy spending in his state. He accused Meyer of having sectional preferences that were detrimental to the South.[30] A fifteen-year senator and an increasingly influential member of the Senate naval committee, Tillman unabashedly demanded a larger share of the national budget for the South in general, and South Carolina in particular. Both the naval station at Port Royal and the Navy yard at Charleston owed their development to Tillman. He publicly acknowledged his motivation to help his state and expressed little concern for the larger view of national defense. Meyer necessarily provided a detailed account of the high cost of maintaining inefficient shipyards, in response to Tillman's Senate resolution relative to plans for closing Southern facilities.[31]

While the outgoing Congress continued to debate tariff reform, its naval committees concerned themselves with Navy organization, increases, and shipyard efficiencies. By the end of January, the House naval committee presented its list for naval growth. It recommended more warship construction than proposed by the Secretary of the Navy but less than endorsed by the General Board of the Navy. Meyer had asked for two battleships and a few auxiliaries while the board had asked for four battleships and several smaller combatants. The committee compromised, deciding on a budget for two battleships and an increase in destroyers and submarines. The Senate agreed. Congress as a whole continued to control the composition of the Navy's strategic fleet.[32] In line with Congress' philosophy of national defense, its Naval Appropriations Act of March 1911 showed congressional preference for a mix of large and small warships while retaining its pork-barrel attachment to local shore facilities.[33]

The outgoing legislature did not take action to disestablish Meyer's organization of aides, allowing him by default to extend the test of the aide structure. But the substantial changes in the makeup of the incoming Congress intensified Meyer's dilemma of directing Navy expansion while seeking economies in Navy facilities. Its majority also did not accept reductions in shore installation spending. The stage was now set for deeper conflicts in the incoming legislature between Southern Democrats even more attached to the pork-barrel aspects of naval legislation and the president's expectation of continued new capital-ship construction within a limited budget.

Once again Taft decided to call a special legislative session to reexamine tariff schedules. The new Sixty-second Congress would take up the issue in early April. Prior to the start of the special session of Congress, Taft faced a developing crisis in Mexico. Its president, Porfirio Díaz, was in a critical situation dealing with an escalating revolution against his autocratic regime. Concerned with the effect on significant U.S. economic interests in Mexico, Taft ordered 20,000 troops to conduct maneuvers in Texas but not intrude into Mexican territory without congressional authority. Independently, the Navy at the same time sent a few small warships to refuel in Mexican ports. The Navy Department publicly stated that "there was no intention to patrol the coast." The ship movement "merely covered a change of station" to Panama. However, Taft disagreed with the timing and implications of the Navy's action. He counteracted Meyer's orders and told him to keep the "maneuvers north of the borderline." The president made the point that he, not the Secretary of the Navy, dictated government policy.[34] By the end of March, communications between Mexico and Taft returned to normalcy for a while.

As the new Congress met in its special session, Taft remained active in pursuing executive-office business while laying the groundwork for his 1912 reelection campaign. He also showed a renewed interest in international diplomacy. Specifically, he began to push for the settlement of international disputes through international courts rather than by the threat of force. While peace advocates praised his efforts, Taft could not get much traction from Congress for any proposal that could undermine U.S. sovereignty. His jurist position on international courts had a negative effect on his political standing while Congress remained in session.

Independent of Taft's politics, Meyer continued to take action to improve efficiency by introducing scientific management in Navy yards. He followed the track developed by Frederick Taylor for large civilian industries, especially Bethlehem Steel Company during the late 1890s and early 1900s. Trained management experts, rather than workers and foremen, would determine the most efficient methods for production by using techniques such as time and motion studies of piecework.[35] However, shipyard artisans saw this scientific rationalization as a threat to age-old, proven methods. Although scientific management had been in place for more than a decade in selected large industries, members of Congress and unions doubted the value of its application to Navy yards. Their combined resistance was formidable. Hundreds of citizen groups and unions petitioned the legislature against adopting "Taylorism" in government facilities.[36] Congressmen with Navy repair operations in their districts expressed concern that the Navy Department would use "Taylorism" as an excuse to reduce the work force. The legislators' regard for the welfare of their voting constituents held priority over faceless, money-saving scientific reorganization.

The power of the Democratic Party majority caucus in the House of Representatives was a new political phenomenon in Congress. For many years of Republican Party rule, power had been vested in the Speaker, who controlled the Committee on Rules and steered the legislative agenda. The House Democrats of the Sixty-second Congress, however, reinstituted a caucus system of majority rule. Its caucus gave party leadership to the Ways and Means chairman, Oscar Underwood, and granted him authority to make all committee assignments. James "Champ" Clark of Missouri, ascending in political power, took over the somewhat downgraded position of Speaker.[37] Clark would be a serious Democratic candidate for president and held his Speaker position for the next eight years.

In early August 1911, while the Sixty-second Congress was still in its special session, Meyer embarked on a scheduled five-week tour of England. The British admiralty granted him a high level of access to both its government and private warship production facilities. On his return to the United States in mid–September, he especially praised the combined Navy and civilian out-put in England and the resultant construction of large and fast combatants. Focusing on efficiency, he concluded from his visit that the U.S. Navy could similarly do all its necessary work in a fewer number of yards.[38]

Before Meyer's return, Congress passed a tariff reciprocity agreement with Canada to decrease some local tariffs. Taft approved Canadian reciproc-ity but, faithful to his cadre of conservative republicans, vetoed the internal tariff reductions. He continued to maintain that lowering such tariffs hurt business. Taft also vetoed a joint resolution to admit Arizona as a state. He dis-agreed with a provision in the Arizona constitution that permitted judicial recall if the voters in the state disagreed with a judge's decision. Taft saw this as a violation of constitutional separation of powers. Unfortunately, progressives led by former president Roosevelt supported judicial recall as being a right of the people. The issue helped set the stage for widening the gap between Taft and Roosevelt during the impending Republican presidential nomina-tion process.

To Taft's great disappointment, barely a month later in September, Canada rejected tariff reciprocity. As a result of his vetoes and Canada's rejection, the five-month special session of Congress from April to August 1911 produced little effective legislation but did lay the groundwork for some of the major issues of the 1912 election season. As an aside during the session, two Southern Democrats introduced House resolutions to prevent the sale of intoxicating liquors on board vessels and in Navy buildings.[39] Although the resolutions died in committee, this was a portent of growing prohibition sentiments that came to fruition in the Navy within three years.

Taft boarded a train for another national tour beginning on September 15, 1911. At the time, the liberal socialist senator William La Follette of Wiscon-sin was the only announced Republican candidate for the approaching 1912 presidential campaign. Roosevelt continued to remain in the background, uncommitted but at growing odds with Taft and his conservative backers. Democratic candidates also began to line up, with Speaker Clark holding a commanding lead and New Jersey governor Woodrow Wilson slowly gather-ing supporters. As Taft proceeded across the states he justified his tariff vetoes and policies, helping to build powerful local organizations of similarly minded conservative Republicans. Upon his return to Washington, he began preparing his third account for the legislature's opening regular session in early December.

A few days prior to Taft's message, the House of Representatives received Meyer's lengthy annual report. He began by again praising the efficiency of his system of aides and the repair of the fleet without exceeding annual appropriations. Commenting on his recent visit to the mostly civilian shipyards in England and in spite of known Southern opposition, Meyer proposed abolishing small, inefficient U.S. government facilities. For increases in the Navy, he recommended building two battleships and two colliers. He also stated a future need for battle cruisers, larger and faster than dreadnoughts with similar big guns but with less armor, of the type being constructed by foreign navies.[40]

Instead of delivering a traditional annual message, Taft chose to send four separate parts to Congress during "the interval between the opening of its regular session and its adjournment for the Christmas holidays." He devoted his first part, delivered on December 5, 1911, solely to support antitrust legislation in accordance with recent Supreme Court decisions. The second part of his message, dated December 7, recounted the positive state of foreign relations and the "crying need for an American Merchant Marine to supplement the Navy with an adequate reserve of ships and men." His brief third part of December 20 concerned his recommendations to revise tariff schedules. Finally, on December 21 he sent his fourth and final part, which contained the status of his departments including the Navy.[41]

Taft agreed that the Navy's fleet was deficient in smaller combatants while also supporting Meyer's building plan for two battleships and two colliers, with the coda that smaller ships could be built more rapidly in times of crisis. He also renewed his endorsement of the previous year to recognize the Navy aides by statute. Additionally, Taft referred to a bill before Congress to establish a Council of National Defense to coordinate recommendations for military and naval requirements, and hoped that it would pass during the upcoming session. Also, in order to have U.S. Navy officers equal in precedence with foreign navies, Taft asked for the creation of flag rank positions above rear admiral. Finally, he concurred with Meyer's proposal to close inefficient Navy yards and wrote that the Navy would make a full report in the near future regarding government facilities.

With the shift of power from the Speaker to the Democratic caucus, the new majority in the House of Representatives was now directly accountable for the course of naval legislation. A relatively small oligarchy of Republicans could no longer bury unwanted naval bills in committee or use the power of rules to block amendments. As the Sixty-second Congress began its regular session in December, House Democrats would not endorse executive-branch naval plans that preferred private industries at the expense of constituents working in government facilities. Over the years, an industrial complex favoring private enterprise had solidified in Republican-dominated regions from New York to the lower Great Lakes. The new majority in the House insisted on continuous Navy-yard work in government shipyards. Accordingly, they also would not tolerate closing yards in Charleston, Pensacola, and New Orleans.

ELECTION SEASON

In early January as the 1912 election season barely got under way, Charles Hilles, Taft's private secretary and chief campaign adviser, warned of the "great dissatisfaction" with the labor situation in the yards. He told Taft that too many men were out of work and that the Navy must modify its system pending a congressional investigation.[42] Four hundred shipyard workers at the Norfolk Navy Yard protested the drive for scientific management and went on strike rather than help the Navy Department gather information for a system that could cost them their jobs. The workers refused to fill out work slips tracking time and material used for specific tasks. Taft felt pressure from both political parties against the possibility of either labor cutbacks or closing naval facilities. By the end of January, Taft told Meyer that the mere proposition of shutting down the Portsmouth, New Hampshire, yard would cost 12,000 Republican Party votes in that state.[43] Other members of the legislature also criticized the Navy for any attempt to reduce the numbers of its civilian employees.

The discontent took shape in congressional proposals. The Democratic House focused on reducing both battleship construction and naval appropriations while maintaining government shipyards. Its caucus also agreed not to authorize any battleships, focusing on maintaining a strong naval defense by building destroyers and torpedo boats. Lemuel Padgett (D-TN), an experienced four-term member and now chairman of the House naval committee, advocated a less strident path than directed by his caucus. He prompted the

House to at least review its position on military preparedness and consider approval of one battleship as part of an annual replacement policy.[44] The debates continued without resolution throughout the spring and summer months.

Meanwhile the presidential election campaign heated up. Taft concentrated on piling up delegates for the nominating convention to be held in June 1912. Throughout the month of January, Roosevelt had continued to deny that he had any desire to run for president. But he also refused to unequivocally state that he would not seek the nomination, explaining to his associates that he only would run in response to a genuine popular movement. Finally during the last week of February, in full disagreement with Taft's campaign, he responded collectively to the exhortation of seven governors that he would in fact "accept the nomination for President."[45] His announcement to run closely followed his speech again supporting judicial recall by the states. This bothered some of his fellow progressives, who then defected to Taft.

Separate from campaign issues, Meyer appeared before the House of Representatives for eight days in March to defend his warship construction recommendations of early December, his shipyard efficiency proposals, and his management structure of aides. Naval committee chairman Padgett countered that there was a shortage in the Navy of two thousand officers and four thousand enlisted men, meant the Navy would be unable to man any new warships. Throughout the following months of May and June, the Democratic caucus continued to refuse the approval of any new battleships.

The Republican Party convention met in Chicago from June 18 to June 21. At the time, only twelve states had open Republican primaries while thirty-six still had delegates selected by state conventions rather than by voters. Roosevelt had gathered the majority of the open primary votes while the state convention delegates, approved by the Republican National Committee, favored Taft. As a result of Taft's strong state organization, he received more than five times the votes cast for Roosevelt in Chicago and handily won the Republican nomination. La Follette remained a distant third. An angry Roosevelt considered the committee's decision not to seat many of his delegates as fraudulent. Prior to the closing of the convention he separated himself and his supporters from the Republican Party proceedings. He then made his decision not only to run for office separately, but to rapidly form a viable third party with an organization and candidates to compete at all levels of government.

Five days later the Democratic Party met in Baltimore. Newly elected Speaker of the House Champ Clark rapidly gathered the majority of votes. However, according to party rules, a contender needed a two-thirds mandate to win the nomination. Over the course of the next few days, supporters of the scholarly Governor Woodrow Wilson chipped away the backing of the self-styled "good ole boy" from Missouri. With William Jennings Bryan backing Wilson, the majority saw him as the more electable national candidate than Clark. On July 2 Wilson's total reached two-thirds, and he became the Democratic presidential candidate. Clark reluctantly returned to his speakership.

As the Democratic convention settled on its candidate, Roosevelt energetically labored to establish quickly a competitive third party with himself as its presidential nominee. Within the course of just a few weeks in July, he organized his followers to prepare a national convention of the Progressive Party. Although his developing platform covered liberal issues of the day including social justice and more power to the government, his foremost motivation was his current hatred of Taft and his strong desire to see him defeated.[46] Taft formally accepted the Republican Party nomination on August 1 and less than a week later the Progressive Party commenced its convention in Chicago to coronate Roosevelt. While shunning Southern black support, he heartily endorsed the burgeoning movement for women's rights and arranged for future Nobel Prize winner Jane Addams to give a resounding seconding speech at the convention. Roosevelt accepted his party's nomination on August 7, the same day that Wilson formally accepted his Democratic Party nomination.

The legislature continued to sit in its regular session until August 22. Secretary Meyer had been at home in Massachusetts from mid-June to mid-August for treatment of a serious bout of typhoid fever. He remained loyal to Taft but was mostly unable to contribute to the final congressional debates concerning naval appropriations. However, he apparently had enough energy to pen a lengthy article for the widely read New York periodical *The Independent*, laying open his views on needed changes to the organization of the Navy.[47] At the end of its session Congress approved naval appropriations of $2.5 million less than the previous year. The act authorized construction for one battleship, two fuel ships, six destroyers, eight submarines, and a tender. The legislature showed its preference for only replacing aging battleships while increasing the number of smaller defensive warships to protect the U.S. coasts.[48]

Shortly after Congress adjourned, the U.S. Navy established what would become a continuous occupation of Nicaragua until 1933. Beginning in early August 1912, the Navy sent about one hundred sailors to the capital at Managua to protect American and foreign citizens and their property from the depredations of an escalating revolution. On August 28, Rear Adm. William Southerland, commander of the Pacific Fleet, arrived on scene, took charge of all U.S. efforts in the area, and assumed the additional title of commander, Nicaragua Expeditionary Force. By mid-September the United States had 2,350 sailors and Marines ashore and had suffered 7 casualties.[49] Although the revolution subsided, except for a nine-month period in 1925, U.S. forces remained ashore for the next twenty-one years.

Meanwhile, Wilson led the presidential campaign, gathering momentum during the months of September and October. Taft's efforts at the same time were somewhat lackadaisical, whereas Roosevelt energetically continued to push his liberal social justice agenda. Overall, his platform managed to maintain a solid Progressive Party constituency, which sustained the Republican split. The major excitement of the campaign occurred in Milwaukee on October 14 when John Schrank, a religious drifter, shot Roosevelt as he entered an auditorium to give a campaign speech. Schrank claimed to have received a vision from the deceased William McKinley to kill Roosevelt to prevent him from serving a third presidential term. The bullet went through Roosevelt's jacket and a folded copy of his speech and hit a rib. Roosevelt afterward gave a rousing hour-and-a-half speech and then spent the next several days recovering in a hospital.

On the day Roosevelt was shot, Taft was in New York City on board the presidential yacht USS *Mayflower* to review the greatest assembly of U.S. Navy vessels in history. The total of 123 warships of the Atlantic Fleet, including 31 battleships, had begun arriving in New York Harbor 8 days earlier; they were greeted by an estimated 250,000 visitors. Meyer accompanied a "beaming Taft" as they boarded the flagship USS *Connecticut* (BB 18) to begin inspecting the armada. The review ended with an impressive salute from more than one thousand naval guns.[50] Unfortunately for Taft, the spectacular Navy event did not contribute significantly to his reelection campaign. Three weeks later on November 5, due to the Republican-Progressive split, Wilson won the election with less than 50 percent of the popular vote but with a majority of the electoral vote. Democrats also won a majority of both houses of Congress.

With such a total turnaround of political power, Taft and Meyer could only attempt a futile last-ditch effort with the outgoing Congress to make up for lost ground in the Navy's program. Meyer began his fourth annual report by justifying his aide program as essential in order to have experienced senior Navy officers in high departmental positions to support inexperienced civilian leadership. He also again urged passage of bills separate from appropriations to create a council of national defense and to provide for increasing flag ranks above rear admiral. Considering new construction, he forwarded the ambitious recommendations of the General Board for four battleships, two battle cruisers, and numerous smaller combatants and support ships. Meyer contended that at least three battleships were needed this coming year and that if Congress authorized only two per year the U.S. Navy's worldwide ranking would fall from second to fourth. Finally he expressed a need for a reserve force of 50,000 men.[51]

Once again Taft sent lengthy separate messages on different dates to the opening lame-duck session of Congress rather than deliver a traditional single account. His second part on "Fiscal, Judicial, Military, and Insular Affairs," included the state of the Navy. According to Taft, "reduced expenditures in the Navy means reduced military strength." He "urgently recommended that this Congress make up for the mistake of its last session" by authorizing construction of three battleships. Taft also repeated almost line-by-line Meyer's requests for aides, a Council of National Defense, additional levels of flag ranks, the construction schedule of the Navy's General Board, and a naval reserve force.[52]

The outgoing Congress would not reverse itself. Instead, at the end of its session in March 1913, it again held the line at one new battleship and authorized fewer small combatants than requested by Meyer and Taft. However, it also increased naval funding significantly for the first time in four years. Annual appropriations rose from $128.9 million to $141 million but reduced the level of new shipbuilding programs. The increase in funding put additional millions of dollars into government shore facilities throughout the coastal states. The one new battleship would be built in a government facility. Overall, the annual construction of new warships fell to its lowest level in seven years.[53]

Although congressional alignments on naval appropriation issues moved unevenly from regional to party solidarity, control of naval administration remained a bipartisan affair. The temporary Navy staff organization of aides reduced the authority of the Navy bureaus and increased the executive branch's span of control, giving the president more power. Not surprisingly, House and Senate bills that attempted to legitimize the aide system languished. What is surprising is that the failed bills, held over from the first regular session, were reintroduced by luminaries of both parties. Padgett, chair of the naval committee and a twelfth-year Democratic congressman, introduced a House version. Senator Lodge, a powerful Republican figure in his twenty-sixth year in the legislature, introduced a Senate version. Padgett's and Lodge's clout was insufficient to gain congressional approval for any weakening of the Navy's long-standing bureau organization.[54]

The ships authorized during the eighth four-year period of new naval growth under President Taft from 1909 to 1913 consisted of six battleships, twenty-six destroyers, two gunboats, two colliers, two tenders, and twenty submarines.[55] The total was roughly compatible with the authorizations of the previous four-year period of Roosevelt's second presidential term. Taft's Sixty-first and Sixty-second Congresses favored government shipyards, not ships, and continued to block efforts to streamline the Navy's business management.

13

NEUTRALITY, 1913–15

With their sweep of the 1912 elections, Democrats gained the majority in both houses of Congress for the first time in eighteen years. As a result, the legislature underwent a major change in its orientation toward the Navy. Control of naval statutes shifted further toward the populist concerns of the South and Midwest.[1] The new majority expressed interest in Navy Department business rather than in appropriations to expand a fleet already ranked among the top few in the world. Champ Clark retained his position as Speaker of the House and James Clarke of Mississippi became the president pro tempore of the Senate. Democrats also chaired the appropriation and naval committees of both houses. During the period of Republican control from 1895 to 1913, annual naval appropriations had risen from $29.5 million to $141 million.[2] At stake was control of the very large annual disbursement of naval treasuries.

In the presence of a large crowd on the morning of March 4, 1913, Wilson took his oath of office on a platform in front of the Capitol. His relatively brief inaugural address consisted of high-minded rhetoric about change for human good within the great system of U.S. government. He remarked that issues needing congressional action included tariffs, the banking system, industrial operations, agricultural activities, waterway development, forest care, and mine-waste reclamation. However, he did not offer specific solutions and ended his speech with a call for dedication.[3] Wilson had a significant academic background with a substantial list of scholastic credentials. However, his actual experience in U.S. politics consisted only of his recent two-year term as governor of New Jersey. He was not particularly attentive to international policy and had even less familiarity with the operations of the Navy, whose potential growth was in the hands of Congress.

Thomas Woodrow Wilson was born in Staunton, Virginia, five years before the outbreak of the Civil War. As an adult in law school, he dropped his first name in favor of his mother's maiden name, Woodrow, a practice not uncommon at the time.[4] His father Joseph, a second-generation American whose Scots-Irish parents had emigrated from Northern Ireland, was a successful Presbyterian minister in Virginia. His mother, Jessie Woodrow, had immigrated with her family to the United States from Carlisle, England. During the Civil War Joseph Wilson took up the cause of the South and joined the General Assembly of the Presbyterian Church in the Confederate States of America. After the war, his church discontinued its reference to the Confederacy but did not rejoin the Northern denomination. Woodrow also maintained an affinity for the South throughout his life. Wilson attended a progression of private schools as his successful father moved upward in the Presbyterian ministry. At the age of eighteen he enrolled at Princeton University, New Jersey, where he blossomed as a scholar of government and politics. After graduating, he chose to attend the law school of the University of Virginia. Although he was an excellent student, he found the work in law school to be uninspiring and decided to leave the university and study law on his own. Soon afterward, he joined the firm of a friend in Atlanta and passed the Georgia bar exam. But he found the law profession too narrow and returned to academia. He entered graduate school at Johns Hopkins University to pursue a career as a college professor.

Wilson's full-time college employment began in 1885 at Bryn Mawr College, Pennsylvania, followed by Wesleyan College, Connecticut, in 1888, and Princeton University in 1890, where he became its president in 1902. He remained a well-spoken political theorist, a highly sought-after lecturer, and an excellent university leader. Over the years he gained a cadre of allies who encouraged him to become active in politics rather than remain in academia. He accepted essential patronage from leading conservatives in the state of New Jersey and handily won its gubernatorial election in November 1910.

During his two years as governor, to the dismay of his conservative supporters, he embraced liberal progressivism in government, and emerged victorious in the fractious three-way presidential campaign of 1912.[5]

After the election, Wilson had four months to choose his cabinet. Realizing that this was truly a daunting task, he turned to Col. Edward House of Texas to help sort out who needed to be rewarded and who had the competency to fill his presidential needs. Independently wealthy, House had been given the honorary title of "Colonel" by Texas governor James Hogg for his help in getting Hogg elected in 1890. House had likewise been a key player in Wilson's presidential election and became his principal adviser for the next seven years. In mid-November, prior to departing to Bermuda for a month's vacation, President-elect Wilson announced that he would call a special session of Congress to meet in April to deliver the recent campaign promises to the people of the United States. Upon returning from his vacation, Wilson got down to business with House and on December 21 agreed to appoint William Jennings Bryan secretary of state because of his definitive contributions to the recent election. He then waited until late February to announce the remainder of his appointments.

Wilson chose Josephus Daniels, a North Carolina newspaper publisher and a dauntless ally in his run for the presidency, to be his Secretary of the Navy. He had briefly considered rewarding Daniels with the patronage-laden postmaster general position but House pointed out that Daniels was neither aggressive enough nor in touch with Congress and thus would leave Congress to its own devices. Instead Wilson selected him for the Navy Department with no apparent concern for his espousal of anti-imperialism and his unrepentant racist demagoguery.[6] Daniels' only prior experience in national government consisted of one year of service as an assistant to the secretary of the interior in the second administration of President Grover Cleveland in 1893. As was the case for most of his predecessors, Daniels had no association with the Navy when he took office.

He was born in North Carolina of Scots-Irish heritage during the beginning of the Civil War and raised by his mother after the death of his father in 1865. For several years she worked diligently to make ends meet. With some financial help Daniels succeeded in private schools, purchased his first newspaper at the age of eighteen, attended law school at the University of North

Carolina, and passed the bar exam. However, he chose the newspaper business rather than law as his life's work. He moved upward in society when he married Adie Bagley, the granddaughter of former North Carolina governor Jonathan Worth. For the next twenty-four years he continued to expand his newspaper enterprises while becoming a major figure in his state's Democratic Party. Daniels was not well traveled beyond Washington, D.C., and had virtually no experience with ocean expanses, the arduous life of a sailor, and the necessarily independent decision-making of those who commanded ships at sea. He was also not attuned to long-standing U.S. naval traditions and came to resent the supposed high-born status of the officers now in his charge. He saw Navy officers as part of a closed aristocracy and resented their purported life of privilege while not comprehending the rigors of years of sea duty throughout the world and the Navy's historical role in U.S. diplomacy.

Daniels promptly accepted guidance from Senator Tillman and Representative Padgett as the de facto leaders on naval issues and never seriously contested the power of Congress to shape the Navy according to its will.[7] With the new, solid Democratic majority in the Senate, the boisterous Ben "Pitchfork" Tillman, in his nineteenth year in the Senate, assumed the chair of his naval committee. Padgett, now in his thirteenth year in the House, had become chairman of its naval committee in the previous Congress. Together they unabashedly used their positions to shape the Navy according to the needs of their pork-barrel agendas. Each of them presented their requirements and the compliant Daniels generally reacted favorably to them. Tillman made demands on Daniels' very first day of work in Washington. The senator wanted fleet activity in Charleston, South Carolina, in order to reap the economic benefits of having ships in port, and called on the Navy to use Charleston Bay for fleet target practice.[8] Although Daniels did not have an immediate opportunity to alter fleet movements, some months later he installed a manufacturing plant for naval uniforms at the Charleston Navy Yard. Afterward, he disingenuously asserted that this action would not adversely affect the uniform shops in Philadelphia and New York City.[9]

Wilson's first order of presidential business concerned international events in Mexico that had begun prior to his presidency. In late February 1913 General Victoriano Huerta conducted a successful coup against the weak democratic government of President Francisco Madero to become the thirty-fifth president of Mexico since 1821. Soon afterward Madero died in his presumed attempt to escape from prison. President Taft decided not to recognize Huerta's dictatorship and to let Wilson make his own executive decision after the forthcoming inauguration. In mid-March, on the basis of maintaining an anti-imperialist position, Wilson opted to do nothing, leaving the question of recognition unresolved pending further investigation and deliberation.

As he settled into his office Wilson entertained hundreds of guests at each of forty-one official functions from his inauguration in March through May.[10] The White House took on the aura of a relaxed Southern manor. Wilson preferred short working days with time to play golf in the late afternoons. Five of his cabinet members were Southerners and within a month of taking office Secretary of the Treasury William McAdoo and Postmaster General Albert Burleson segregated their department facilities, disallowing African Americans from having positions of authority, especially positions directing women. Burleson also received approval from the president to segregate the railroad mail-delivery system. As a result, Wilson faced immediate, strident protests from civil rights leaders and met with Oswald Villard, a cofounder of the NAACP (National Association for the Advancement of Colored People) in 1909, and William Trotter, the African American editor of the *Boston Guardian*. To the chagrin of the leaders, Wilson did not take action to stop the segregation and allowed his departments to follow the lead of Burleson and McAdoo throughout the city of Washington, D.C.[11]

Wilson's primary and most pressing activity concerned his mandates to the special session of Congress, which met in early April. First, he devoted himself solely to the domestic issue of tariffs. In his opening address to the legislature, he explained that in accordance with the results of the recent elections the government must answer to the will of the majority and alter existing tariff duties. Therefore, Congress needed to lighten the burden of the people and inform business interests of the necessary adjustments.[12] The recent passage of the Sixteenth Amendment in February 1913, allowing the federal government to collect income taxes, radically altered the requirements for revenue and protective tariffs. Congress would now occupy itself fully with this single financial issue until October.

As Congress met, Daniels relied on the politicians of the new majority to determine which senior officers were best for key Navy bureau positions. In his first month in office Daniels removed Capt. Philip Andrews from his position as chief of the Bureau of Navigation and forced Capt. Templin Potts, Meyer's aide for personnel, to retire. Ostensibly, Daniels claimed that neither had sufficient recent sea duty. But at the same time he also desired to comply with the necessities of political patronage as well as to eliminate Meyer's system of senior aides coordinating bureau chief activities. According to Postmaster General Burleson, Andrews had been a "pet" of Meyer, and his appointment by Taft was an outrage.[13] Andrews went back to sea and continued his successful career as a fleet commander and rear admiral. Potts was forced to retire by the "plucking board" of Navy examiners because he did not qualify for promotion or reassignment. His offense was his assignment as an aide. Daniels would eliminate the positions of the remaining three aides by simply not replacing them when their terms expired.

The special session of Congress was barely underway when relations with Japan took a serious downward turn again. President Roosevelt's informal 1907 Gentlemen's Agreement with Japan limited visas for Japanese workers in return for allowing Japanese businesses to continue in California and permitting their children to attend non-segregated schools. The informal agreement was never signed into law by Congress and in the spring of 1913 the California legislature, on its own authority, considered restricting Japanese who were not citizens from owning land. Japan reacted strongly by threatening to use its Navy against California. Wilson discussed the unanticipated crisis with his Army and Navy secretaries and on April 22 sent an official letter to the California governor explaining why the proposed restriction was a bad idea.[14]

A day later, Daniels learned that his large printing plant in Raleigh had been seriously damaged by fire beyond the amount covered by insurance. Handing Navy business to his aide for operations, Rear Adm. Bradley Fiske, Daniels departed for North Carolina. Tillman almost immediately sent a note of condolence to Daniels while taking the opportunity to question the loyalty of his Navy staff, with a warning that advised: "You are surrounded by a naval clique which is ever on the watch to control your actions and movements and thoughts."[15] A few weeks later, Daniels returned to Washington and met with Fiske who informed him that the Joint Army-Navy Board, as instructed, had prepared a plan for war with Japan that a short time after Daniels' return was leaked to the press. Wilson immediately disavowed any plans for war and disbanded the joint board. He then sent an ameliorating note to the Japanese ambassador in Washington explaining that California's action was not approved by the president and, more importantly, that he had disbanded the Joint Army-Navy Board. Wilson's diplomacy in disbanding the board resonated with the Japanese government and the affair rested.[16]

AT HOME AND ABROAD

As Congress continued in its special session to resolve tariff issues, members reopened the subject of the cost of armor for Navy ships. Regional preferences to conduct manufacturing in government facilities gained support once again. In previous administrations, influential senior Navy officers and secretaries had generally expressed a preference for private contractors, for reasons of both cost-effectiveness and quality. Daniels took the opposing position in agreeing with the new congressional majority. Rep. Silas Barton of Nebraska and Sen. Henry Ashurst of Arizona introduced bills to study the feasibility of establishing a government manufacturing plant for warship armor plate. The plan would be presented at the beginning of the regular session in December 1913.[17]

Ordnance bureau chief Rear Adm. Nathan Twining's initial testimony advised the Senate naval committee that operating government armor plants would cost considerably more than having work done by private contractors. Tillman, among others, strongly objected to his counsel and called for his removal as bureau chief. According to Tillman, the ordnance bureau "was in collusion with the armor thieves" of private industry.[18] Daniels, already vigorously promoting the notion of establishing a government armor factory, could not tolerate Twining's lack of support. Accordingly, he replaced Twining with Rear Adm. Joseph Strauss, who agreed with Congress in the rush to establish a government steel plant.[19] Strauss took over the ordnance bureau and established good relations with key congressmen. Twining continued a successful career at sea.

By the end of May 1913 Wilson could no longer ignore the volatile revolutionary disorder in Mexico. Significant and long-standing U.S. business interests in that country needed stability to ensure their financial survival. But Mexico was becoming a failed state, agitated with rebellions in its various states and territories. Wilson kept to his course of not taking sides and sent William Hale, a journalist friend, to Mexico to evaluate the state of affairs. Hale did not support Huerta's dictatorial government, but neither did he embrace Venustiano Carranza, the principal leader of the Constitutionalist Army opposing Huerta.

Hale's on-scene evaluation helped Wilson decide on a course of action. In early August he recalled Henry Lane Wilson, the U.S. ambassador to Mexico, a Taft appointee and a Huerta supporter in favor of big business. Next, Wilson sent John Lind, former governor of Minnesota, to Mexico as a special envoy. Lind's mission was to negotiate four conditions necessary for U.S. recognition: cession of fighting, free elections, Huerta's consent not to be a candidate, and agreement of all parties to accept election results. At the end of August, Wilson reported to Congress that Huerta had, unsurprisingly, rejected all four conditions, compelling the United States to continue accepting the unresolved status quo.[20]

Domestically, throughout the summer and early fall, Wilson continued to press Congress to remove the long-standing U.S. protective tariffs. He not only used his influence with the majority in the legislature, he also appealed directly to the people by blaming their lawmakers for acting in their own self-interests rather than for the greater good of the country. His strong-arm tactics were effective as his congressional allies gradually drew up resolutions to further his agenda. Finally in early October 1913, Wilson signed the Underwood-Simmons Tariff Act as the first step in inaugurating his New Freedom plan. Without a break, Congress ended its special session at the end of November to reconvene in December for its first regular session and continue working on banking and antitrust legislation.

Prior to Daniels submitting his first annual report, Tillman asked him to prod the president to assist in strengthening his party in its upcoming regular session. He wanted Wilson to urge the Senate leadership to put Democratic freshman James Hamilton Lewis of Illinois on the naval committee.[21] Lewis had been a one-term congressman in the late 1890s, and served as inspector general in Puerto Rico during the Spanish-American War. When he joined the Senate in March 1913, he became the first "majority whip," a significant position of party leadership. Tillman expressed his anxiety to Daniels that, in spite of the recent elections, Democrats on the Senate naval committee had a tenuous majority of one and needed to add another member of their party. He also knew that Wilson was closely involved in the complicated party patronage in Lewis' state of Illinois.[22] With the president's personal intervention, Senate Democratic leaders appointed Lewis to an expanded naval committee as it got down to business.

Daniels' first annual report recommended considerably fewer warship increases than advocated by the General Board of the Navy.[23] The nonstatutory board, now in its thirteenth year with Admiral Dewey as its first and only head, continued to call for a long-term shipbuilding schedule that included the construction of four battleships. Both Tillman and Padgett ignored the Navy board's recommendations while taking a public position of utmost respect for Dewey and his staff of experienced senior officers. Prior to the commencement of the session, Daniels had received assurance from Padgett that it would be easier to get two battleships rather than three.[24] In his report, Daniels also presented the Navy department's position of promoting work in government facilities and establishing an armor plant. He was already on the record stating that it was the administration's policy to build all warships in government yards. His stance was in line with the majority of Southern Democrats in Congress against Northeastern Republican industrialists, who had been receiving the bulk of the Navy shipbuilding and steel manufacturing contracts.

Appearing in person before the opening joint session of Congress, Wilson broke tradition by giving an oral account rather than a written presentation for his first State of the Union address. In his succinct and well-received speech, Wilson noted the lack of a legitimate government in Mexico and declared that the United States would continue its international "policy of watchful waiting." On national issues, he did not embellish on the reports of his department heads and simply let them speak for themselves.[25] Allowing Daniels to point the way for naval administration, Wilson did not seek any Navy advances that differed from those sponsored by the Democratic congressional naval committees. A few weeks after the opening of its session, Congress passed the Federal Reserve Act, establishing a national banking system that had been dormant since the presidency of Andrew Jackson. This legislation was the second major element of Wilson's New Freedom platform that he had been vigorously pursuing since calling the special congressional session in April. The third component consisted of antitrust and monopoly legislation. Wilson laid out his arguments for the necessity of establishing reasonable controls on business before another joint session of Congress in January. Throughout the next several months, he would closely involve himself in the debates.

Early in the session, Congress again faced the issue of armor plate contracting for new warships. After the House naval committee submitted legislation favoring government steel facilities, many congressmen rushed forward with site proposals in their districts. Enthusiastic members introduced twenty-one separate bills for armor plant surveys.[26] The possibility of advancing this new government enterprise now became a major issue in forming the 1914 naval appropriations bill. But Congress procrastinated again. Rather than take action, it authorized yet another committee to report to its December lame-duck session the cost and recommended locations for a government plant. The three-member Armor Plant Committee of Congress consisted of Senator Tillman, Representative Padgett, and Rear Admiral Strauss, the friendly new chief of the Bureau of Ordnance. All three members were already on record strongly supporting government steel manufacturing.

In spite of Wilson's national focus to advance his New Freedom program, he could no longer ignore the situation in Mexico. By proclamation he revoked his arms embargo of the previous year and allowed U.S. businesses to trade with the rebelling Constitutionalist Party led by Carranza.[27] In April 1914, in a move that was unrelated to Carranza's activities but that still escalated the situation, Huerta's soldiers arrested unarmed U.S. sailors who were ashore in Tampico to pick up supplies for the U.S. Navy. The sailors were soon released, but Rear Adm. Henry Mayo, commander of the U.S. forces in the area, demanded an apology and a twenty-one-gun salute honoring the U.S. flag. (Gun salutes were a serious part of international protocol at the time.)

When Huerta's government refused to salute, Wilson sent additional naval forces to the area and asked Congress to authorize the use of force if necessary to exercise U.S. international trading rights. Shortly afterward, Huerta's soldiers fired at U.S. sailors and Marines who were attempting to occupy a customs house at Vera Cruz. With congressional authority, the Navy then proceeded to land more than 3,000 sailors, Marines, and soldiers to face Huerta's federal forces. After two days of fighting, 19 Americans were killed. Mexican casualties were estimated to be as high as 175. Wilson then accepted an offer from the ambassadors of Argentina, Brazil, and Chile to negotiate a mutual withdrawal. Losing principal Latin American support, Huerta went into exile. Carranza then entered Mexico City to govern the country while continuing to face remaining splinter revolutionary groups.[28] Without fanfare, the United States departed Vera Cruz.

At the end of June, a month before Europe plunged into the First World War, Congress passed its annual appropriation acts. Prior to the crisis of 1914 unfolding in Europe, the legislature approved an increase of $5 million in the Navy budget, a relatively small raise in the annual naval allocation, which now totaled $146 million.[29] The level of approved warship construction, which included two battleships, was less than half of the recommendations of the General Board. However, due to the impending sale to Greece of the outdated battleships USS *Mississippi* (BB 23), commissioned in February 1908, and USS *Idaho* (BB 24), commissioned in April 1908, Congress authorized the Navy to construct a third new battleship from the profits. In keeping with the congressional practice of the previous decades, one of the new battleships would be built in a government shipyard.[30]

Not all Navy officers agreed with Daniels and Congress on the financial details of government shipbuilding. According to Rear Adm. Thomas Cowie, supplies and accounts bureau chief, government manufacturing did not result in actual savings. When Daniels took office in the spring of 1913, Tillman had pushed to have Cowie replaced. Now, a year later, Daniels finally agreed with the senator and in early July he relieved Cowie and appointed Rear Adm. Samuel McGowan to the Navy's top financial position.[31] McGowan had previously been stationed at Port Royal and then at Charleston, South Carolina. Tillman again successfully maneuvered a Navy officer unsympathetic to Northern private manufacturing enterprise into a strategic position for reviewing contracts. For the next six years of Daniels' tenure McGowan kept his post as bureau chief in charge of all Navy finances.

The immediate chain of actions in Europe leading to the long and devastating First World War began on June 28, 1914. In Sarajevo, a Serbian nationalist assassinated both Archduke Franz Ferdinand, the heir presumptive to the throne of the Austro-Hungarian Empire, and his wife Sophie. After a month of international alignments, with approval from Germany, Austria-Hungary declared war against Serbia. To assist and protect its ally, Germany then declared war against Russia on August 1 and against France on August 3. Reacting to Germany's advancement through neutral Belgium, Great Britain joined the

fray and declared war against Germany on August 4. President Wilson immediately delivered a formal proclamation of U.S. neutrality to all nations. Two
days later he issued a gag order to all active and retired U.S. military officers
to restrict comment on the situation in Europe.[32]

As the momentous events unfolded beyond the United States, Wilson
was absorbed in caring for his wife Ellen, who was dying of kidney failure.
She succumbed on August 6, the same day he issued his gag order. Her private and simple funeral service took place on August 10 in the White House,
attended by her family, cabinet members, select heads of congressional committees, and Supreme Court justices. On the following day, accompanied by
Wilson and a small group of close acquaintances, her casket traveled by train
to Rome, Georgia, for interment in her family's plot. The grieving president
was back on duty in Washington late in the afternoon two days later to guide
the course of U.S. neutrality. Without fanfare on August 13, the first ship
traveled through the Panama Canal. The formal opening with international
participation remained scheduled for the spring of 1915.

With the Navy act on the books since June, Congress stayed in session
until it passed the Clayton Antitrust Act in October 1914. Only the regulation of trusts and monopolies remained as Wilson's New Freedom third priority. In spite of the war in Europe, the legislature did not make any additions
to its annual Navy or Army appropriations prior to its adjournment in late
October. Its more immediate interest was the November congressional elections. In the House of Representatives, the Democratic Party lost sixty seats,
but maintained a majority of 230 to 190. In the Senate, due to the Nineteenth
Amendment, all seats up for election were selected by popular vote for the
first time. Democrats gained four Senate seats for a majority of fifty-one to
forty-four. Both congressional naval committees maintained a Democratic
Party majority.

READINESS

Throughout the months of August to December the war in Europe accelerated
rapidly while Wilson retained his isolationist stance. Almost simultaneously,
Germany fought the French, the British, and the Belgians while engaging
Russia along the eastern border of Prussia. At the same time Austria-Hungary
attacked Serbia to its south and Russian forces to its north in Galicia. Because

of modern, accurate, rapid-fire weapons, long-range cannon, new levels of high explosives, and mechanized transportation, the battle intensity was unlike anything previously experienced. Warring nations each fielded hundreds of thousands of soldiers in the first few weeks of combat and soon doubled and tripled their armies' strength. Initial casualty counts were mostly rough estimates, while the total losses reported on all fronts over the next five months totaled more than one million. President Wilson and the American public received daily war reports. Japan declared war against Germany at the end of August. In mid-October Great Britain recorded that it had lost one-sixth of its Army officer corps.[33] At sea in September, a German submarine sank three British cruisers in the North Sea. A month later German ships sank two additional British warships off the Pacific coast of South America. Britain won the next significant at-sea encounter in early December by sinking four German cruisers in a running big-gun battle in the vicinity of the Falkland Islands.

As a war measure Britain decided to intercept all cargo of neutral nations destined for Germany and its allies. Wilson objected to Britain's disruption of U.S. shipping as a violation of international freedom of the seas laws concerning blockades and contraband, but he took no action. By doing nothing throughout the winter of 1914, he quietly favored Britain rather than maintaining strict nonalignment. Secretary of State Bryan and Secretary of the Navy Daniels vigorously protested to Wilson that not demanding freedom of the seas violated the rules of neutrality and would lead the United States into war with Germany. Wilson held his ground in the interest of peace and let the British take the lead in restricting cargo bound for the European Central Powers. Bryan was not appeased and continued his stance of strict neutrality in opposition to the president.

While the war stalemated in Europe, a highly vocal Republican minority in Congress charged that the Navy was glaringly unprepared for the defense of the United States. Led by Rep. Augustus "Gussie" Gardner, a progressive Republican from Massachusetts and a son-in-law of Senator Lodge, this minority vociferously faulted the Navy Department and Daniels for not leading the way toward making the Navy "second to none." Gardner had previously been an avid ally of Secretary Meyer and immersed himself in a running feud with Daniels over the Navy's state of training and readiness. The representative and his colleagues stood for increased intervention in global affairs and were dissatisfied with the shift of power to the localism of Southern states, as well as with the visible issue of unpreparedness. In early November, Gardner unsuccessfully petitioned Robert Lee Henry, chairman of the Committee on Rules, to appoint a committee to investigate the adequacy of the military. Daniels testified shortly after the opening session that the Navy was fine and that newspapers' claims were not correct.[34] In reality, the Navy was sufficiently prepared to meet the needs of peace-seeking President Wilson, but fell short of the expectations of those who saw necessary and proximate U.S. involvement in the European conflict.

Daniels delivered his second annual report on December 1. His fifty-six-page tome did not include any proximate preparations for involvement in the ongoing war. Rather, his estimates for the next fiscal year, due to efficiencies in Navy yards and stations, showed a modest reduction of a little more than a half a million dollars from the recent appropriations act of the regular session that had ended in June. His proposals included new construction costs for two battleships, six destroyers, one seagoing submarine, seven coastal submarines, one gunboat, and one oiler. Daniels' shipbuilding program included approximately one-third of the recommendations of the General Board, which he listed in an appendix. He expressed a need for a government armor plant, increased funds for the naval militias, and the establishment of a Navy reserve. Additionally, ignoring the reality of the European navies being fully engaged in war, he naively wrote that a number of the "great maritime powers of the world" would participate in the official opening of the Panama Canal in February–March 1915. He also devoted four pages to explaining his issuance of General Order No. 99 prohibiting liquor on board all Navy vessels and stations.[35]

Wilson again appeared in person to present his second State of the Union address to the opening joint session of the lame-duck legislature. He began by praising the work of the Sixty-third Congress for virtually completing his program of business regulation for the good of the nation. Regarding the war in Europe, Wilson spoke of the serious disruption of trade and the associated need to develop a strong U.S. Merchant Marine, which Congress had "hindered" in the past. He asked the legislature to do its best in its upcoming short session to correct this deficiency. Speaking of national defense, he questioned the notion that "preparedness" required a large standing army ready to protect the Unites States from attack. Wilson said that the country was at peace and had no reason to fear that U.S. territory was threatened. However, he considered it within U.S. tradition to continue developing a reasonable National Guard of the States and a powerful Navy for defense, with no thoughts of aggression or of conquest. According to Wilson, the United States would sensibly agree on a defense policy "perfectly consistent with the peace of the world."[36]

At the time the U.S. Army numbered less than its authorization of 100,000 men, which was considerably fewer than the millions of soldiers of the various nations facing each other in Europe. American soldiers were stationed in the Philippines, China, Puerto Rico, and Cuba. Within the United States, cavalry regiments served on border security duty and artillery units maintained U.S. coastal defense stations. The U.S. Navy listed 66,500 officers and men, compared to the 150,000 of Great Britain's navy and the 79,000 of Germany's navy when war broke out in 1914.[37] Additionally, not all capable U.S. Navy warships were fully manned. Rather, several stood in a nondeployable readiness status awaiting crews.

In the ongoing war in Europe, none of the combatant nations could imagine seeking peace rather than victory. In mid-December, Germany expanded its naval war by bombarding cities on the northeast coast of England. A few weeks later, while remaining fully engaged against Austria, Russia conducted a massive attack against the Ottoman Empire's army in the frozen Caucasus Mountains. The combined losses in the east were estimated to be well into the tens of thousands, including deaths due to frostbite and disease. Less than a week prior to Christmas, the French and the British commenced their first offensive attempt against the German army since the stalemate of the fall. The ensuing battles in northern France continued for more than two months, with heavy losses of French, British, and German soldiers. The *New York Times* cynically but accurately reported that the territorial gains of the French in the last days of December were measured in feet, not miles. Germany reported that from all fronts it held a total of 586,000 prisoners from France, Russia, Belgium, and Britain. On the first day of the new year, a German submarine in the English Channel sank the British battleship, HMS *Formidable*. A few weeks later, the British sank a German armored cruiser during a running engagement at Dogger Bank in the North Sea. The U.S. public received almost real-time news of these events.[38]

In mid-January, Wilson faced a burgeoning financial crisis that had been looming over the past several months. Oscar Underwood, influential chairman of the House Ways and Means Committee, urged additional economy. He advocated a reduction of the Navy appropriations bill that the outgoing Congress would pass in early March. A powerful ally of Wilson, Underwood had recently been elected U.S. senator of the state of Alabama and would continue to be a forceful conservative voice in the next Congress. He maintained that the Navy was strong enough for national defense and that at least one battleship should be removed from the program.[39] As the legislature continued its debates, Wilson acted in late January by cutting the Army and Navy budgets. This was a blow to Daniels, who now had to alter his battleship plan and schedule the construction of one, vice two, dreadnoughts for that year. As result of his adjustments, he would again face the growing ire of congressmen and those in the public who continued to blame Daniels and the Navy loudly for being unprepared for war. According to the press, the cutback moved the French navy up to third place and dropped the U.S. Navy to fourth.[40]

In an article published in the beginning of February in the *North American Review*, former Secretary of the Navy Meyer reflected on conditions in the Navy Department. He expressly blamed local politics for hindering Navy development and preparedness. Yet politics had always been an essential ingredient in the separation of powers of the executive and legislative branches. Congressmen necessarily considered the needs of both their party and their constituents. Nonetheless, in his article, Meyer vigorously complained that it was not "realized to what extent political influences have misdirected the appropriations of the past twenty-five years."[41] He showed that keeping all government shipyards employed caused a significant waste of funds. He echoed the long-standing complaint of Secretary Long more than a decade before that compared to civilian enterprise they were grossly inefficient and expensive. Meyer's solution focused on eliminating redundancy by closing unnecessary yards and creating an autonomous Navy general staff to oversee construction priorities and properly manage expenditures.

In early February 1915 Kaiser Wilhelm II escalated the war in Europe by declaring that all of the waters around Britain were a war zone where ships could be sunk without warning. After a two-week waiting period, all neutrals were legitimate targets. Germany was reacting to its naval losses at sea and its significant economic shortages caused by Britain's extended blockade. It decided to intensify its *guerre de course* operations by using its submarine force to destroy merchant shipping. Germany's action was contrary to the international rules of the sea concerning commerce raiding, which required warnings and safe passage for crews and passengers prior to any sinking. Its chancellor, Bethmann-Hollweg, expressed concern to German leaders about the possible adverse reaction of neutrals, specifically the United States and Italy. But he was overruled by his admirals and his emperor.[42] President Wilson responded by sending a carefully worded note to Germany expressing that the United States would hold it to "strict accountability" for its actions.[43] He did not elaborate further and instead worked on an international peace proposal while Germany slowly began its new phase of naval warfare with a small number of U-boats capable of high-seas operations.

In its final session ending in early March 1915, the Sixty-third Congress authorized the establishment of a Navy Reserve force separate from the naval militias of the states. The reserves could serve as a source of manpower for idle warships. The force would consist of men with prior naval service to be available for duty when ordered by the president in time of war or national emergency. Congress also established provisions for a military position of CNO (Chief of Naval Operations). The officer, selected by the president for a four-year term with the consent of the Senate, would be next in succession to act as the Secretary of the Navy in the absence of both the secretary and his assistant. As the Navy had grown considerably over the years, the legislature pragmatically recognized the need for coordinating responsibilities in order to coherently carry out naval operations. Historically, the chief of the Bureau of Navigation controlled fleet movements. But since the advent of Meyer's aides in 1909, the Bureau of Navigation had been reduced in importance and the aide for operations assumed the duties of directing fleet operations.

The operations aide at the time, Rear Adm. Bradley Fiske, was a strong director in the Navy Department as well as a prestigious inventor of shipboard optical and electrical equipment. He also was a well-known contributor of leadership and technical writings. His many deployments over the years included operations in Asian, Pacific, Mediterranean, and Atlantic waters. He had participated in the Navy's initial movement out of the doldrums of post–Civil War neglect into its revitalization. Commissioned in 1875, after serving on remnants of the old Navy, he supervised the installation of modern ordnance on board the protected cruiser *Atlanta*, one of the ABCDs authorized in 1883. He later saw action in the war with Spain as executive officer of a gunboat in the Battle of Manila Bay. His subsequent sea duty included commanding a scouting cruiser, a training ship, and a major protected cruiser. As a rear admiral, he commanded three different Atlantic Fleet battle divisions before receiving his appointment as operations aide in February 1913, just prior to Meyer leaving office. Fiske was a vocal proponent of increased Navy preparedness and of the necessity for a general staff to properly command the Navy.[44]

Against Daniels' wishes, Fiske had helped draft initial legislation for the House of Representatives naval committee to create the office of a powerful CNO. His proposal prescribed the foundation of an autonomous military staff to oversee virtually all aspects of Navy administration and business. Rep. Richmond P. Hobson of Alabama, longtime advocate of a Navy general staff, agreed with Fiske and introduced bills for the new position.[45] Strongly objecting to Fiske's plan, Daniels sent his own draft to Tillman's Senate naval committee. Daniels' arrangement limited the CNO to responsibility for fleet operations only, without oversight of ship construction and repairs activities. His deposition subordinated the new office to the civilian secretary in all matters.[46] The full legislature of both houses agreed with Daniels' version of reduced military influence of the position as advanced by the Senate and passed the act that established the office separate but equal to the Navy bureau chiefs. Under the Secretary of the Navy, the CNO would carry out naval warfighting strategy but did not have authority over Navy business.[47] Congress reorganized the Navy Department without creating an overarching Navy general staff or a chief of staff and without reducing its access to the bureau chiefs.

Concurrent with Navy Department organizational changes, the Naval Appropriations Act of March 1915 totaled $150 million, a modest 3 percent increase over the authorization of the previous year.[48] As the war in Europe raged on, Congress approved two new battleships, the same number it had funded in its previous session prior to the outbreak of war in Europe. In addition to the dreadnoughts, the legislature also approved Daniels' moderate request for destroyers and submarines rather than accept the significantly higher warship construction recommendations of the General Board of the Navy. Once again, the legislature put off a decision on building a government armor plant and extended the congressional Armor Plant Committee to report to the newly elected Sixty-fourth Congress, which would not meet until December.

14

SECOND TO NONE,
1915–21

A few days prior to the Sixty-third Congress' adjournment on March 4, 1915, Wilson made it known that, because of the European situation demanding his attention, he probably would not be able to leave Washington for his planned springtime visit across the country.[1] American newspapers provided daily coverage of the war in Europe and the public was well aware of the depth of the conflict. Germany and Austria-Hungary had recently conducted forays against Russia in the freezing cold of the Carpathian Mountains. While suffering heavy losses, the Russian army managed to temporarily hold its ground. But eventually, by the end of February, the German and Austro-Hungarian armies had soundly crushed Russian forces in the vast Masuria Lakes area in northeastern Prussia. During the same month, Britain had begun a massive land and sea campaign in the Dardanelles that eventually involved tens of thousands of its colonial soldiers facing the armies of the Ottoman Empire. Along the western front of Europe, France and Britain reopened their campaigns against Germany in Ypres and Champagne, with both sides experiencing high casualties.

Wilson monitored the world events from his Washington residence and continued to develop peace plans to end the devastating warfare. His chief adviser, Colonel House, was then on an extended trip throughout Europe visiting belligerent capitals as the president's personal representative.[2] While Wilson was maintaining his self-imposed homebound routine of morning business and afternoon golf, his cousin Helen Bones introduced him to her widowed friend Edith Galt. The unmarried Bones had been the social secretary of Wilson's wife, and after Helen Wilson's death she had remained a resident of the White House. An immediate mutual attraction arose between the fifty-eight-year-old president and the forty-four-year-old Galt, who would be married to each other nine months later.

In early April Daniels continued to disband the Navy Department's organization of military staff aides established by Secretary Meyer. At considerable odds with Daniels' management of the Navy and with the knowledge that he was not being considered for the newly created post of CNO, Admiral Fiske resigned from his soon-to-be defunct position of aide for operations. Shortly thereafter, Daniels reassigned Fiske from his Washington duties to the Naval War College in Newport, Rhode Island. Fiske retired eleven months later after an illustrious forty-three-year career as a sailor, influential naval officer, and prominent president of the U.S. Naval Institute.[3]

For the first CNO, Daniels convinced Wilson to pass over twenty-six rear admirals and five senior captains and appoint Capt. William Benson to the new office.[4] Benson came from a background of extensive sea duty and had recently commanded the Navy's newest battleship, USS *Utah* (BB 31). He was at the time commandant of the important Philadelphia Navy Yard proximate to Washington, D.C., where he came to Daniels' attention as a steady administrator as well as a fellow Southerner. Until the Civil War, Benson's slave-owning family maintained a successful plantation near Macon, Georgia. After the war, ten-year-old William experienced the economic struggles of Reconstruction while being schooled at home. His parents moved to the city of Macon in 1870 where he attended high school for a few years and then, through family connections, managed to receive an appointment to the U.S. Naval Academy. With the nickname "Judge," he began his years at sea, which included an around-the-world cruise on the gunboat *Dolphin*, the first ship of the new steel Navy. Daniels saw Benson as a dependable and compliant leader separated from the supposed clique of high-society Navy officers.

On Friday, May 7, 1915, world events took center stage for President Wilson when a German submarine sunk the British ocean liner RMS *Lusitania*, resulting in the loss of 1,198 persons, including 120 Americans. He was truly

shocked, and deliberated for days over an appropriate response while outwardly retaining his regular routine. He played a round of golf on Saturday
followed by an automobile ride, attended church services on Sunday, met
with Secretary of State Bryan on Monday, and called for his cabinet to meet
on Tuesday.[5] Finally, on Thursday, May 13, Wilson sent a communiqué to
Germany demanding an apology, along with a vague warning that the United
States would take unspecified action to protect its citizens. Upon receiving a
noncommittal response three weeks later, he prepared a stronger diplomatic
note of complaint. At this juncture, in order to maintain neutrality and keep
the United States out of the war, Secretary of State Bryan strongly advised
Wilson not to directly confront Germany. After many discussions, the president maintained his position. Bryan reacted by resigning as Wilson sent a second and firmer message of protest to Germany on June 9. Shortly thereafter,
Wilson moved to his summer residence in Concord, New Hampshire, and
awaited further developments.

Carrying on his reorganization of the Navy, Daniels expanded the management system run by his congressionally accessible bureau chiefs. He was
responding to the requirements of the growing Navy as well as to the increasing level of criticism concerning the Navy's lack of preparedness. With the
new office of CNO limited to fleet activities, Daniels formed a body of con-
sultants called the Secretary's Advisory Council. The council consisted of the
civilian Assistant Secretary of the Navy Franklin Roosevelt, the CNO, and the
eight bureau chiefs. Although the council itself did not have statutory approval
from Congress, Daniels publically legitimized the members as holding positions "created by act of Congress, charged with certain statutory duties,
appointed by the President and confirmed by the Senate."[6] In the newly established position of CNO, recently promoted Rear Admiral Benson became a
member of a senior advisory group equal to the bureau chiefs. As the Navy's
leader, Daniels remained aligned with congressional requirements.

Meanwhile, outspoken congressmen, led by Gussie Gardner, continued
to consider the state of Navy preparedness as grossly inadequate and blamed
the weaknesses squarely on Daniels.[7] In reality, several deficiencies highlighted
by Gardner were actually a product of congressional manning decisions. Congress controlled the end strength of naval personnel, requiring the Navy to place
ships in reserve status without maintaining a full complement of crew members. This practice had been common in pre-war Europe where reserves awaited

a call-up to round out ship crews in an emergency. Opponents in Congress such as Gardner blamed naval leadership and the executive branch for some of the shortcomings that the legislature itself had created. However, according to Daniels, the size of the Navy and the appropriations for its support were determined by a democratic process involving the desires of the people properly carried out by a responsive Congress.[8] He held that the Navy, as an executive branch department, contained the technical expertise and therefore was accountable for design, inspection, and operations of the fleet but not its composition.[9]

Germany gave an evasive response in mid-July to Wilson's second diplomatic note. This moved the president to take a considerably firmer stand and to increase military readiness significantly. His reaction was a definitive turning point, moving him toward national preparedness and away from maintaining the semblance of international neutrality. Returning from his respite in New Hampshire and secretly engaged to Edith Galt, Wilson called a cabinet meeting to deal with Germany and then proceeded to put together specific military plans for the immediate future. Colonel House, his unofficial adviser, had completed his recent sojourn to Europe and promoted a strong pro-British stance. Germany was now clearly Wilson's adversary. His subsequent third diplomatic note to Berlin, sent on July 21, was his strongest to date. In fact it was a barely veiled ultimatum that the United States regarded any further comparable aggressions as "deliberately unfriendly."[10]

Wilson then took direct control of his administration's policy to strengthen both the Army and the Navy. A day after he sent his third letter of protest, he charged Daniels to consult with Navy experts and determine what the Navy must be in order "to stand upon an equality" with the best in the world.[11] Rather than call a special session of Congress in July, Wilson decided to assess his options and wait until the opening of the regular session in December to present his Navy and Army programs. Without articulating a specific strategy for naval forces, he fully embraced updated plans of the General Board of the Navy for an unprecedented five-year program of shipbuilding. He then charged Daniels to develop the annual naval estimates for the Sixty-fourth Congress.

The land battles in Europe remained stalemated throughout the remainder of the summer and fall of 1915. Germany had introduced the use of poison gas against combatants bogged down in trenches just a few hundred yards from each other. Italy had joined the war against Austria and was engaged in debilitating trench warfare along its northern border. In late summer Germany stopped torpedoing passenger liners but unceasingly continued U-boat construction for future deployment. This temporary easement reflected Germany's internal policy struggles regarding the propriety of undersea warfare against neutral shipping, as well as being a reaction to Wilson's ultimatum.[12] As the war continued on the land, French and German casualties during the renewed campaign in the Champagne area during September and October numbered more than one hundred thousand.

Navy preparedness complaints by some legislators fixated on Daniels' slowness in awarding building contracts for ships already authorized. However, the naval appropriation acts of the past few years had required the construction of at least one battleship in a government shipyard. Carrying out this congressional mandate, Daniels aligned with the legislative majority and rejected bids from private firms, which he accused of price fixing as members of steel trusts. For the time being, the Brooklyn Navy Yard was the only government facility that had the capacity to build large dreadnoughts and could build only one at a time.[13]

The legislature, not the Navy, continued to direct both the composition and manufacture of the Navy's fleet. In 1903 the General Board of the Navy had developed a long-range, twenty-year plan that would eventually make the U.S. Navy equal to the most powerful in the world. However, in spite of the board's recommendations, successive legislatures chose lesser options each year, allowing the Navy to fall behind the board's benchmark schedule. In the absence of a coherent long-range goal, congressional authorizations were not based on a course to make the Navy equal or better than any other. As the "peace president," Wilson knew he could not now insist on a single radical increase to make the U.S. Navy instantly number one in the world. Instead, he sanctioned Daniels to present a proposal to Congress that would spread increases in construction beyond the current annual appropriations cycle.[14] Because of the huge outlays required, the new Congress that would meet in December could not finance a long-term, multi-year program with appropriations from its two annual sessions. A long-range plan would therefore require significant appropriations from successive Congresses not yet elected.

Three weeks prior to sending his annual report to the president, Daniels' printing press in Raleigh, North Carolina, once again suffered from a devastating fire. Daniels immediately traveled to North Carolina to survey the damage and returned to Washington shortly thereafter with his newspaper amazingly back in circulation.[15] He then forwarded to Congress his recommendations for an updated five-year shipbuilding schedule prepared by the Navy's long-standing General Board. Accordingly, Daniels proposed a total of 191 various vessels to be built with the fiscal year funding of 1917 through 1921.[16]

Following Daniels' report Wilson delivered his State of the Union message, again in person, to a joint session of Congress. His lengthy speech was deliberate and professorial, pronouncing his specific mandate of national defense through preparation.[17] His principal points concerned the necessity of U.S. neutrality, guardianship of the Americas in accordance with the Monroe Doctrine, military readiness without resorting to a standing army, and the financial requisites for the immediate future. He urged a greater than one-third increase in the manpower of each service, raising the Army to 142,000, the Navy to 83,000, and the Marine Corps to 13,000, plus the establishment of a citizen army of 400,000 reserves. According to Wilson the increases, totaling 560,000 men, would come from volunteers who desired to serve their country in a time of need. Considering the Navy to be the country's first line of defense, he approved verbatim Daniels' five-year warship construction program. In order for the United States to maintain its independence Wilson also again called for a greatly expanded merchant marine to be initially subsidized by the government. Finally, he laid out his plan to pay for preparedness with various internal taxes that he considered to be reasonable and which would spread the burden without incurring great national debt.

As the Sixty-fourth Congress had barely begun its opening session in December 1915, Rep. Clyde Tavenner (D–IL) took the floor of the House of Representatives to excoriate the wasteful record of naval preparedness. He presented a scathing indictment of what he considered to be gross long-term profiteering by the civilian manufacturers of naval war materials. He specifically condemned the membership of the newly revived civilian Navy League as being complicit in excessive price-fixing since its founding in 1903. Covering many pages in the Congressional Record, Tavenner named organizations such as Bethlehem Steel, Carnegie Steel, Midvale Steel, Harvey Steel, and International Nickel as leveraging obscene profits from the government while building the Navy's fleet. He contended that Congress needed to scrutinize its past and not be taken in by the jingoism behind the current clamor for additional naval preparedness.[18] Tavenner had the support of a vocal minority and set the tone for the polemic debates of the upcoming long winter-spring-summer congressional session.

While Congress proceeded with its business, Wilson married Edith Galt on December 19, 1915. The small, private ceremony took place in her Washington, D.C., home. She had been the president's almost constant companion since the spring. Born in Wytheville, Virginia, in 1872 to a family struggling to recover from the loss of its plantation and slaves, she was mostly schooled at home by her father and grandmother.[19] Her formal education consisted of two years at a boarding school during her mid-teenage years. At the age of twenty-three she married Norman Galt, who had a jewelry and silverware business in Washington, D.C. Upon his death in 1908, Edith successfully ran the business for several years and after selling it to her employees lived comfortably on her investments. Immediately following their wedding, the Wilsons traveled by train to Hot Springs, Virginia, for a three-week honeymoon.[20] Although Galt did not have a background in national or international politics, by the time of her marriage to Wilson she had become his confidante.

The newlyweds returned to Washington a week earlier than planned due to the submarine sinking of the British liner SS *Persia*, which resulted in the death of two American civilians. At first Austria-Hungary and Turkey were blamed for torpedoing the civilian ship. After almost two weeks Germany revealed that one of its submarines had been in the area and its commander had considered that the *Persia* was fair game as a warship because it had a mounted cannon. In spite of recommendations from Secretary of State Robert Lansing (Bryan's replacement) to strongly condemn such U-boat activities, Wilson decided against taking immediate diplomatic action that would risk breaking relations with Germany. Intensely desiring to avoid war, he embarked on a one-week speaking tour to present his policy of peace and preparedness to his American constituents. From January 27 to February 4, 1916, he traveled by train across the friendly progressive crescent of the Midwestern states as far as Iowa and returned via Kansas, Missouri, and Illinois. He and his wife were met by large crowds who approved his message of preparedness for national defense, not international war. In Wilson's speech in St. Louis, he called for a naval service that "ought, in my judgment, to be incomparably the greatest navy in the world."[21]

Daniels continued his work in Washington by authorizing the government shipyard at Mare Island in San Francisco to build a battleship, even though necessary dredging remained incomplete. Also, the inclined building structures, known as the "ways," for launching the dreadnoughts at Mare Island were inadequate and needed renovation. Daniels decided to put off for a year the construction of the two battleships, authorized by the previous Congress, until the ship currently being built in Brooklyn was launched and the Mare Island Yard improvements were completed. Critics, led by Representative Gardner, relentlessly spoke out publicly about the incapacity of government yards, while Daniels insisted that both Mare Island and a second battleship dry dock at Brooklyn would soon be available.[22] A compliant Democratic majority in Congress agreed with Daniels and provided extra appropriations to upgrade both the West Coast and East Coast facilities. Part of the bid differences between private and government cost estimates stemmed from the government practice of not including shipyard improvements in the costs of its warship construction. Private enterprise, unlike Navy Department yards, necessarily included overhead and depreciation costs when submitting the bids, which Daniels judged to be excessive. Congress did not challenge the Navy's fiscal interpretations.

ESCALATION

Shortly after Wilson's return from his well-received speaking tour, Germany announced a new submarine campaign to sink without warning "enemy merchantmen inside the war zone." However, deferring to the previous concerns of the United States, merchant ships outside the war zone "could only be sunk without warning if they were armed, and passenger ships were not to be touched."[23] The new policy put the rules of engagement in the hands of the on-scene submarine commanders, who faced problematic identification requirements. In late March 1916, a German U-boat torpedoed the TSS *Sussex,* a French cross-channel ferry boat. Although the explosion tore off most of the ship's bow, it remained afloat and was eventually towed into a French harbor. Of its 350 passengers, several Americans were injured and many passengers of other nationalities either died in the explosion or drowned in capsized lifeboats. Wilson was clearly disturbed but again took no immediate action, taking counsel not only from Colonel House but also from his wife Edith, who was now his closest adviser.

He deliberated over a period of a few weeks before sending his demands via a lengthy diplomatic note to Germany's foreign minister on April 18, in which he condemned the unrestricted submarine warfare that violated the rights of neutrals and noncombatants. Rather than immediately break with Germany, he issued an ultimatum: "Unless the Imperial Government should now immediately declare and effect an abandonment of its present methods of submarine warfare against passenger and freight carrying vessels, the United States can have no choice but to sever diplomatic relations with the German Empire altogether."[24] Two weeks later on May 4, the German minister responded to the United States that Germany rescinded its submarine policy and ordered its naval forces to act according to international law regarding the safe passage of merchant vessels "both within and without the area declared to be a naval war zone."[25] The document became known as the Sussex Pledge. For the second time in a year Germany modified its unrestricted submarine warfare strategy as a result of U.S. protests.

Wilson had considerably more than the European war to worry about. He had recently decided to stop U.S. support for Pancho Villa in northern Mexico in order to allow President Carranza to establish a stable government. In mid-January, in retaliation against the new U.S. policy, Pancho Villa attacked a train in the Mexican state of Chihuahua and killed eighteen U.S. citizens. Then on March 9, he crossed the U.S. border and attacked the town of Columbus, New Mexico. The on-scene American army quickly responded and killed about thirty of Villa's men, while suffering the loss of eleven civilians and nine of its soldiers. Carranza "insisted that his own soldiers would punish the Villistas and that the United State should not interfere."[26] Continuing to act in accordance with U.S. interests, Gen. John Pershing invaded Mexico on March 15 with approximately four thousand U.S. soldiers to stop Villa's activities. Telegraph communications allowed the White House to receive updates from New Mexico within a few hours and authorize cross-border operations.

Throughout the remaining days of March and into early April, President Carranza's Mexican army and Pershing's soldiers separately engaged the revolutionaries and chased remnants of Villa's troops scattered throughout the local mountains in Chihuahua. On April 12, in a remonstration of the continued, unwanted U.S. presence, Carranza's army ambushed unsuspecting American soldiers. In late May, after several encounters between U.S. and Mexican forces that resulted in the loss of lives on both sides, Carranza sent a strong note of protest to the United States. Wilson reacted on June 18 by calling on the National Guard to mobilize and prepare to assist at the border as necessary. Two days later, he responded to Carranza's note by criticizing his attacks on the U.S. Army.[27] To avoid further escalation, both sides agreed to a conference to settle differences, which eventually ended the confrontations. However, Pershing and his army remained in Mexico until early 1917.

With little connection to the conflict with Mexico, Congress debated the level of Navy appropriations throughout the spring and again turned its attention to the cost of private ship-armor manufacturing. At this time the public generally sided with the legislature in favor of government facilities.[28] The recommendations of the still-extant congressional Armor Plant Committee of Senator Tillman, Representative Padgett, and Rear Admiral Strauss led the naval committees in both the Senate and House to sponsor legislation establishing a government steel plant.[29] Supporters of the bills claimed that a government factory would halt excessive profit-taking and also reduce militarism, as civilian contractors would lose the incentive to manufacture unneeded warfare matériel. Detractors countered that the legislature was simply shifting the pork from private enterprise to a larger and noncompetitive congressional trough. By the end of its session a solid majority overcame the critics and incorporated the provisions of the armor-manufacturing bill as an amendment to the annual naval act.

The president's plan for the "greatest navy in the world" was a bigger issue than armor manufacturing. The House naval committee, led by Padgett of Tennessee, initially attempted to abandon the five-year shipbuilding program, which the president had declared essential to make the Navy equal to any in the world. By late spring, the House majority opposed adding dreadnoughts to the Navy, preferring instead to reduce appropriations by authorizing fewer battle cruisers as being sufficient.[30] Battle cruisers were a new class of capital ship, larger and faster than dreadnoughts with comparable firepower but with less armor. The Senate naval committee disagreed with their House counterparts and backed the full proposal of the administration's combination of battleships and battle cruisers to command all the seas. In pointed reaction to wartime developments, including the devastating naval battle between Britain and Germany at Jutland on May 31, the Senate also demanded that the Navy's timetable for fleet expansion be accelerated.[31] The House eventually acquiesced to the demands of the upper chamber for both battleships and battle cruisers. Nevertheless, it was a long and substantial fight that continued throughout the spring and summer.

While Congress was still in session, both political parties met in June to select their presidential candidates for the November elections. Republicans held their convention in Chicago and needed to quell the great split between conservatives and progressives that had caused them to lose the campaign of 1912. This time around, antagonists Taft and Roosevelt chose not to run again and joined in solidarity with party luminaries to settle on the candidacy of Charles Evans Hughes, popular associate justice of the Supreme Court and former governor of New York State. Less than a week later, the Democrats met in the friendly territory of St. Louis. With his peace platform, Wilson managed to draw together a majority of isolationists and international activists and was renominated without opposition.

In spite of the summer heat in Washington, Congress continued to convene until September 8. At the end of August it passed, on its own terms, the long-term Naval Appropriations Act of 1916.[32] The act was substantially more ambitious than the five-year plan submitted by Daniels and Wilson to the opening congressional session in December. Instead, the Sixty-fourth Congress authorized a three-year plan for unprecedented growth to make the U.S. Navy number one in the world. Following the prolonged floor debates and conferences, Congress authorized Navy appropriations of $313 million for fiscal year 1917, more than double the record $150 million naval budget of the previous year. The three-year plan provided for the construction of 156 vessels:[33]

Fiscal Yr. 1917:	*Fiscal Yr. 1918:*	*Fiscal Yr. 1919:*	*Total:*
4 battleships	3 battleships	3 battleships	10
4 battle cruisers	1 battle cruiser	1 battle cruiser	6
4 scout cruisers	3 scout cruisers	3 scout cruisers	10
20 destroyers	15 destroyers	15 destroyers	50
30 submarines	18 submarines	19 submarines	67
4 auxiliaries	2 auxiliaries	7 auxiliaries	13
66 total	42 total	48 total	156 total

Prior to Congress' adjournment, congressmen once again scrambled to introduce bills to survey locations in their districts for the approved $11 million government armor plant. To settle the issue, the legislature charged the General Board of the Navy to approve suitable places "with the especial reference to considerations of safety in time of war."[34] For security reasons the board recommended eliminating areas within two hundred miles of the coast. After much congressional logrolling, six months later in March 1917, Daniels used his authority as Secretary of the Navy to select Charleston, West Virginia, for the plant's location. The construction of the armor plate factory remained incomplete when the First World War ended in 1918. Without a wartime priority, and in an environment of reduced shipbuilding, the government armor project was abandoned after Wilson and Daniels left office.[35]

In addition to its three-year plan, Congress authorized the president to increase the enlisted strength of the Navy to 87,000 when in his judgment a sufficient national emergency existed. The legislature also increased the strength of the newly created organization of Navy Reserves, and defined six categories of volunteers who could commit to serve in the Navy during war or emergencies declared by the president.[36] This action significantly bolstered the national reserve force of the Navy, which had been authorized the previous year, without changing the status of the separate active-duty naval militias of the states, which were composed mostly of watermen performing local coastal maritime duties. Much to Wilson's chagrin, Congress did not create a similar national organization of Army reserves. Instead the legislature approved increasing the strength of the existing National Guard, which remained as a state militia. The Navy now could build its own large national reserve force while the Army remained dependent on state-organized minutemen.

Soon after Congress adjourned in September both political parties embarked on the serious business of election campaigning. Wilson began his crusade by moving to a rented estate called Shadow Lawn, in Long Branch, New Jersey, reconnecting with his old Democratic Party friends. He then made reelection speeches from his temporary quarters and on campaign trips.[37] Judge Hughes stumped for his own election across the country, pressing his uncompromising position against Germany's submarine warfare and his firm pro-business stand. The Republican Party held together in the populous northeast and gained some western votes from wary progressives who moved toward the conservative judge. The election was very close, but Wilson survived for another term, primarily on the determining platform of: "He kept us out of war."

Daniels settled back into his Washington office after contributing to the successful election campaign. His very detailed annual report, forwarded to the outgoing lame-duck Congress in December, reiterated and praised all the provisions of the recent Navy act passed in August. He stressed the wellness of the Navy and discussed the challenges that the Navy faced in managing the large surge of shipbuilding in both government and private shipyards. Concurrently, he noted the need for experienced naval officers and praised the development of a national naval reserve force that would be trained and ready for active duty. He recommended a status quo building program for fiscal year 1918 that would continue the second year of the three-year congressional plan.[38]

In the meantime, since his reelection Wilson had totally immersed himself in developing a closely-held peace initiative for the belligerent nations.[39] While continuing with the final touches on his diplomatic endeavor, he delivered a rather detached State of the Union address in person to a joint session of the lame-duck Congress. His relatively short speech covered a few domestic issues, mostly involving ICC railroad regulations and requesting the granting of presidential authority "to control railroad operations in time of war or other public necessity."[40] Beyond that statement, he made no reference to the state of the worldwide war. Less than two weeks later, on December 18, he sent a peace proposal to European capitals and then released the contents of his diplomatic note to the press. The essence of his correspondence concerned the tragedy of war and the proclaimed realization of the belligerents that they had essentially similar objectives. Wilson did not call for a formal peace conference. Rather he simply asked the nations to state their terms for ending the war.[41] The initial national response was virtually universal, praising Wilson's initiative and hopeful that an international conference to end the war would be forthcoming.[42]

However, upon further examination, Wilson's plan was soon questioned by various national leaders. Senator Lodge and Senator William Borah, a well-known isolationist Republican from Idaho, expressed concern that U.S. involvement in a peace process could lead to an unwanted commitment of involvement in any future worldwide conflict. Internationally, Germany stood firm on its a priori proposal for a peace conference before discussing its war objectives. Concurrently, Great Britain and France would not consider participating in a peace conference until Germany agreed to return territory gained by war. U.S. senators pessimistically expressed that neither side would settle on a peace that did not involve military victory.[43] Wilson was sorely disappointed by the impasses preventing peace initiatives. Continuing his labors, he decided in mid-January 1917 to send a note again to the heads of the belligerent nations with a more detailed and hopefully acceptable path toward ending the war. He again kept his new round of diplomacy secret for a few days until the European capitals had time to consider his proposition. Wilson then addressed the Senate on January 22, presenting his notion of an "honorable peace without victory" to end the current crisis and explaining his concept of a future international community organized for common accord.[44]

Notwithstanding his efforts for peace, the war took a decidedly more deadly turn. Throughout the winter, German leaders had been debating the efficacy of resuming unrestricted submarine warfare. They were well apprised of the rise in the number of ships sunk in spite of their recent Sussex Pledge policy. With an increased number of submarines in operation, monthly totals for the second half of 1916 had risen from 163,000 tons in August to 355,000 tons in December. Admiral Henning von Holtzendorff, chief of the German naval staff, predicted that with a change in policy his submarine force could sustain a sinking rate of 600,000 tons per month. This would economically break Britain and bring victory prior to potential U.S. involvement. At a conference in Pless, Prussia, on January 9, Kaiser Wilhelm II and Chancellor Bethmann-Hollweg agreed with their military staff to commence unrestricted submarine warfare effective February 1.[45]

On January 31 the German ambassador to the United States, Johann Heinrich von Bernstorff, delivered to the U.S. secretary of state a formal notification of his empire's new submarine policy. Wilson conferred with his cabinet and on February 3 met with Congress in a joint session to announce his actions. Accordingly, he stated to the legislature that "all diplomatic relations between the United States and the German Empire are severed" and that he had recalled the U.S. ambassador in Germany and expelled the German ambassador in Washington. However, despite the gravity of the situation, Wilson still held out hope in his discourse to the legislature that the German navy would not actually carry out a program to willfully destroy American ships and take American lives.[46]

On February 23 Wilson learned from British intelligence sources of a deciphered telegram sent in January by Germany's recently appointed secretary of foreign affairs, Alfred Zimmerman, to its ambassador in Mexico, Heinrich von Eckhardt. The note declared that Germany was about to begin unrestricted submarine warfare and proposed an alliance with Mexico if the United States did not remain neutral. Zimmerman instructed Eckhardt to inform President Carranza that Germany would give him financial support, and invited Mexico to reconquer its lost territory in New Mexico, Texas, and Arizona. Zimmerman also suggested that Carranza "on his own initiative, should communicate with Japan suggesting adherence with the plan" and "offer to mediate between Germany and Japan."[47] Japan was at the time in the process of sending a destroyer squadron to the Mediterranean in support of the Entente alliance against Germany and Austria. Unrelated to the Zimmerman telegram, the last of the U.S. expedition in Mexico had withdrawn in early February. Carranza did not reply to the telegram and did not contact Japan.

As Germany intensified its undersea *guerre de course* naval warfare, some U.S. merchants reacted by keeping their ships in port, further denying American economic support to Britain, while allied and neutral losses eventually rose to 540,000 tons for the month of February. Prior to its imminent termination, Wilson called another joint session of Congress on February 26 in order to obtain an "immediate assurance of authority" for the possible recourse to "armed neutrality" by supplying merchant ships with defensive arms.[48] A day later Wilson authorized the release of the Zimmerman telegram to a subsequently enraged American public, making it aware of the need to arm U.S. merchant vessels and illuminating the proximity of war with Germany.[49]

The Sixty-fourth Congress adjourned on Sunday, March 4, having approved appropriations for the forty-two vessels previously authorized as part of the second year of the outgoing legislature's three-year plan. Showing its continuing preference for government facilities, it authorized $13 million for the Secretary of the Navy to provide government shipyards with machinery, building ways, and equipment for warship construction. Additionally, it added twenty coastal submarines to be built on the Pacific coast and included a Naval Emergency Fund of $115 million to be used at the discretion of the president for additional destroyers, submarine chasers, other naval small craft, and aircraft.[50] The total naval appropriation of $535 million was 70 percent higher than the record-breaking $313 million authorized by its previous session in August 1916. However, to Wilson's great disappointment, due to a lengthy filibuster by ardent pacifist Sen. Robert La Follette, the legislature did not act on his request for authority to arm U.S. merchant ships.

On the day after Congress dissolved, Wilson gave a relatively brief inaugural address marking the official beginning of his second presidential term. He opened with a paragraph praising recent U.S. economic and industrial reforms and then turned to America's awareness of the nations at war. Although Wilson stated that "we have been deeply wronged upon the seas," he did not call for retaliation. Rather, he stood for peace with armed neutrality as "a more active assertion of our rights." He continued with a high-minded assessment that "all nations are equally interested in the peace of the world and in the political stability of free peoples." Wilson did not identify any international friends or foes and held to his sentiment that all nations must stand together for liberty and justice.[51]

Concerned about the lack of congressional action to implement his policy of armed neutrality at sea, Wilson decided to use his executive authority to put Navy guns and sailors on merchant ships.[52] He also called both houses of the newly formed Congress to meet in special session on April 16. Throughout the month of March, allied shipping losses rose to a new high. This included U.S. merchant ships sunk with the loss of their American crews. Wilson now faced the reality that having U.S. Navy men on merchant ships actually fire on German submarines would in fact be an act of war rather than armed neutrality. He decided on March 21 to upgrade Navy operations at sea by authorizing Daniels to take antisubmarine actions as necessary against German submarines, and called Congress to come to Washington and meet on Monday, April 2, instead of two weeks later that month.[53]

WAR AND THEN PEACE

On Monday evening of the somewhat chaotic opening day of the special session, Wilson addressed both houses of Congress and proclaimed that the conduct of German submarine warfare was in fact war against the people of the

United States. He called for Congress to declare war to bring down the government of Germany and end the worldwide conflict.[54] In order to accomplish this, he requested that the Navy be immediately equipped to deal with German submarines and that the Army be increased to five hundred thousand men. Both houses of the legislature debated the president's address at considerable length for the remainder of the week until noon on Friday, April 6, 1917, when it formally declared war between the United States and Germany.

The die was cast and Wilson would take the lead. Unfortunately, in spite of huge congressional appropriations for warship construction, the Navy was unprepared to contend with German submarines. A year and half previously, in mid-summer 1915, Wilson had expressed deep apprehension concerning the course of German warfare and charged Daniels with organizing a plan to make the U.S. Navy the best in the world. Daniels in turn requested advice from the General Board of the Navy, whose duty since 1900 had consisted of making Navy policy recommendations. With Wilson's approval, Daniels forwarded the board's proposals as an appendix to the Navy's annual report of December 1915. Members of Congress then spent the next several months arguing about the necessary capabilities and quantities of battleships and battle cruisers. Although the German naval fleet had been bottled up in the North Sea since the Battle of Jutland in late May 1916, Congress funded a comprehensive three-year construction plan in September 1916 for capital ships to command the seas. Preparations for antisubmarine warfare remained latent until a month before the United States entered the war in April 1917.

In the absence of a general staff, senior Navy officers performed as fleet commanders and as bureau chiefs with no single leader other than the civilian secretary. Admiral Dewey's position was unique in that he had been rewarded for his great victory in the 1898 Battle of Manila with a permanent non-statutory assignment to lead an advisory General Board of the Navy, which was not the same as being a hands-on chief of staff. Congress and the executive branch always eschewed development of a functional general staff and successfully held off any senior officers' attempts to speak with a single voice. Over the years presidents, secretaries of the Navy, and members of Congress had politely accepted Dewey's policy recommendations and proceeded to reduce, delay, or change them according to their own agendas.

Dewey, however, was not isolated from Navy officer leadership. His three-year proposal of December 1915 spelled out his endorsement of the philosophy of Mahan and the Naval War College, which required control of the seas. In spite of the alarming German submarine successes, Navy thinkers did not challenge Dewey's lack of consideration for antisubmarine-warfare vessels. According to Dewey's report, the submarine was useful as an auxiliary but not an instrument capable of dominating warfare. He stated that fast battle cruisers were well equipped to provide sea lane protection using heavy guns and torpedoes.[55] Congress agreed and scheduled a total of ten battleships and six battle cruisers to be constructed during fiscal years 1917 through 1919.

Upon the U.S. declaration of war, Daniels necessarily put the construction of capital ships on hold and immediately concentrated on the undersea menace. In April 1917, enemy submarines sank 881,000 tons of Allied shipping. American destroyers arrived in western European waters a month later to assist in defensive operations against the submarines. Navy enrollment increased from 66,000 to 497,000 men and women.[56] Under duress, the United States and Britain together developed a successful joint convoy system, using small, fast escorts to protect both troop transports and merchant ships. Within a year, using its emergency fund of $115 million, the Navy had built 355 highly maneuverable 110-foot wooden submarine chasers.[57] As a result, monthly shipping losses due to submarine attacks gradually decreased over the next year and a half to below 100,000 tons per month when the war ended.[58] During that period the British and U.S. navies moved more than two million American soldiers safely across the Atlantic Ocean. The war ended when an exhausted and defeated Germany agreed to stop fighting on November 11, 1918.

Three weeks after the armistice, Daniels submitted his annual report to the president and, in spite of the recent cease-fire, requested a second three-year construction program that duplicated the act of 1916. He recommended adding an additional 156 warships, which included ten battleships and six battle cruisers, to be built during fiscal years 1920 to 1922. President Wilson "earnestly recommended pursuit" of the Navy's plan on December 2, when he gave his annual State of the Union address to Congress.[59] Two days later he departed for France to participate in the war settlement.

In Europe, the president met separately with various heads of state until the conference opened at the Quai D'Orsay, Paris, on January 18, 1919. The first order of business was to "take up the question of the League of Nations."[60] The leaders decided to create a committee to determine penalties for the past acts of war and the level of future international cooperation. Over the course of the next several weeks, members developed the structure of the League charter that included a requirement for members to defend another member under attack. Wilson was aware that, although he could agree to such a treaty while in Paris, final approval required a two-thirds vote of the U.S. Senate.

Wilson came home on February 23 to sign bills by the outgoing Sixty-fifth Congress and proselytize in favor of joining the proposed League of Nations. He spent the next ten days making his case to the public and the legislature that joining the League would not curtail national autonomy.[61] He then called a special session of the incoming Sixty-sixth Congress to meet in April and departed the United States again for four more months of negotiations in Paris. Germany accepted the harsh terms of the Treaty of Versailles and the victorious nations established the League of Nations on June 28, 1919. Wilson signed the treaty and returned to Washington on July 8.

A few days later, the Sixty-sixth Congress, in special session, signed a Navy appropriations act reinstating previously approved funding for six battleships, five battle cruisers, and an assortment of scout cruisers, submarines, and auxiliaries. This was a continuation of the 1916 war-delayed three-year program of 1917–19.[62] At this time Wilson did not bring up his previous support of additional Navy increases and another three-year plan. Rather, he remained fully focused on getting the League of Nations Treaty approved, and strove to convince the new Republican Senate that the United States needed to be a part of the international organization. Senator Lodge, chairman of the Senate Committee on Foreign Relations and a vociferous opponent of the treaty, held his own hearings in relation to the presumed loss of national sovereignty under the League's charter.

Wilson reacted to Lodge's actions by taking his cause to the people and embarking on an exhausting three-week train tour of the nation. After a long speech in Pueblo, New Mexico, on September 25, 1919, he became sick and returned to Washington. Six days later, he suffered a stroke that left him disabled.[63] Although he eventually received visitors he was no longer able to direct governmental affairs or alter the path of the Senate, which finally voted against the Treaty on March 1, 1920. Wilson retained his ineffective presidency until the inauguration of Warren G. Harding.

By the end of 1920 the governments of the United States, Britain, and Japan were at loggerheads over the necessity for continued naval armament. In early March 1921, Senator Borah introduced a resolution to solve the conflict by negotiating arms limitations. However, members of the House naval committee and Navy leaders instead argued that completing the 1916 program could compel disarmament because of the resultant depth of U.S. sea power.[64] In Harding's subsequent inauguration address of March 4, 1921, he disagreed with the Navy and spoke of the need for disarmament by mediation.[65] In July, the White House announced that it was negotiating with the major powers to convene meetings on arms limitations. Commencing on November 12, 1921, representatives gathered in Washington. A group of nations consisting of the United Kingdom, United States, Japan, France, and Italy focused on the ongoing naval arms race in a meeting that became known as the Washington Naval Conference.

Secretary of State Charles Evans Hughes headed the U.S. delegation, which included Senator Lodge, Senate Minority Leader Oscar Underwood, and distinguished former government official Elihu Root. Navy experts who advised the U.S. delegates were Assistant Secretary of the Navy Theodore Roosevelt Jr., Chief of Naval Operations Adm. Robert Coontz, and General Board member Rear Adm. William Pratt.[66] To settle disputes about capabilities, delegates agreed to use tonnage displacement as the measure of a ship. At the close of the conference the United States, Britain, and Japan agreed to retain a ratio of 5:5:3 capital ships. The State Department's maximum figure for U.S. Navy capital ships stood at 500,650 tons. Led by Lodge, the Senate of the Sixty-seventh Congress passed the Washington Naval Treaty on March 29, 1922.[67]

As a result, the United Sates scrapped seventeen operational battleships and thirteen others either contracted or under construction. The U.S. Navy did not become number one, but by being equal to the British navy it had achieved "second to none" status. It would take another war for the United States to build the largest Navy in the world. The reality remains, however, that the Navy's order of battle continues to rest on the appropriation decisions of 435 representatives and 100 senators in the U.S. Congress.

ACKNOWLEDGMENTS

I thank George Baer, Chris Harmon, William Fuller, and John Maurer, my colleagues in the Strategy and Policy Department of the U.S. Naval War College, who encouraged me to pursue further academic involvement in the study of history. Also, I am indebted to the patience and guidance of Michael Barnard, my adviser at Stony Brook University. I thank J. Charles Schencking of the University of Hong Kong for his critical recognition of my Stony Brook work. I also thank Richard McCully of the Center for Legislative Archives for his personal assistance over the course of my many trips from Texas to Washington, D.C., as I prepared this book. I especially appreciate the erudite and unflinching direction of Martha Dawson, Florida Memorial University, throughout the slow process of developing my manuscript.

As ever, I am truly indebted to the corps of professional librarians of my Stony Brook alma mater, the National Archives Center for Legislative Archives, the Library of Congress Manuscript Collections, the New York Public Library, the Massachusetts Historical Society, Bowdoin College, the University of North Carolina, and the University of Houston. I also value the work of the many historians, past and present, who painstakingly put together detailed biographies, which I used in this work. Over the years, this pursuit has sometimes suffered from the slings and arrows of modernity. But without a doubt, the biographer's craft has been invaluable for me in determining my approach and completing my exposition of the political dynamics that developed a modern U.S. Navy.

NOTES

ABBREVIATIONS

ANB—Garraty, John A. and Mark C. Carnes, eds. *American National Biography.* 24 vols. New York: Oxford University Press, 1999.

ARSN—*Annual Report of the Secretary of the Navy:* cites with Congressional session and serial number. The Secretary sent the summary of Navy activity to the president who forwarded it to the House of Representatives, and it is recorded as an H. Ex. Doc. or an H. Doc.

DAB—Malone, Dumas, ed., *Dictionary of American Biography.* 22 vols. New York: Charles Scribner's Sons, 1937.

DAN—Cogar, William B., ed., *Dictionary of Admirals of the U.S. Navy.* 2 vols. Annapolis: Naval Institute Press, 1989.

DANFS—*Dictionary of American Naval Fighting Ships,* online: http://www.haze gray.org/danfs.

LC—Library of Congress, Manuscript Division, Washington, D.C.

Messages of the Presidents—Richardson, James D., ed., *A Compilation of the Messages and Papers of the Presidents.* 10 vols. New York: Bureau of National Literature, 1914.

MHS—Massachusetts Historical Society, Boston.

NA—National Archives, Washington, D.C.

Navy Yearbook 1916—B. R. Tillman Jr., comp. 64th Cong., 2d sess., 1916, S. Doc. 555, serial 7115. Washington, D.C.: Government Printing Office, 1916.

NHHC—Naval History and Heritage Command Photographs, online: http://www.history.navy.mil/our-collections/photography.html.

NYT—*The New York Times.*

Papers of Woodrow Wilson—Peters, Gerhard, and John T. Wooley, comp. The American Presidency Project, http://www.presidency.ucsb.edu/woodrow _wilson.php.

Papers of Warren Harding—Peters, Gerhard, and John T. Wooley, comp. The American Presidency Project. http://www.presidency.ucsb.edu/warren_ harding.php.

Roosevelt Letters—Morison, Elting. *The Letters of Theodore Roosevelt.* 8 vols. Cambridge: Harvard University Press, 1951.

s.v.—(an organizing principle of dictionaries) *sub verbo,* meaning "under the word."

UNCL—University of North Carolina Library, Chapel Hill, NC.

CHAPTER 1. THE FIRST HUNDRED YEARS

1. Paullin, *Paullin's History of Naval Administration,* 91.
2. Ibid., 97 and 113.
3. Ibid., 118.
4. *Messages of the Presidents,* February 10, 1807, 1:407–409.
5. Hagan, *This People's Navy,* 85.
6. Ibid., 89.
7. *DANFS,* s.v., "The 'Old Navy,' Ships of the Line: *'Independence,'*" accessed October 20, 2015, http://www.hazegray.org/danfs.
8. *Messages of the Presidents,* December 7, 1819, 1:631.
9. Hagan, *This People's Navy,* 109; U.S. Navy Ships-Index, NA., s.v., "Early Ships, Sail and Steam Ships, *Mississippi and Missouri,*" accessed October 20, 2015, https://www.archives.gov.
10. Paullin, *Paullin's History of Naval Administration,* 280; Hagan, *This People's Navy,* 163.

CHAPTER 2. A BEGINNING, 1881–82

1. Peskin, *Garfield,* 510–13.
2. Ibid., 17–20.
3. Ibid., 92.
4. *Naval Appropriations Act, U.S. Statutes at Large* 21 (1881): 331–39.
5. Hunt, *The Life of William H. Hunt,* 19.
6. Ibid., 158.
7. Ibid., 116, 135, 151, and 243.

8. Quote of Whitthorne in "House of Representatives," *NYT*, January 25, 1881. Whitthorne also clamored for an expanded merchant marine.

9. An editorial response, expressing a popular opinion that a Navy buildup was not necessary, rebutted an article by Commo. Robert Shufeldt proposing naval increases: "A Plea for the Navy," *NYT*, March 15, 1881.

10. Paullin, *Paullin's History of Naval Administration*, 406; Albion, "The Administration of the Navy," 294.

11. Paullin, *Paullin's History of Naval Administration*, 328; Beers, "The Bureau of Navigation," 12.

12. Peskin, *Garfield*, 575.

13. "Secretary Hunt's Visit," *NYT*, April 15, 1881.

14. *ANB*, s.v., "Morgan, John Tyler."

15. "Naval Academy Exercises," *NYT*, June 11, 1881.

16. Hunt, *The Life of William H. Hunt*, 222; Harold and Margaret Sprout, *The Rise of American Naval Power*, 186–87.

17. Long, *The New American Navy*, 1:17; "A Board of Officers to Consider the Needs of the Navy," *NYT*, July 1, 1881.

18. Reeves, *Gentleman Boss*, 178–82.

19. Ibid., 246–47.

20. The quote and disparaging cartoon from *Puck*, September 14, 1881, is reprinted in Hunt, *The Life of William H. Hunt*, 253.

21. *ARSN*, 47th Cong., 1st sess., H. Ex. Doc. 1, Part 3, November 28, 1881, serial 2016, 37.

22. Ibid., 3.

23. *Messages of the Presidents*, December 6, 1881, 6:4638.

24. One year later, Rep. William H. Calkins (R–IN) recounted on the floor of Congress the story of the Navy's weakness in Chile on January 20, 1883, 47th Cong., 2d sess., Cong. Rec. 14, pt. 2:1404.

25. Howarth, *To Shining Sea: A History of the United States Navy*, 223.

26. Reeves, *Gentleman Boss*, 391–411; *DAB*, s.v., "Frelinghuysen, Frederick Theodore."

27. Thomas (R–IL) argued against Whitthorne (D–TN), George Robeson (R–NJ), Benjamin Harris (R–MA), and Abram Hewitt (D–NY) on January 17, 1882, 47th Cong., 1st sess., Cong. Rec. 13, pt. 1:455–56.

28. Swann, *John Roach: Maritime Entrepreneur*, 159–64.

CHAPTER 3. POLITICS VERSUS PROGRESS, 1882–83

1. Leon Richardson, *William Chandler "Republican,"* 52.

2. Ibid., 185–99.

3. *Senate Journal*, S 689 (January 5, 1882) and *House Journal*, HR 249 (January 9, 1882) and HR 5274 (March 20, 1882), 47th Cong., 1st sess.

4. *House Journal*, HR 4775 (March 2, 1882) and HR 5001 (March 8, 1882), 47th Cong., 1st sess.

5. General correspondence for April–June 1882, especially S.S. Cox to Chandler, April 30, 1882, and J. L. Morris to Chandler, June 15, 1882, Chandler Papers, LC.

6. Boutelle to Chandler, May 30, 1882, Chandler Papers, LC.

7. Wicks, *New Navy and New Empire: The Life and Times of James Grimes Walker*, 52–58 and 65–69; "That Pull of Walker," *NYT*, September 9, 1891. Also see *DAB*, s.v., "Walker, John Grimes."

8. Gorringe, "The Navy," *North American Review* 134 (May 1882): 486–502.

9. Roach to Chandler, June 2, 1882, Chandler Papers, LC. Also see Chandler to S. S. Cox, February 11, 1884, NA, Files of the House Committee on Naval Affairs, RG 233, file 48A-F23.1.

10. *Senate Journal*, S 55 (December 5, 1881) and *House Journal*, HR 1215 (December 16, 1881), 47th Cong., 1st sess.

11. Senators argued to reduce officer accessions on July 27, 1882, 47th Cong., 1st sess., Cong. Rec. 13, pt. 7:6544–48.

12. *Naval Appropriations Act, U.S. Statutes at Large* 22 (1882): 285–86.

13. John Thomas (R–IL) complained of the ambition of younger naval officers on January 20, 1883, 47th Cong., 2d sess., Cong. Rec. 14, pt. 2:1418. Also see "Two Committees at Odds" and "Top Heavy Navy," *NYT*, July 28, 1882.

14. *Naval Appropriations Act, U.S. Statutes at Large* 22 (1882): 291.

15. *DAN*, vol. 1, *1862–1900*, s.v., "Shufeldt, Robert Wilson."

16. Drake, *The Empire of the Seas*, 261 and 307.

17. Leon Richardson, *William Chandler "Republican,"* 289–90.

18. Swann, *John Roach, Marine Entrepreneur*, 171–72.

19. Long, *The New American Navy*, 1:29–30. Also see Leon Richardson, *William Chandler "Republican,"* 290.

20. Reeves, *Gentleman Boss*, 342.

21. *Naval Appropriations Act, U.S. Statutes at Large* 22 (1882): 289–90.

22. Paullin, *Paullin's History of Naval Administration*, 405–6.

23. *Legislative, Executive, and Judicial Act, U.S. Statutes at Large* 22 (1882): 243.

24. Senators argued about the necessity for a civilian assistant secretary on February 4, 1886, 49th Cong., 1st sess., Cong. Rec. 17, pt. 2:1121.

25. Chandler to Frank Hiscock (R–NY), January 16, 1883, entered on January 5, 1887, 49th Cong., 2d sess., Cong. Rec. 18, pt. 1:384–85.

26. *Legislative, Executive, and Judicial Act, U.S. Statutes at Large* 22 (1883): 550.

27. Senator John R. Logan (R–IL), 47th Cong., 2d sess., 1883, Cong. Rec. 14, pt. 4:3278.

28. *Naval Appropriations Act, U.S. Statutes at Large* 22 (1882): 297 and (1883): 481.

29. *ARSN*, 47th Cong., 2d sess., H. Ex. Doc. 1, Part 3, November 29, 1882, serial 2097, 40.

30. Ibid., 54–55.

31. *Naval Appropriations Act, U.S. Statutes at Large* 22 (1883): 477.

32. Swann, *John Roach, Marine Entrepreneur*, 178–82; Leon Richardson, *William Chandler, "Republican,"* 295–296.

33. Reeves, *Gentleman Boss*, 343.

CHAPTER 4. INCUBATION, 1883–85

1. Gleaves, *Life and Letters of Rear Admiral Stephen B. Luce*, 8–9.

2. Ibid., 6–7.

3. Ibid., 57.

4. Herrick, *The American Naval Revolution*, 10 and 21; Howarth, *To Shining Sea: A History of the United States Navy*, 234–35.

5. Gleaves, *Life and Letters of Rear Admiral Steven B. Luce*, 227–28.

6. An unsigned article attributed to Luce criticized Navy management in "Our Naval Policy," *United Service*, May 1882, 501–21. For a summary of the article see Hayes and Hattendorf, eds., *The Writings of Stephen B. Luce*, 189–91.

7. *Report of commission on navy-yards*, 48th Cong., 1st sess., 1883, S. Ex. Doc. 55, serial 2165; extracts entered on June 17, 1886, 49th Cong., 1st sess., Cong. Rec. 17, pt. 6:5833–34.

8. Leon Richardson, *William Chandler "Republican,"* 308–9.

9. *ARSN*, 48th Cong., 1st sess., H. Ex. Doc. 1, December 1, 1883, serial 2188. Chandler repeated his request the following year in *ARSN*, 48th Cong., 2d sess., H. Ex. Doc. 1, December 1, 1884, serial 2284.

10. Chief Engineer Benjamin Isherwood to Chandler, January 21, 1884 and Commodore English, Chief of the Bureau of Equipment, to Chandler, February 6, 1884, in NA, Files of the House Committee on Naval Affairs, RG 233, file HR 48A–F23.1. Calkins (R–IN) supports consolidation and Samuel Randal (D–PA) backs the corps of naval constructors, 48th Cong., 1st sess., 1883, Cong. Rec. 15, pt. 2:1069–74.

11. *House Journal*, HR 3399 (January 14, 1884), 48th Cong., 1st sess. (died in committee).
12. Wicks, *New Navy and New Empire*, 76.
13. Walker to Allison, October 27, 1883, and Informal Memorandum for the Secretary of the Navy, May 13, 1885, Walker Papers, LC.
14. *DAB*, s.v., "Cox, Samuel Sullivan."
15. Cox (D-NY) speaking in favor of a reduced Navy only for defense of the country on March 4, 1884, 48th Cong., 1st sess., Cong. Rec. 15, pt. 2:1592–93.
16. *Messages of the Presidents*, March 20, 1884, 6:4796.
17. Nevins, *Grover Cleveland*, 22–33.
18. Ibid., 177.
19. "An Unfortunate Coincidence," *NYT*, October 20, 1884.
20. *House Journal*, HR 7771 (December 18, 1884), 48th Cong., 2d sess.
21. *Naval Appropriations Act, U.S. Statutes at Large* 23 (1885): 433.
22. Nevins, *Grover Cleveland*, 194–95.
23. *DAB*, s.v., "Whitney, William Collins."
24. Hirsch, *William C. Whitney*, 236, 238–39, 248, 252–55; Herrick, "William C. Whitney," *American Secretaries of the Navy*, 1:405–6.
25. Frank Jones to Whitney, December 15, 1884, Whitney Papers, LC.
26. "The New War Ships," *NYT*, October 6, 1885.
27. Cooling, *Grey Steel and Blue Water Navy*, 36 and 48.
28. William Calhoun to Whitney, April 2 and 21, 1885, Whitney Papers, LC. Also see Hirsch, *William C. Whitney*, 365.
29. "Reform in the Navy Department," *NYT*, August 3, 1885.
30. Nevins, *Grover Cleveland*, 219.

CHAPTER 5. SOME MOVEMENT, 1885–89

1. Leonard White, *The Republican Era*, 50.
2. Statistics compiled from the *Congressional Record* and *House Journals* show naval committee membership.
3. "The Labors of the Speaker," *NYT*, December 15, 1883; "Mr. Carlisle's Troubles," *NYT*, December 18, 1883; "Speaker Carlisle's Work," *NYT*, December 25, 1883.
4. "Senate Committee Changes," *NYT*, December 11, 1883.
5. *House Journal*, Amend Rule XI, 49th Cong., 1st sess., December 9, 1885, 108.
6. Albion, "The Naval Affairs Committees," 1230.

7. Hammett, *Hilary Abner Herbert*, 109. Also see "Mr. Randall," *NYT*, December 28, 1885 and "Ways and Means Committee," *NYT*, January 8, 1886.

8. Woodrow Wilson, *Congressional Government*, 92; Goodwin, *The Little Legislatures*, 8.

9. Hammett, *Hilary Abner Herbert*, 9.

10. Ibid., 28–33.

11. Herbert and Zebulon B. Vance, *Why the Solid South?*, 51–55.

12. *ARSN*, 49th Cong., 1st sess., H. Ex. Doc. 1, November 30, 1885, serial 2376.

13. *Messages of the Presidents*, December 8, 1885, 6:4936.

14. *Senate Journal*, S 672 (December 8, 1885) and Frye (R-ME) speaking about Navy bureau chiefs on December 18, 1885, 49th Cong., 1st sess., Cong. Rec. 17, pt. 1: 2994. Also see "Our Faulty Naval System," *NYT*, December 5, 1885, and "Mr. Frye's Bureau Bills," *NYT*, January 24, 1886.

15. Testimony of February 17, 1886, NA, Files of the House Committee on Naval Affairs, RG 233, file 49A-F24, 1.

16. Walker to Hilary Herbert, February 19, 1886, Walker Papers, LC.

17. *House Journal*, HR 7635, with H. Rep. 1469 (April 6, 1886), serial 2439, 49th Cong., 1st sess. Also see "Bill Consolidates Certain Bureaus," *NYT*, December 13, 1886.

18. Boutelle (R-ME) called for a reading of the minority report supporting the status quo of the bureaus, on January 5, 1887, 49th Cong., 2d sess., Cong. Rec. 18, pt. 1:382–85.

19. Sayers (D-TX), Reed (R-ME), Boutelle (R-ME), and McAdoo (D-NJ) on January 6, 1887, Goff (R-WV), Thomas (R-IL), and Lore (D-DE) on January 8, 1887, 49th Cong., 2d sess., Cong. Rec. 18, pt. 1:406–20, 462–64, and 470–72.

20. Reed (R-ME) on January 31, 1887, 49th Cong., 2d sess., Cong. Rec. 18, pt. 2:1216–17.

21. Herbert (D-AL) and McAdoo (D-NJ) on June 17, 1886, 49th Cong., 1st sess., Cong. Rec. 17, pt. 6:5832–36.

22. Paullin, *Paullin's History of Naval Administration*, 380.

23. Nevins, *Grover Cleveland*, 199.

24. Ibid., 304.

25. *Naval Establishment Act, U.S. Statutes at Large* 24 (1886): 215.

26. *ARSN*, 49th Cong. 2d sess., H. Ex. Doc. 1, December 1, 1886, serial, 2466.

27. *Naval Appropriations Act, U.S. Statutes at Large* 24 (1887): 592.

28. *Naval Appropriations Act, U.S. Statutes at Large* 22 (1883): 474.

29. *Report of Gun Foundry Board*, 48th Cong., 1st sess., 1883, H. Ex. Doc. 97, serial 2204; *Report of Gun Foundry Board, supplement*, 48th Cong. 2d sess., 1884, S. Ex. Doc. 13, serial 2261.

30. *ARSN*, 50th Cong., 1st sess., H. Ex. Doc. 1, December 6, 1887, x–xi, serial 2539.

31. Ibid., xvi.

32. "Republican Senators and Committees," *NYT*, December 8, 1887.

33. *Senate Journal*, S 1428 (January 13, 1888) with S. Rep. 233 (February 13, 1888), serial 2519, and *House Journal*, HR 5024 (January 16, 1888), HR 5702 (January 23, 1888), and HR 7314 (February 16, 1888) with H. Rep. 531, serial 2599, 50th Cong., 1st sess.

34. *DAB*, s.v., "Thurman, Allen Granberry."

35. *ANB*, s.v., "Quay, Matthew Stanley."

36. Nevins, *Grover Cleveland*, 415–16.

37. *Naval Appropriations Act, U.S. Statutes at Large* 25 (1888): 472 and 463. Congress authorized $20,000 for expenses for the two commissions.

38. Calhoun, *Benjamin Harrison*, 13.

39. Ibid., 21.

40. *ARSN*, 50th Cong., 2d sess., H. Ex. Doc. 1, December 1, 1888, serial 2634.

41. *Naval Appropriations Act, U.S. Statutes at Large* 25 (1889): 808.

42. *DANFS*, s.v., "*Texas*-I" (second-class battleship) and "*Maine*-I" (second-class battleship), accessed October 20, 2015, http://www.hazegray.org/danfs.

CHAPTER 6. A TURNING POINT, 1889–93

1. Cooling, *Benjamin Franklin Tracy*, 4–5 and 8–9.

2. Ibid., 20–22.

3. Gillespie, *Andersonvilles of the North*, 199–200 and 203–210.

4. Cooling, *Benjamin Franklin Tracy*, 38 and 160.

5. Ibid., 44 and 66.

6. *Messages of the Presidents*, March 4, 1889, 7:5445 and 5447.

7. Roosevelt to Charles Bonaparte, May 14, 1889, *Roosevelt Letters*, 1:161 and 161n.

8. Cooling, *Benjamin Franklin Tracy*, 63–64.

9. Long, *The New American Navy*, 1:121.

10. Navy Department General Order 372, June 1889; "Secretary Tracy's Orders," *NYT*, June 28, 1889; "The Navy Bureaus," *NYT*, July 12, 1889.

11. Stephen B. Luce, "Our Future Navy," *North American Review* CXLIX, July 1889.

12. *ARSN*, 51st Cong., 1st sess., H. Ex. Doc. 1, November 30, 1889, serial 2721; *Messages of the Presidents*, December 3, 1889, 7:5479.

13. *DAN*, s.v., "Mahan, Alfred Thayer;" NavSource Naval History, s.v., "Old Navy, Steam and Sail, *Wachusett*-I," accessed October 20, 2015, http://www .navsource.org.

14. *Senate Journal*, S 538 (December 5, 1889), 51st Cong., 1st sess.; Cooling, *Benjamin Franklin Tracy*, 80.

15. Chandler (R-NH) and others spoke against Navy officer lobbies on December 19, 1889, 51st Cong., 1st sess., Cong. Rec. 21, pt.1:300.

16. *Secretary of the Navy Letter*, March 19, 1890, 51st Cong., 1st sess., Cong. Rec. 21, pt. 3:2373–74. Also see "Organizations Among Naval Officers," *NYT*, March 21, 1890.

17. *House Journal*, HR 428 (December 18, 1889), 51st Cong., 1st sess. Also see "The Cowie Bill," *NYT*, November 15, 1889.

18. "Report of the Policy Board," U.S. Naval Institute *Proceedings* 16 (1890): 207–73.

19. Cooling, *Benjamin Franklin Tracy*, 83.

20. *Assistant Secretary of War, U.S. Statutes at Large* 26 (1890): 17.

21. *Legislative, Executive, and Judicial Appropriations Act, U.S. Statues at Large* 26 (1890): 254.

22. McPherson (D-NJ) criticized the policy board on May 22, 1890, 51st Cong. 1st sess., Cong. Rec. 20, pt. 2:5138–5139.

23. *Naval Appropriations Act, U.S. Statutes at Large* 26 (1890): 204.

24. Luce to Secretary of the Navy Tracy, July 7, 1890, Tracy Papers, LC.

25. *ARSN*, 51st Cong., 2d sess., H. Ex. Doc. 1, November 26, 1890, serial 2838.

26. *Messages of the Presidents*, December 1, 1890, 7:5551–5552.

27. *House Journal*, HR 8794 (March 29, 1890) and HR 9286 (April 12, 1890), 51st Cong., 1st sess.

28. *Senate Journal*, S 2664, with S. Rep. 1864 (December 12, 1890), serial 2826, 51st Cong., 2d sess.

29. *Naval Appropriations Act, U.S. Statutes at Large* 26 (1891): 814–15.

30. "To Reorganize the Navy," *NYT*, October 3, 1891.

31. Cooling, *Benjamin Franklin Tracy*, 118.

32. *ARSN*, 52d Cong., 1st sess., H. Ex. Doc. 1, December 3, 1891, serial 2931.

33. Commander Davis to Senator Hale, March 29, 1892, NA, Files of the Senate Committee on Naval Affairs, RG 46, file 52A-F17.

34. *Senate Journal*, S 2664 (March 22, 1892) and *House Journal*, HR 7683 (March 29, 1892), HR 8980 (May 25, 1892), 52d Cong., 1st sess.

35. *Senate Journal*, S 2667 (March 22, 1892), with S. Rep. 481, serial 2913 and *House Journal*, HR 9515 (July 12, 1892), 52d Cong., 1st sess.

36. Holman (D-IN), Simpson (P-KS), Watson (P-GA), and McMillin (D-TN) speak against increases on April 30, 1892, 52d Cong., 1st sess., Cong. Rec. 23, pt. 4:3710, 3800 and 3801.

37. *Naval Appropriations Act, U.S. Statutes at Large* 27 (1892): 251.

38. *ARSN*, 52d Cong., 2d sess., H. Ex. Doc. 1, December 1, 1892, serial 2931.

39. *Messages of the Presidents*, December 6, 1892, 7:5744.

40. *Navy Engineer Corps Act, U.S. Statutes at Large* 27 (1892): 405.

41. *Naval Appropriations Act, U.S. Statutes at Large* 27 (1893): 717 and 731.

CHAPTER 7. REASONABLE PROGRESS, 1893–97

1. Herrick, "Hilary A. Herbert," *American Secretaries of the Navy*, 1:425.

2. *Messages of the Presidents*, March 4, 1893, 8:5821–25.

3. Hammett, *Hilary Abner Herbert*, 147.

4. Nevins, *Grover Cleveland*, 515–16; *Grandfather's Talks About His Life Under Two Flags*, 316–18, Herbert Papers, UNCL, Chapel Hill, N.C.

5. "Two Cabinet Assistants," *NYT*, March 16, 1893.

6. Hammett, *Hilary Abner Herbert*, 151–52.

7. "The Lesson of the Naval Review," *The North American Review* 156 (June 1893): 644.

8. Nevins, *Grover Cleveland*, 528–29.

9. *ARSN*, 53rd Cong., 2d sess., H. Ex. Doc. 1, November 18, 1893, serial 3207.

10. *Messages of the Presidents*, December 4, 1893, 8:5875.

11. *Senate Journal*, S 1564 (February 4, 1894) with S. Misc. Doc. 76 (September 6, 1894), serial 3167, 53rd Cong., 2d sess.

12. *Senate Journal*, S 276 (August 14, 1893) and *House Journal*, HR 162 (September 6, 1893), HR 3462 (September 25, 1893), 53rd Cong., 1st sess.

13. *Resolution to form joint committee to reorganize the personnel of the Navy*, H. Misc. Doc. 39, December 13, 1893, 53rd Cong., 1st sess., Cong. Rec. 26, pt. 1:209, serial 3151.

14. Cummings (D-NY), Boutelle (R-ME), and Baker (P-KS) on May 11, 1894, 53rd Cong., 2d sess., Cong. Rec. 26, pt. 5:4508, 4621–29.

15. *Naval Appropriations Act, U.S. Statutes at Large* 28 (1894): 140.

16. Paymaster Gen. James Fulton to Herbert, March 7, 1888, NA, Files of the House Committee on Naval Affairs, RG 233, file 50A-F16. Also see "Our Well Managed Navy," *NYT*, November 21, 1894.

17. *Naval Appropriations Act, U.S. Statutes at Large* 28 (1894): 132.
18. Wicks, *New Navy and New Empire*, 76.
19. William McAdoo, "Reorganization of the Personnel of the Navy," 457–66.
20. *Senate Journal*, S 1564 (February 5, 1894) and *House Journal*, HR 8045 (August 28, 1894), 53rd Cong., 2d sess.
21. "Hichborn Will Be in Control," *NYT*, October 13, 1894.
22. *ARSN*, 53rd Cong., 3rd sess., 1894, H. Ex. Doc. 1, November 17, 1894, serial 3303.
23. *Messages of the Presidents*, December 3, 1895, 8:5972–73.
24. Nevins, *Grover Cleveland*, 663.
25. *House Journal*, HR 8476, with Rep. 1573, 53rd Cong., 3rd sess., January 12, 1895, serial 3345.
26. Hammett, *Hilary Abner Herbert*, 175–76.
27. *Naval Appropriations Act, U.S. Statutes at Large* 28 (1895): 842.
28. *ARSN*, 54th Cong., 1st sess., H. Doc. 3, November 27, 1895, serial 3379.
29. *Messages of the Presidents*, December 2, 1895, 8:6058–87.
30. Ibid., 8:6090.
31. Brodsky, *Grover Cleveland*, 373.
32. *Senate Journal*, S 735 (December 10, 1895), and *House Journal*, HR 3618 (January 10, 1896), 54th Cong., 1st sess.; Herbert to Senator Cameron, January 30, 1896, NA, Files of the Senate Committee on Naval Affairs, RG 46, file 54A-F19.
33. *Naval Appropriations Act, U.S. Statutes at Large* 29 (1896): 378.
34. Hammett, *Hilary Abner Herbert*, 179.
35. *ARSN*, 54th Cong., 2d sess., 1896, H. Doc. 3, December 2, 1896, serial 3486.
36. *Messages of the Presidents*, December 7, 1896, 8:6146–77.
37. *House Journal*, HR 10135 (January 27, 1897), 54th Cong., 2d sess. Also see "Naval Personnel Legislation," *Army and Navy Journal* 34 (December 12, 1896): 253.
38. *Naval Appropriations Act, U.S. Statutes at Large* 29 (1897): 665.

Chapter 8. War and Imperialism, 1897–99

1. Morgan, *William McKinley and His America*, 9.
2. Ibid., 7.
3. Ibid., 195.
4. Coletta, "John Davis Long," *American Secretaries of the Navy*, 1:431–32

5. Leonard White, *The Republican Era,* 166.

6. *Messages of the Presidents,* March 4, 1897, 8:6236.

7. Roosevelt to Bellamy and to Maria Storer, August 10, 1896, and December 5, 1896, *Roosevelt Letters,* 1:556 and 569; Roosevelt to Henry Cabot Lodge, December 4, 1896, March 19, 1896, and March 29, 1898, *Roosevelt Letters,* 1:567, 585, and 590.

8. Quote from Mrs. Bellamy Storer, "How Theodore Roosevelt Was Appointed Assistant Secretary of the Navy," *Harper's Weekly* 66 (June 1, 1912): 8–9.

9. Proctor to McKinley, March 23, 1897, Long Papers, MHS; Roosevelt to Lodge, March 23, 1897, *Roosevelt Letters,* 1:590.

10. "Secretary Long," *Army and Navy Journal* 34 (April 10, 1897): 579–80.

11. "Navy Yard Investigation," *NYT,* May 13, 1897; "Roosevelt on Hand Early," *NYT,* May 14, 1897; "Roosevelt's Second Day," *NYT,* May 15, 1897.

12. "Roosevelt on the Navy Yard," *NYT,* May 18, 1897.

13. Morgan, *William McKinley and His America,* 213.

14. Ira Hollis, "A New Organization for the Navy," *The Atlantic Monthly* 80 (September 1897): 309–19.

15. *ARSN,* 55th Cong., 2d sess., H. Doc. 3, November 15, 1897, serial 3638.

16. *Messages of the Presidents,* December 6, 1897, 8:6251.

17. *Report of Assistant Secretary of Navy on proposed personnel bill,* 55th Cong., 2d sess., 1897, S. Doc. 97, serial 3593. Also see Roosevelt to Long, December 9, 1897, *Roosevelt Letters,* 1:726.

18. *Senate Journal,* S 3404 (January 26, 1898) and *House Journal,* HR 7443 (January 29, 1898), replaced by HR 10403 (May 19, 1898) with H. Rep. 1375, 55th Cong., 2d sess.

19. Trask, *The War with Spain,* 9.

20. *House Journal,* HR 8348 (February 18, 1898), 55th Cong., 2d sess.

21. Roosevelt to Dewey, February 25, 1898, *Roosevelt Letters,* 1:784.

22. *An Act making appropriations to supply urgent deficiencies, U.S. Statutes at Large* 30 (1898): 273; Morgan, *William McKinley and His America,* 275. Also see "A Great Peace Measure," *NYT,* March 8, 1898.

23. Trask, *The War with Spain,* 82.

24. *Messages of the Presidents,* March 28, 1898, 8:6277–80.

25. Ibid., April 11, 1898, 8:6281–93.

26. Ibid., April 25, 1898, 8:6296–98; *An Act declaring that war exists between the United States of America and the Kingdom of Spain, U.S. Statutes at Large* 30 (1898): 364.

27. Morgan, *William McKinley and His America*, 289.

28. Ibid., 293.

29. *Naval Appropriations Act, U.S. Statutes at Large* 30 (1898): 389–90.

30. Roosevelt to Long, May 6, 1898, *Roosevelt Letters*, 2:825.

31. Ibid., 2:820n.

32. Roosevelt to Paul Dana, April 18, 1898, *Roosevelt Letters*, 2:816.

33. Mahan to Long, May 10, 1898, in Seager and Maguire, *Letters and Papers of Alfred Thayer Mahan*, 2:551–52.

34. Lodge to Rear Admiral Luce, May 27, 1898, in Gleaves, *Life and Letters of Stephen B. Luce*, 235.

35. "Rear Adm. J. C. Walker," *Army and Navy Journal* 35, April 23, 1898; Rear Adm. French Chadwick to Long, April 30, 1898, Long Papers, MHS.

36. Long to Henry Bingham, April 26, 1898, and Long to Senator Redfield Proctor, April 28, 1898, Long Papers, MHS.

37. Long to Senator Elkins, April 30, 1898, Long Papers, MHS.

38. Long to Allen, May 4, 1898, Allen to Long, two letters, May 5, 1898, Long Papers, MHS.

39. Trask, *The War with Spain*, 115–16.

40. Ibid., 156.

41. Ibid., 162.

42. Ibid., 385.

43. Morgan, *William McKinley and His America*, 296.

44. Strait, *Alphabetical List of Battles*, 180.

45. Long, *The New American Navy*, 2:1–50.

46. Morgan, *William McKinley and His America*, 299.

47. Phillips, *William McKinley*, 98.

48. Morgan, *William McKinley and His America*, 301.

49. Strait, *Alphabetical List of Battles*, 188.

50. Trask, *The War with Spain*, 385–86.

51. Strait, *Alphabetical List of Battles*, 177.

52. "Report of the Naval War Board of 1898," Mahan to Adm. George Dewey, October 26, 1906, Mahan Papers, Naval Historical Foundation Collection, Manuscript Division, LC.

53. Phillips, *William McKinley*, 100.

54. *ARSN*, 55th Cong., 3rd sess., H. Doc. 3, November 15, 1898, serial 3753.

55. *Messages of the Presidents*, December 5, 1898, 8:6344–45.

56. Morgan, *William McKinley and His America*, 317.

CHAPTER 9. REORGANIZATION AND GROWTH, 1899–1901

1. Crowninshield to Long, NA, January 7, 1899, Files of the House Committee on Naval Affairs, RG 233, file 55A.F26.5.

2. For Crowninshield's presumed importance see "The New Secretary of the Navy," *Army and Navy Journal* 34, (April 24, 1897): 623. For his influence see Platt to Tracy, December 23, 1890, January 15, 1891, and June 18, 1891, Tracy papers, LC.

3. *Navy Personnel Bill* on January 13, 1899 and January 17, 1899, 55th Cong., 3rd sess., Cong. Rec. 32, pt. 1:657–73 and pt. 1:706–725.

4. *Personnel of the Navy and Marine Corps*, February 17, 1899, 55th Cong., 3rd sess., Cong. Rec. 32, pt. 2:1969–82.

5. *Naval Personnel Act, U.S. Statutes at Large* 30 (1899): 1004–1009.

6. Skocpol, *Protecting Soldiers and Mothers*, 151.

7. Hollis, "A New Organization for the Navy," *Atlantic Monthly* 80 (September 1897): 318–19.

8. *Roosevelt Letters*, 1:617n.

9. *Senate Journal*, S 4972 (December 12, 1899), 55th Cong., 3rd sess.; Park Benjamin, "The National Naval Reserve Bill," *The Independent* 46, January 19, 1899, 183–86. Also see Roosevelt's discussion of the dangers of having makeshift Navy crews, "Military Preparedness and Unpreparedness," *Century Magazine*, November 1899, 183–86.

10. *Naval Appropriations Act, U.S. Statutes at Large* 30 (1898): 1045.

11. "Navy Supply Bill Passes," *NYT*, March 2, 1899; "Armor Plate in Congress," *NYT*, March 3, 1899.

12. "Platt Praises McKinley," *NYT*, May 25, 1899.

13. *ARSN*, 56th Cong., 1st sess., H. Doc. 3, November 22, 1899, serial 3912.

14. *Messages of the Presidents*, December 5, 1899, 8:6386 and 6393.

15. Long, *The New American Navy*, 1:122 and 2:183.

16. Taylor to Long, January 30, 1900, Long Papers, MHS; "Memorandum, on General Staff for the Navy," U.S. Naval Institute *Proceedings* 95 (Sept. 1900): 441–48.

17. *House Journal*, HR 117 (December 4, 1899), 56th Cong., 1st sess.; "Immediate Naval Needs," *Forum*, April 1900, 161–70.

18. *House Journal*, HR 12126 (June 5, 1890), 56th Cong., 1st sess. Many petitions favoring reserves from the American Association of Masters and Pilots of Steam Vessels are bundled in Files of the Senate Committee on Naval Affairs, RG 46, file SEN 56A-F26.6.

19. *Dry Dock Act, U.S. Statutes at Large* 31 (1900): 1; *Naval Appropriations Act, U.S. Statutes At Large* 31 (1900): 706.

20. Underwood (D-AL), Charles Wheeler (D-KY), William Kitchin (D-NC), and William Vandiver (D-MO), April 16, 1900, 56th Cong., 1st sess., Cong. Rec. 33, pt. 5, 4226, 4256, 4321–22, and 4338–39.

21. Testimony of Secretary Long, April 16, 1900, 56th Cong., 1st sess., Cong. Rec. 33, pt. 5:4230.

22. *Naval Appropriations Act, U.S. Statutes at Large* 31 (1900): 706–7.

23. Morgan, *William McKinley and His America*, 358–360.

24. *ARSN*, 56th Cong., 2d sess., H. Doc. 3, November 17, 1900, serial 4098.

25. *Messages of the Presidents*, December 13, 1900, 8:6452.

26. *House Journal*, HR 13103 (January 3, 1901), 56th Cong., 2d sess. Also see the Navy amendment in Long to George Foss, December 24, 1900, NA, Files of House Committee on Naval Affairs, RG 233, file HR 56A-F26.6.

27. "Plan for A Naval Reserve," *NYT*, December 5, 1900.

28. *Senate Journal*, S 5111 (December 10, 1900), with S. Doc. 33, serial 4029, 56th Cong., 2d sess.

29. *Naval Appropriations Act, U.S. Statutes at Large* 31 (1901): 1132–33.

30. *Messages of the Presidents*, March 4, 1901, 8:6465–69.

31. Morgan, *William McKinley and His America*, 392.

32. Ibid., 393.

33. Miller, *Theodore Roosevelt: A Life*, 349.

34. Morris, *Theodore Rex*, 7.

35. Ibid., 13–14. Roosevelt's first inaugural address is not contained in *Messages of the Presidents*, but is quoted in several other sources.

36. Miller, *Theodore Roosevelt: A Life*, 163.

37. Morris, *Theodore Rex*, 55.

38. *Messages of the Presidents*, December 3, 1901, 8:6639–78.

39. Ibid., 8:6663.

40. *ARSN*, 57th Cong., 1st sess., 1901, H. Doc. 3, November 4, 1901, serial 4286.

41. *House Journal*, H. 5834 (December 13, 1901) and *Senate Journal*, S 1947, S. 2824 with S. Doc. 122, serial 4230, and S. 2825, 57th Cong., 1st sess., 1901.

42. The regular Navy showed indifference to naval militias and reserves: "Is the Naval Militia to Go," *NYT*, January 6, 1902, and "Naval Reserves and Naval Militia," *NYT*, January 20, 1902.

CHAPTER 10. AN OFFENSIVE NAVY, 1902–5

1. Morris, *Theodore Rex*, 83.
2. Ibid., 103–4.
3. Paul Heffron, "William H. Moody," *American Secretaries of the Navy*, 1:461–62.
4. *Naval Appropriations Act, U.S. Statutes at Large* 32 (1902): 691.
5. "Republicans Rebel on the Naval Bill," *NYT*, May 20, 1902.
6. Rappaport, "Certification of Incorporation," *The Navy League of the United States*, 213.
7. James Terry White, ed., *National Cyclopedia of American Biography*, s.v., "Satterlee, Herbert Livingston."
8. "For National Navy League," *NYT*, November 6, 1902.
9. *ARSN*, 57th Cong., 2d sess., H. Doc. 3, November 19, 1902, serial 4455.
10. *Messages of the Presidents*, December 2, 1902, 8:6762.
11. Roosevelt first used the proverb in January 1900 according to Miller, *Theodore Roosevelt: A Life*, 337. Also see Roosevelt to Henry L. Sprague, January 26, 1900, *Roosevelt Letters*, 2:1141.
12. Baer, *One Hundred Years of Sea Power*, 36–40.
13. *Naval Appropriations Act, U.S. Statutes at Large* 32 (1903): 1197 and 1202.
14. *House Journal*, HR 16875 and HR 16876 (January 19, 1903), 57th Cong., 2d sess.
15. *An act to promote the efficiency of the militia, U.S. Statutes at Large* 32 (1903): 775. For development of the Militia Act of 1903 see Skowronek, *Building a New American State*, 216–18.
16. Coetzee, *For Party or Country*, 28–37.
17. "A Good Thing: 'Push it Along'," *The Bookman* 17, April 1903, 129. Also see Herwig, *"Luxury" Fleet*, 40–41.
18. Carlos de Zafra, "The Needed Increase of Our Navy," *Scientific American* 88 (February 7, 1903): 95.
19. Morris, *Theodore Rex*, 275.
20. *Messages of the Presidents*, November 10, 1903, 8:6781.
21. *Messages of the Presidents*, December 7, 1903, 9:6880; *ARSN*, 58th Cong., 2d sess., H. Doc. 3, November 23, 1903, serial 4642.
22. *ANB*, s.v., "Cannon, Joseph Gurney"; "Scandals May Affect the House Committees," *NYT*, November 29, 1903; and "Shake-Up in the House," *NYT*, December 9, 1903.
23. *ANB*, s.v., "Frye, William Pierce."

24. *ANB*, s.v., "Hale, Eugene."

25. Morris, *Theodore Rex*, 311.

26. Evans and Peattie, *Kaigun*, 95–105.

27. *Naval Appropriations Act, U.S. Statutes at Large* 33 (1904): 350–51.

28. *House Journal*, HR 10137 and HR 10138 (January 18, 1904), 58th Cong., 2d sess.

29. *An act to provide for the temporary government of the Canal Zone at Panama, the protection of the canal works, and for other purposes, U.S. Statutes at Large* 33 (1904): 429.

30. Roosevelt to Taft, May 9, 1904, *Roosevelt Letters*, 4:786.

31. Paul Heffron, "William H. Moody," *American Secretaries of the Navy*, 1:469–73.

32. Roosevelt to Morton, June 25, 1904, *Roosevelt Letters*, 4:847.

33. *ARSN*, 58th Cong., 3rd sess., H. Doc. 3, November 23, 1904, serial 4795.

34. *Messages of the Presidents*, 9:7053–56.

35. *Roosevelt Letters*, 4:1081n.

36. Roosevelt to Nicholas Murray Butler, December 2, 1904 and December 9, 1904, *Roosevelt Letters*, 4:1055 and 1062.

37. Roosevelt to Meyer, December 26, 1904, *Roosevelt Letters*, 4:1078.

38. Roosevelt to Foss, January 10 and 13, 1905, and to Cannon, January 13, 1905, *Roosevelt Letters*, 4:1097 and 1101.

39. *Naval Appropriations Act, U.S. Statutes at Large* 33 (1905): 1116.

40. *Navy Yearbook 1916*, 618–620, and also in the individual naval appropriation acts of 1898–1905.

41. *House Journal*, H. 10137 with H. Rep. 3148 (December 21, 1904), 58th Cong., 3rd sess., serial 4760.

42. *Army Appropriations Act, U.S. Statutes at Large* 32 (1903): 942; *Navy Yearbook 1916*, 547.

43. Morris, *Theodore Rex*, 380.

44. Roosevelt to Taft and to Hermann Speck von Sternburg, April 20, 1905; to Taft, April 27, 1905; and to Hay, May 6, 1905, *Roosevelt Letters*, 4:1161, 1165, 1167, and 1168.

45. Evans and Peattie, *Kaigun*, 124.

46. Roosevelt to Lodge, June 5, 1905, *Roosevelt Letters*, 4:1202.

47. Roosevelt to Joseph Bucklin Bishop, June 15, 1905, *Roosevelt Letters*, 4:1219.

48. Bishop, *Charles Joseph Bonaparte*, 95–96.

49. Roosevelt to Bonaparte, August 1, 1905, *Roosevelt Letters*, 4:1294.

50. Bonaparte to Roosevelt, August 2, 1905, Bonaparte Papers, LC.

51. *ARSN*, 59th Cong., 1st sess., H. Doc. 3, December 4, 1905, serial 4956.

52. Morris, *Theodore Rex*, 417.
53. *Messages of the Presidents*, December 5, 1905, 9:7371.
54. Ibid., 7382.

CHAPTER 11. POWER PROJECTED, 1905–9

1. *House Journal*, HR 10858 (January 8, 1906) with Rep. 2680 (March 28, 1906), serial 4907, and HR 17626, 59th Cong., 1st sess.
2. "Coal Economy in Navy: Congress delays Action," *NYT*, February 26, 1906; "House Members Angry Over Navy Complaints," *NYT*, February 27, 1906.
3. *An Act Making appropriations to supply deficiencies, U.S. Statutes at Large* 34 (1906): 634.
4. Roosevelt to Bonaparte, December 20, 1905, *Roosevelt Letters*, 5:121.
5. *Naval Appropriations Act, U.S. Statutes at Large* 34 (1906): 554.
6. Roosevelt to Kaneko, October 26, 1906, *Roosevelt Letters*, 5:473.
7. Roosevelt wrote a "strictly private" letter to Hale crediting him as being the most influential man in the Senate. Roosevelt to Hale, October 27, 1906, *Roosevelt Letters*, 5:473.
8. *ARSN*, 59th Cong., 2d sess., H. Doc. 3, November 28, 1906, serial 5115.
9. *Messages of the Presidents*, December 3, 1906, 9:7447.
10. Morris, *Theodore Rex*, 473; Roosevelt to Kermit Roosevelt, December 5, 1906, *Roosevelt Letters*, 5:520n1, 5:521.
11. S 529, 59th Cong., 2d sess., Cong. Rec., pt. 4:4000–4378 and 4430–4653.
12. *Naval Appropriations Act, U.S. Statutes at Large* 34 (1907): 1203; *Navy Yearbook 1916*, 581.
13. Various unions sent many petitions to Congress asking for work in government yards, NA, RG 233, file HR 60A-F38.
14. Calvin Davis, *The United States and the Second Hague Peace Conference*. The failure to limit arms is detailed throughout.
15. *Messages of the Presidents*, 9:7494, December 3, 1907.
16. Roosevelt to Lodge, October 1, 1906, *Roosevelt Letters*, 5:437.
17. Morris, *Theodore Rex*, 467; *Roosevelt Letters*, 5:489n1.
18. Henry and Margaret Sprout, *The Rise of American Naval Power*, 264–70.
19. Rixey to Metcalf, November 6, 1907, and Brownson to Metcalf, November 18, 1907, in House, 60th Cong., 1st sess., 1908, H. Doc. 552, 17 and 21, serial 5375.
20. Roosevelt to Hart Lyman, editor-in-chief of the *New York Tribune*, December 26, 1907; Roosevelt to Metcalf, January 2, 1908, *Roosevelt Letters*, 6:876

and 891; Mahan to Luce, January 27, 1908, Seager and Maguire, *Letters and Papers of Alfred Thayer Mahan*, 3:236; also see Rear Adm. Chauncey Thomas in Reckner, *Teddy Roosevelt's Great White Fleet*, 66–67.

21. H. Res. 120, 60th Cong., 1st sess., January 7, 1908.

22. NavSource Naval History, s.v., "Auxiliaries & Service Ships, AH 1 *Relief*," accessed October 20, 2015, http://www. navsource.org.

23. "Attacks on Navy Called Groundless," *NYT*, December 22, 1907, and "Unharmonious Working of Separate Bureaus," *NYT*, December 29, 1907.

24. Harold and Margaret Sprout, *The Rise of the American Navy*, 277–78.

25. Henry Reuterdahl, "The Needs of Our Navy," *McClure's Magazine* 30 (January 1908): 251–63; "The Reuterdahl Attack on the Navy," *Scientific American* 98 (January 18, 1908): 38–39; Benjamin Baker, "The Needs of Our Navy," *McClure's Magazine* 30 (February 1908): 517–20; "The Navy' and Naval Criticism," *Scientific American* 98 (February 22, 1908):122.

26. "Sims Causes Strife By Criticizing Navy," *NYT*, March 3, 1908, and "15 Naval Men to Testify," *NYT*, March 8, 1908.

27. Reckner, *Teddy Roosevelt's Great White Fleet*, 21.

28. *House Journal*, HR 245, HR 526, HR 3902, HR 6146, HR 6212, HR 6230, HR 10570, and HR 11813, 60th Cong., 1st sess.

29. Ibid., 9–12.

30. *Reduction in Skilled Labor Force in Navy Yards*, 60th Cong., 1st sess., H. Doc. 710, February 22, 1908, serial 5377.

31. Members argued over appropriation provisions of HR 20471, 60th Cong., 1st sess., Cong. Rec. 42, pt. 5:4604 and 4789.

32. Several members presented extensive arguments concerning HR 20471 in April 1908, 60th Cong., 1st sess., Cong. Rec.42, pt. 5:4581, 4596, 4598, 4606, 4647, 4779, 4790, 4799, 4800, 4801, and 4802.

33. *Messages of the Presidents*, April 14, 1908, 9:7528.

34. On the floor of the House of Representatives, William Willet (D-NY) quoted Roosevelt and then apologized for Roosevelt's gaffe, 60th Cong., 1st sess., Cong. Rec. 42, pt. 5:4801.

35. "Only Two Battleships" and "The President's Defeat," *The Independent* 64, April 23, 1908, 887–88 and 927–28; "The Controversy over the Battleships," *The Nation* 86, April 23, 1908, 368; "The Progress of the World: Shall We Maintain the Navy?," *The American Review of Reviews* 37, May 1908, 515–21.

36. *Naval Appropriations Act, U.S. Statues at Large* 35: 127. Appropriations increased from $100 million to almost $123 million. *Navy Yearbook 1916*, 581.

37. The public building bill is "scandalous" in "Where the Money Goes," *The American Review of Reviews* 37, May 1908, 518; Senate dominance and patronage in the Navy budget is criticized by George K. Turner, "The Greatest Waste of National Treasure in the History of the United States," *McClure's Magazine* 32, February 1909, 397–411.

38. *ARSN*, 60th Cong., 2d sess., H. Doc. 1045, November 30, 1908, serial 5449.

39. *Messages of the Presidents*, December 8, 1908, 10:7616–17.

40. Roosevelt to Mahan, January 27, 1909, *Roosevelt Letters*, 6:1487–88n1.

41. *Message of the President on Navy Reorganization*, 60th Cong., 2d sess., S. Doc. 740, serial 5409; *Final Report of Naval Reorganization Commission*, 60th Cong., 2d sess., S. Doc. 743, serial 5409.

42. *Army General Staff Corps Act, U.S. Statutes at Large* 32 (1903): 830–31.

43. For the struggle to reconstitute the Army, see Skowronek, *Building a New American State*, 218–22.

44. *Naval Appropriations Act, U.S. Statutes at Large* 35, (1909): 777 (for two battleships, five torpedo boat destroyers, four submarine torpedo boats, one destroyer, and two small vessels).

45. Roosevelt to Governor James Gillet, February 6, 1909, *Roosevelt Letters*, 6:1505.

46. *Navy Yearbook 1916*, 620–21.

CHAPTER 12. STEADY AS SHE GOES, 1909–13

1. The story of the Taft family's lives, society, and successes is nicely told by Ishbel Ross in *An American Family: The Tafts, 1678 to 1964*.

2. Because of a complaint from Germany concerning the improper use of "von" inferring nobility, Meyer explained that his grandmother's maiden name was Johanna van Lengerke in Meyer to Gustave Dirks, October 4, 1911, Meyer Papers, MHS.

3. Howe, *George von Lengerke Meyer*, 412.

4. *DAB*, s.v., "Perkins, George Clement." Also see "Vote on Four Ships in Senate on Monday," *NYT*, April 26, 1908, and "Agree on Two Battleships," *NYT*, February 10, 1909.

5. *Messages of the Presidents*, March 4, 1909, 10:7749–50.

6. Harold and Margaret Sprout, *The Rise of American Naval Power*, 296–97; George Davis, *A Navy Second to None*, 188.

7. Quoted from "The New Plans for the Reorganization of the Navy," *Harper's Weekly* 53 (December 4, 1909). Almost the exact wording is attributed to Cdr. William Sims in Howe, *George von Lengerke Meyer*, 459.

8. Meyer to Roosevelt on safari in Africa, July 9, 1909, Meyer Papers, MHS; Howe, *George von Lengerke Meyer*, 437–40.

9. The Sixteenth Amendment made the rounds of the states and passed in February 1913 as Taft left office.

10. Gould, *The Taft Presidency*, 61–63.

11. *ARSN*, 61st Cong., 2d sess., 1909, H. Doc. 106, December 4, 1909, serial 5740.

12. *Messages of the Presidents*, December 7, 1909, 10:7809–10. Also see "Plans to Make U.S. First Naval Power," *NYT*, February 27, 1910.

13. Gould, *The Taft Presidency*, 97; Miller, *Theodore Roosevelt*, 504.

14. Gould, *The Taft Presidency*, 86–8.

15. "We Have Too Many Yards," *Outlook* 94 (January 8, 1910): 48–9. Also see Casper F. Goodrich, "The Navy from the Business Standpoint," *The Independent* 66 (May 6, 1909): 944–47.

16. Congress supported bureau chiefs who were "fighting for their lives," in Luce to Meyer, May 2, 1910, Meyer Papers, MHS. Also in Gleaves, *Life and Letters of Rear Admiral Stephen B. Luce*, 301.

17. Meyer, "Reorganization Statement for the Associated Press," February 3, 1910; Meyer to Roosevelt on safari in Africa, March 10, 1910; Meyer to Lodge, March 31, 1910, and Meyer to Hale, April, 11, 1910, Meyer Papers, MHS. Also see Howe, *George von Lengerke Meyer*, 469.

18. Numerous petition memorials are in *Senate Journal* and *House Journal*, 61st Cong., 2d sess., 1909–1910. Also see "Meyer Still in Trouble," *Boston Transcript*, April 30, 1910.

19. 61st Cong., 2d sess., 1910, Cong. Rec. 45, pt. 3:4340 and pt. 4:5027.

20. *House Journal*, HR 17759 with Rep. 1712 (June 23, 1910), 61st Cong., 2d sess.

21. *Navy Yearbook 1916*, 581.

22. *Naval Appropriations Act, U.S. Statutes at Large* 36 (1910): 628.

23. Roosevelt to Lodge, May 5, 1910, *Roosevelt Letters*, 7:79; Roosevelt to Pinchot, June 28, 1910, *Roosevelt Letters*, 7:95; Roosevelt to Lodge and to Arthur Lee, July 19, 1910, *Roosevelt Letters*, 7:102–103.

24. Gould, *The Taft Presidency*, chap. 8.

25. Howe, *George von Lengerke Meyer*, 471–81.

26. "Meyer Plans Naval Changes," *NYT*, November 7, 1910. Meyer had no plans for new locations on the Gulf Coast: Meyer to Congressman George Taylor (D–AL), November 14, 1910, Meyer Papers, MHS. Also see "Naval Yard Reform," *The Nation* 91 (November 24, 1910):489–90.

27. *ARSN*, 61st Cong., 3d sess., 1910, H. Doc. 1005, November 30, 1910, serial 572.

28. *Messages of the Presidents*, December 6, 1910, 10:7887, 7909–11.

29. For Tillman as an agrarian radical and reactionary see Simkins, *Pitchfork Ben Tillman*, 456. For a history of his racism and his leading role in maintaining segregation see *ANB* and *DNB*, s.v., "Tillman, Benjamin Ryan."

30. Tillman to President Taft, December 6, 1910, Meyer Papers, MHS.

31. *Senate Journal*, 61st Cong., 3d sess., Resolution by Tillman for a report from the Secretary of the Navy, S. Res. 327 (January 26, 1911), and letter from Meyer to the Senate, S. Doc. 830 (February 11, 1911), serial 5944.

32. The differences between the General Board of the Navy, the Secretary of the Navy, and the House committee are shown in "$34,270,816 in Bill for New Warships," *NYT*, January 29, 1911.

33. *Naval Appropriations Act, U.S. Statutes at Large* 36 (1911): 1287. Also see "Will Congress Put Our Navy on the Sea?" *McClure's Magazine* 36 (March 1911): 523–35.

34. "20,000 Troops and Two Naval Divisions to Mobilize Near Mexican Border," *NYT*, March 8, 1911; quotes are from Gould, *The Taft Presidency*, 145, and from "Diaz a Sufferer from Sclerosis" with a sub-heading of "Warships to Stop at Mexican Ports Only Long enough to Coal," *NYT*, March 14, 1911.

35. Buenker and Kantowicz, eds., *Historical Dictionary of the Progressive Era*, s.v., "Scientific Management" and s.v., "Taylor, Frederick." Also see Casper F. Goodrich, "Mr. Newberry and Navy Yard Management," *The Independent* 69 (September 15, 1910): 589–92.

36. *Senate Journal*, "Memorials against the introduction of the so-called Taylor System by citizens" (May 4, 11, 15, 16, 23, and July 11, 1911), 62d Cong., 1st sess., 48, 58, 63, 66, 74, and 115.

37. Robert Wickliffe Woolley, "Underwood, Democracy's New Chieftain," *American Review of Reviews* 44 (September 1911): 296–99.

38. "Would Revive Rank of Vice Admiral," *NYT*, September 18, 1911.

39. *House Journal,* "To prevent the sale of intoxicating liquors on board vessels, etc.," HR 1308 (April 4, 1911), and "To prevent the sale of intoxicating liquors in buildings, etc.," HR 5971 (April 17, 1911), 62d Cong., 1st sess.

40. *ARSN,* 62d Cong., 2d sess., 1911, H. Doc. 119, December 1, 1911, serial 6219.

41. *Messages of the Presidents,* December 5, 1911, 10:8024–78 with quotes from pages 8024 and 8054.

42. Telegram from Hilles to Taft, January 3, 1912, Meyer Papers, MHS. Also see "Economy Plan Leads to Navy Yards Strike," *NYT,* January 4, 1912 and "Privileged Workers in Revolt," *NYT,* January 5, 1912.

43. Taft to Meyer, January 24, 1912, and March 16, 1912, Meyer Papers, MHS.

44. "Favors A Defensive Navy," *NYT,* February 3, 1912; "May Get Two Battleships," *NYT,* February 29, 1912; "The Navy Not in Politics," *NYT,* May 22, 1912; and "House Democrats Against Big Navy," *NYT,* May 29, 1912.

45. Roosevelt's collective letters to seven governors, February 24, 1912, *Roosevelt Letters,* 7:511.

46. Taft was clearly Roosevelt's enemy in Gould, *Four Hats in the Ring,* 132.

47. "The Reorganization of the Navy," *The Independent* 72 (August 8, 1912): 304–9.

48. *Naval Appropriations Act, U.S. Statutes at Large* 37 (1912): 354–55.

49. Secretary Meyer recounted the Nicaragua operations in his annual report: *ARSN,* 62d Cong., 3d sess., 1912, H. Doc. 932, November 20, 1912, 12–13, serial 6405.

50. Ibid., 15–21. Also see "Fleet's Flagships to Arrive Today," *NYT,* October 6, 1912, and "Fleet Greets Taft with Mighty Salvos," *NYT,* October 15, 1912.

51. *ARSN,* 62d Cong., 3d sess., H. Doc. 932, November 20, 1912, serial 6405.

52. *Messages of the Presidents,* December 6, 1912, 10:8187–88.

53. *Naval Appropriations Act, U.S. Statutes at Large* 37 (1913): 911.

54. *House Journal,* HR 15266 (December 9, 1911) and *Senate Journal,* S 3850 (December 18, 1911), 62d Cong., 2d sess.

55. *Navy Yearbook 1916,* 621–22

CHAPTER 13. NEUTRALITY, 1913–15

1. Judson Welliver, "Leaders of the New Congress," *Munsey's Magazine* 48 (February 1913): 715–28.

2. *Navy Yearbook 1916,* 581.

3. *Messages of the Presidents*, March 4, 1913, 10:8247–51; Cooper, *Woodrow Wilson*, 198–99.

4. Cooper, *Woodrow Wilson*, 35.

5. Ibid., 56, 61, 64, and 121; Craig, *Josephus Daniels*, 215.

6. Cooper, *Woodrow Wilson*, 183; Craig, *Josephus Daniels*, 223.

7. Morrison, *Josephus Daniels: The Small-d Democrat*, 58.

8. Tillman to Daniels, March 5, 1913, Daniels Papers, LC.

9. "Navy to Make Uniforms," *NYT*, November 23, 1913.

10. Cooper, *Woodrow Wilson*, 199.

11. Ibid., 205–6.

12. *Messages of the Presidents*, April 9, 1913, 10:8252.

13. Burleson to Taft, November 1, 1911, Meyer Papers, MHS; Cronon, ed., *The Cabinet Diaries of Josephus Daniels*, 13.

14. *Messages of the Presidents*, April 22, 1913, 10:8255.

15. Tillman to Daniels, April 25, 1913, Daniels Papers, LC.

16. Craig, *Josephus Daniels*, 259–61.

17. *House Journal*, HR 115 (June 2, 1913), 63rd Cong., 1st sess. Also see *NYT*, "Alleges Armor Plate Deal," May 17, 1913; "Plans Armor Plant at $3,000,000 Cost," May 22, 1913; "$1,600,000 for Armor Plant," May 23, 1913.

18. Tillman to Daniels, May 29, 1913, Daniels Papers, LC.

19. Cooling, *Grey Steel and Blue Water Navy*, 196.

20. *Messages of the Presidents*, August 27, 1913, 10:8264–75.

21. Tillman to Daniels, November 5, 1913, and January 27, 1914, Daniels Papers, LC.

22. Link, *Wilson: The New Freedom*, 164.

23. *ARSN* and *Appendix A*, 63rd Cong., 2d sess., 1913, H. Doc. 681, December 1, 1913, serial 6630. Also see Harold and Margaret Sprout, *The Rise of American Naval Power*, 310–12.

24. Padgett to Daniels, October 11, 1913, Daniels Papers, LC.

25. *Messages of the Presidents*, December 2, 1913, 10:8286–93; "The President's First Annual Message," *American Review of Reviews* 49 (January 1914): 9–10.

26. *House Journal*, Index: Navy, Armor Plate, 63rd Cong., 2d sess.

27. *Messages of the Presidents*, February 3, 1914, 10:8309.

28. Cooper, *Woodrow Wilson*, 142–44. Also see *NYT*, "Mediators End Peace Sessions; Their Work Done," July 1, 1914, and "Huerta's Retirement Is Accepted by Deputies," July 16, 1914.

29. *Navy Yearbook 1916*, 581.

30. *Naval Appropriations Act, U.S. Statutes at Large* 38 (1914): 413.

31. Tillman to Daniels, April 8, 1913, April 22, 1914 and Cdr. Richardson to Tillman, July 7, 1914, Daniels Papers, LC.

32. *Messages of the Presidents*, August 4, 1914, 10:8349; "Must Not Discuss War," *NYT*, August 6, 1914.

33. "Loss of Officers Britain's Big Peril," *NYT*, October 12, 1914.

34. Gardner to Henry, November 9, 1914, Gardner to Daniels, November 17, 1914, and Daniels to Gardner, November 25, 1914, Daniels Papers, LC; *House Journal*, H. Joint Res. 372, 63rd Cong., 3rd sess. Also see Roosevelt Letters, 8:862n7.

35. *ARSN*, 63rd Cong., 3rd sess., 1914, H. Doc. 1484, December 1, 1914, serial 6812. Also see "Secretary Daniels's Report," *NYT*, December 12, 1914.

36. *Messages of the Presidents*, December 8, 1914, 10:8403.

37. *Navy Yearbook 1916*, 682, 686, and 689.

38. "Allies Gain by Feet in Steinbach Fight," and "586,013 Prisoners held in Germany," *NYT*, January 2, 1915; "German Fleet Bested in North Sea," *NYT*, January 25, 1915.

39. "Underwood Wants Cut in Navy Bill," *NYT*, January 17, 1915.

40. "Our Navy drops to Fourth," *NYT*, January 31, 1915.

41. George V. L. Meyer, "Are Naval Expenditures Wasted?" *North American Review* 210 (February 1915): 248–53.

42. Hough, *The Great War at Sea*, 172–73.

43. Cooper, *Woodrow Wilson*, 275; Link, *Woodrow Wilson: Revolution, War, and Peace*, 40.

44. *DAN*, s.v., "Fiske, Bradley Allen," 2:90–93.

45. *House Journal*, HR 20641 (January 6, 1915) and HR 21257 (January 30, 1915), 63rd Cong., 3rd sess. Also see note in Cronon, *The Cabinet Diaries of Josephus Daniels*, 93 and 94.

46. Daniels to Padgett, January 28, February 2, and February 27, 1915; Daniels to Senator Lee Overman (D-NC), February 25, 1915, Daniels Papers, LC.

47. *House Journal*, HR 20975 (February 5, 1915), 63rd Cong., 3rd sess., and *Naval Appropriations Act, U.S. Statutes at Large* 38 (1915): 929.

48. *Navy Yearbook 1916*, 581.

CHAPTER 14. SECOND TO NONE, 1915–21

1. "War Keeps President Busy," *NYT*, March 2, 1915.

2. Cooper, *Woodrow Wilson*, 276.

3. "Admiral Fiske Resigns," *NYT*, April 3, 1915, and "Admiral Fiske's Withdrawal," *NYT*, April 4, 1915. Also see *DAN*, s.v., "Bradley Allen Fiske," credited with creating the office of Chief of Naval Operations, 2:91.

4. Klachko, *Admiral William Shepherd Benson*, 29–31; "Names Captain Benson As New Naval Chief," *NYT*, April 26, 1915.

5. Cooper, *Woodrow Wilson*, 286–88.

6. Daniels to Assistant Secretary of the Navy Franklin D. Roosevelt et al, June 28, 1915, Daniels Papers, LC.

7. Gardner to Daniels, April 26, June 25, August 13, and November 9, 1915, Daniels Papers, LC. Also see "Biggest Navy For Us Is Gardner's Plea," *NYT*, October 24, 1915.

8. Daniels, Naval War College Speech, June 25, 1915; Daniels to Padgett, January 10, 1916, Daniels Papers, LC.

9. "As They See Daniels," *Harper's Weekly* 61, July 3, 1915, 16; "National Policy and the Experts," *Nation* 101 (December 30, 1915): 766–67.

10. Harold and Margaret Sprout, *The Rise of American Naval Power*, 332–34.

11. Wilson to Daniels, July 21, 1915, Daniels Papers, LC. Also see Davis, *A Navy Second to None*, 213.

12. Hough, *The Great War at Sea*, 175–76.

13. "Ask $400,000,000 to Begin Defense," *NYT*, October 14, 1915; "Dreadnought Bids Exceeded Legal Limit," *NYT*, November 18, 1915.

14. Davis, *A Navy Second to None*, 213.

15. "Daniels's Plant Wrecked," *NYT*, November 7, 1915; "Mimnermus in Raleigh," *NYT*, November 14, 1915.

16. *ARSN*, 64th Cong., 1st sess., H. Doc., 20, December 1, 1915, 5, serial 6986.

17. *Papers of Woodrow Wilson*, December 7, 1915.

18. Tavenner on December 16, 1915, 64th Cong., 1st sess., Cong. Rec. 53, pt. 1:272–92.

19. *ANB*, s.v., "Wilson, Edith Bolling Galt."

20. Cooper, *Woodrow Wilson*, 306.

21. Ibid., 309–10; Harold and Margaret Sprout, *The Rise of American Sea Power*, 336. Also see "Wilson's St. Louis Speech," *NYT*, February 4, 1916.

22. "Gardner Insists on First Rate-Navy," *NYT*, January 11, 1916; Daniels explained that Mare Island would "shortly be equipped" in Daniels

to Congressman Frederick Britten (D-IL), January 12, 1916, Daniels Papers, LC.

23. Hough, *The Great War at Sea*, 176; Germany announced its new campaign on February 11, 1916.

24. Horne, ed., "Woodrow Wilson," in *Source Records of the Great War*, 95.

25. Ibid., 100–101; for the entire text of Germany's reply see pages 95–101.

26. Ibid., 61.

27. See ibid., 63–80 for statements of President Carranza, Robert Lansing, and Newton Baker.

28. Cooling, *Grey Steel and Blue Water Navy*, 203.

29. *House Journal*, HR 707 and HR 4739; *Senate Journal*, S 1417, 64th Cong., 1st sess.

30. For excellent summaries, see "Report Naval Bill Carrying 5 Battle Cruisers," *NYT*, May 19, 1916, and "Hensley and Kitchen's Navy," *NYT*, May 20, 1916.

31. *House Journal*, HR 15947, with S. Rep 575 (June 30, 1916), serial 6899, 64th Cong., 1st sess.

32. For coverage of the 1916 naval debates in Congress, see Harold and Margaret Sprout, *The Rise of American Naval Power*, 336–44, and Davis, *A Navy Second to None*, 218–27.

33. *Naval Appropriations Act, U.S. Statutes at Large* 39 (1916): 617; *Navy Yearbook 1916*, 581.

34. *U.S. Statutes at Large* 39 (1916): 563.

35. Cooling, *Grey Steel and Blue Water Navy*, 210. Also see Cronon, *The Cabinet Diaries of Josephus Daniels*, 128n.

36. *U.S. Statues at Large* 39 (1916): 587–93.

37. Cooper, *Woodrow Wilson*, 352.

38. *ARSN*, 64th Cong., 2d sess., H. Doc. 1480, December 1, 1916, serial 7156.

39. Cooper, *Woodrow Wilson*, 363–64.

40. *Papers of Woodrow Wilson*, December 5, 1916.

41. Link, *Woodrow Wilson: Revolution, War, and Peace*, 57.

42. "Move Hailed in Congress" and "Notes Prepared on Monday," *NYT*, December 21, 1916.

43. "Wilson Studies Entente's Reply," *NYT*, January 13, 1917.

44. *Papers of Woodrow Wilson*, January 22, 1917.

45. Terraine, *The U-Boat Wars 1916–1945*, 14–15; Davis, *A Navy Second to None*, 235.

46. Horne, ed., "Woodrow Wilson," in *The Great Events of the Great War*, 14–15.

47. Ibid., 42–43.

48. *Papers of Woodrow Wilson*, February 26, 1917.

49. "Plot Awakens Congress," *NYT*, March 2, 1917.

50. *Naval Appropriations Act, U.S. Statutes at Large* 39 (1917): 1172, 1191–94.

51. *Papers of Woodrow Wilson*, March 4, 1917.

52. Link, *Woodrow Wilson: Revolution, War, and Peace*, 69.

53. Cooper, *Woodrow Wilson*, 383.

54. *Papers of Woodrow Wilson*, April 2, 1917.

55. *ARSN*, 64th Cong., 1st sess., H. Doc., 20, December 1, 1915, Appendix A, 74–75, serial 6986.

56. Horne, ed., "Josephus Daniels," in *The Great Events of the Great War*, 170.

57. *ARSN*, 65th Cong., 3rd sess., H. Doc., 1450, December 1918, 33, serial 7495. The wooden sub chasers were all SC-1 class, not to be confused with steel Eagle Boats, which were not launched until after the war.

58. Davis, *A Navy Second to None*, 235.

59. *ARSN*, 65th Cong., 3rd Sess., H. Doc., 1450, December 1918, 32–33, serial 7495; *Papers of Woodrow Wilson*, December 2, 1918.

60. Cooper, *Woodrow Wilson*, 469–71.

61. Ibid., 475 and 479.

62. *Naval Appropriations Act, U.S. Statutes at Large* 41 (1919):156.

63. Cooper, *Woodrow Wilson*, 530–33.

64. Davis, *A Navy Second to None*, 271–72.

65. *Papers of Warren Harding*, March 4, 1921.

66. Baer, *One Hundred Years of Sea Power*, 93; Davis, *A Navy Second to None*, 276.

67. Davis, *A Navy Second to None*, 278, 287, 309.

SELECTED
BIBLIOGRAPHY

Albion, Robert G. "The Administration of the Navy 1798–1945." *Public Administration Review* 5 (1945): 293–302.

———. "The Naval Affairs Committees, 1816–1947." U.S. Naval Institute *Proceedings* 78 (November 1952): 1227–37.

Baer, George W. *One Hundred Years of Sea Power: The U.S. Navy, 1890–1990.* Stanford: Stanford University Press, 1994.

Beers, Henry P. "The Bureau of Navigation, 1862–1942." *American Archivist* (October 1943).

Bishop, Joseph Bucklin. *Charles Joseph Bonaparte: His Life and Public Services.* Reproduction from Georgia University Law Library. New York: Charles Scribner's Sons, 1922.

Brodsky, Alyn. *Grover Cleveland: A Study in Character.* New York: Truman Talley Books, St. Martin's Press, 2000.

Buenker, John, and Edward Kantowicz, eds. *Historical Dictionary of the Progressive Era, 1890–1920.* New York: Greenwood Press, 1988.

Calhoun, Charles W. *Benjamin Harrison.* New York: Henry Holt, 2005.

Coetzee, Frans. *For Party or Country: Nationalism and the Dilemmas of Popular Conservatism in Edwardian England.* New York: Oxford University Press, 1990.

Cogar, William B., ed. *Dictionary of Admirals of the U.S. Navy.* 2 vols. Annapolis: Naval Institute Press, 1989.

Coletta, Paolo E., ed. *American Secretaries of the Navy.* 2 vols. Annapolis: Naval Institute Press, 1980.

Cooling, Benjamin. *Benjamin Franklin Tracy: Father of the Modern Fighting Navy.* Hamden, CT: Archeon Books, 1973.

———. *Grey Steel and Blue Water Navy.* Hamden, CT: Archeon Books, 1979.

Cooper, John Milton, Jr. *Woodrow Wilson: A Biography.* New York: Vintage Books, 2009.

Craig, Lee A. *Josephus Daniels: His Life and Times.* Chapel Hill: University of North Carolina Press, 2013.

Cronon, E. David. *The Cabinet Diaries of Josephus Daniels 1913–1921.* Lincoln: University of Nebraska Press, 1963.

Davis, Calvin deArmond. *The United States and the Second Hague Peace Conference: American Diplomacy and International Organization, 1899–1914.* Durham, NC: Duke University Press, 1975.

Davis, George T. *A Navy Second to None: The Development of Modern American Naval Policy.* Westport, CT: Greenwood Press, 1940.

Dictionary of American Naval Fighting Ships. http://www.hazegray.org/danfs.

Drake, Frederick C. *The Empire of the Seas: A Biography of Rear Adm. Robert Wilson Shufeldt, USN.* Honolulu: University of Hawaii Press, 1984.

Evans, Daniel C., and Mark R. Peattie. *Kaigun: Strategy, Tactics, and Technology in the Imperial Japanese Navy, 1887–1941.* Annapolis: Naval Institute Press, 1997.

Garraty, John A., and Mark C. Carnes, eds. *American National Biography.* 24 vols. New York: Oxford University Press, 1999.

Gillespie, James. *Andersonvilles of the North.* Denton, TX: University of North Texas Press, 2008.

Gleaves, Albert. *Life and Letters of Rear Admiral Stephen B. Luce, U.S. Navy.* New York: G. P. Putnam's Sons, 1925.

Goodwin, George. *The Little Legislatures: Committees of Congress.* Amherst: University of Massachusetts Press, 1970.

Gould, Lewis L. *Four Hats in the Ring: The 1912 Election and the Birth of Modern American Politics.* Lawrence: University Press of Kansas, 2008.

———. *The William Howard Taft Presidency.* Lawrence: University Press of Kansas, 2009.

Hagan, Kenneth J. *This People's Navy: The Making of American Sea Power.* New York: The Free Press, 1991.

Hammett, Hugh B. *Hilary Abner Herbert: A Southerner Returns to the Union.* Philadelphia: American Philosophical Society, 1976.

Hayes, John D., and John Hattendorf, eds. *The Writings of Stephen B. Luce.* Newport, RI: U.S. Naval War College, 1975.

Herbert, Hilary A., and Zebulon B. Vance. *Why the Solid South? Or Reconstruction and Its Results.* Whitefish, MT: Kessinger Publishing, 2007.

Herrick, Walter R., Jr. *The American Naval Revolution.* Baton Rouge: Louisiana State University Press, 1966.

———. "Hilary A. Herbert." In *American Secretaries of the Navy,* edited by Paolo Coletta, 1:425–29. Annapolis: Naval Institute Press, 1980.

———. "William C. Whitney." In *American Secretaries of the Navy,* edited by Paolo Coletta, 1:405–412. Annapolis: Naval Institute Press, 1980.

Herwig, Holger H. *"Luxury" Fleet: The Imperial German Navy 1888–1918.* London: George Allen and Unwin, 1980.

Hirsch, Mark D. *William C. Whitney: Modern Warwick.* New York: Dodd, Mead, 1948.

Horne, Charles F., ed. *Source Records of the Great War.* Vol. 4, *AD 1916.* New York: National Alumni, 1923.

———, ed., *The Great Events of the Great War.* Vol. 5, *AD 1917.* New York: National Alumni, 1923.

Hough, Richard. *The Great War at Sea.* New York: Oxford University Press, 1983.

Howarth, Stephen. *To Shining Sea: A History of the United States Navy, 1775–1991.* New York: Random House, 1991.

Howe, M. A. DeWolf. *George von Lengerke Meyer: His Life and Public Service.* New York: Dodd, Mead, 1920.

Hunt, Thomas. *The Life of William H. Hunt.* Brattleboro, VT: E. L. Hildreth, 1922.

Klachko, Mary. *Admiral William Shepard Benson, First Chief of Naval Operations.* Annapolis: Naval Institute Press, 1987.

Link, Arthur S. *Wilson: The New Freedom.* Princeton: Princeton University Press, 1956.

———. *Woodrow Wilson: Revolution, War, and Peace.* Arlington Heights, IL: Harlan Davidson, 1979.

Long, John D. *The New American Navy.* 2 vols. New York: The Outlook Company, 1903.

Malone, Dumas, ed. *Dictionary of American Biography.* 22 vols. New York: Charles Scribner's Sons, 1937.

McAdoo, William. "Reorganization of the Personnel of the Navy." *North American Review* 159 (October 1894): 457–66.

Miller, Nathan. *Theodore Roosevelt: A Life.* New York: William Morrow, 1992.

Morgan, H. Wayne. *William McKinley and His America*. Rev. ed. Kent, OH: The Kent State University Press, 2003.

Morison, Elting. *The Letters of Theodore Roosevelt*. 8 vols. Cambridge: Harvard University Press, 1951.

Morris, Edmund. *Theodore Rex*. New York: Random House, 2001.

Morrison, Joseph L. *Josephus Daniels: The Small-d Democrat*. Chapel Hill: University of North Carolina Press, 1966.

Naval History and Heritage Command—Photography. http://www.history .navy.mil/our-collections/photography.html.

Nevins, Allan. *Grover Cleveland: A Study in Courage*. New York: Dodd, Mead, 1966.

Paullin, Charles Oscar. *Paullin's History of Naval Administration, 1775–1911*. Annapolis: Naval Institute Press, 1968.

Peters, Gerhard, and John T. Wooley, comp. *Papers of Woodrow Wilson*. The American Presidency Project. http://www.presidency.ucsb.edu/woodrow _wilson.php.

———. *Papers of Warren Harding*. The American Presidency Project. http:// www.presidency.ucsb.edu/warren_harding.php.

Peskin, Allen. *Garfield*. Kent, OH: The Kent State University Press, 1978.

Phillips, Kevin. *William McKinley*. New York: Henry Holt, 2003.

Rappaport, Armin. *The Navy League of the United States*. Detroit: Wayne State University Press, 1962.

Reckner, James R. *Teddy Roosevelt's Great White Fleet*. Annapolis: Naval Institute Press, 1988.

Reeves, Thomas C. *Gentleman Boss: The Life and Times of Chester A. Arthur*. Newtown, CT: American Political Biography Press, 2007.

Richardson, James D., ed. *A Compilation of the Messages and Papers of the Presidents.* 10 vols. New York: Bureau of National Literature, 1914.

Richardson, Leon Burr. *William Chandler "Republican."* New York: Dodd, Mead, 1940.

Ross, Ishbel. *An American Family: The Tafts, 1678 to 1964*. Cleveland and New York: The World Publishing Company, 1963.

Seager, Robert II, and Doris Maguire, eds. *Letters and Papers of Alfred Thayer Mahan*. 3 vols. Annapolis: Naval Institute Press, 1975.

Simkins, Francis. *Pitchfork Ben Tillman; South Carolinian*. Gloucester, MA: Peter Smith, 1944.

Skocpol, Theda. *Protecting Soldiers and Mothers: The Political Origins of Social Policy in the United States.* Cambridge, MA: The Belknap Press of Harvard University Press, 1992.

Skowronek, Stephen. *Building a New American State: The Expansion of National Administrative Capacities, 1877–1920.* New York: Cambridge University Press, 1982.

Sprout, Harold and Margaret. *The Rise of American Naval Power 1776–1918.* 1966 edition. Annapolis: Naval Institute Press, 1939.

Strait, Newton A. *Alphabetical list of battles, 1754–1900; War of the Rebellion, Spanish-American War, Philippine Insurrection, and all old wars with dates; summary of events of the War of the Rebellion, 1860–1865, Spanish-American War, Philippine Insurrection, 1898–1900, troubles in China, 1900, with other valuable information in regard to the various wars; compiled from official records. Washington, 1905.* Detroit: Gale Research, 1968.

Swann, Leonard, Jr. *John Roach, Maritime Entrepreneur 1862–1886.* Annapolis: U.S. Naval Institute, 1965.

Terraine, John. *The U-Boat Wars 1916–1945.* New York: Henry Holt, 1985.

Tillman, B. R., Jr., comp. *Navy Yearbook 1916.* 64th Cong., 2d sess., 1916, S. Doc. 555, serial 7115. Washington, D.C.: Government Printing Office, 1916.

Trask, David F. *The War with Spain in 1898.* New York: Macmillan, 1981.

White, James Terry, ed. *National Cyclopedia of American Biography.* New York: J. T. White, 1910.

White, Leonard D. *The Republican Era: 1869–1901, A Study in Administrative History.* New York: Macmillan, 1958.

Wicks, Daniel. *New Navy and New Empire: The Life and Times of James Grimes Walker.* University of California. Ann Arbor, MI: University Microfilms, 1977.

Wiebe, Robert H. *The Search for Order, 1877–1920.* New York: Hill and Wang, 1967.

Wilson, Woodrow. *Congressional Government: A Study in American Politics,* Boston: Houghton Mifflin Company, 1885.

MANUSCRIPT COLLECTIONS

Maine   Bowdoin College Library, Brunswick
                        Papers of:
                             Reed, Thomas Brackett

Massachusetts   Massachusetts Historical Society, Boston
      Papers of:
        Long, John Davis
        Meyer, George von Lengerke
North Carolina   University of North Carolina Library, Chapel Hill
      Papers of:
        Herbert, Hilary Abner

Washington, D.C.   Library of Congress Manuscript Division
      Papers of:
        Bonaparte, Charles Joseph
        Chandler, William Eaton
        Daniels, Josephus
        Dewey, George
        Luce, Stephen B.
        Mahan, Alfred Thayer
        Melville, George W.
        Moody, William Henry
        Tracy, Benjamin Franklin
        Walker, John Grimes
        Whitney, William Collins

INDEX